FRONT TOWARD ENEMY

FRONT TOWARD ENEMY

War, Veterans, and the Homefront

DANIEL R. GREEN

ROWMAN & LITTLEFIELD
Lanham • Boulder • New York • London

The views expressed in this book are those of the author, not the United States Department of Defense.

Published by Rowman & Littlefield
An imprint of The Rowman & Littlefield Publishing Group, Inc.
4501 Forbes Boulevard, Suite 200, Lanham, Maryland 20706
www.rowman.com

86-90 Paul Street, London EC2A 4NE, United Kingdom

British Library Cataloguing in Publication Information Available

Library of Congress Cataloging-in-Publication Data

Names: Green, Daniel R., author.
Title: Front toward enemy : war, veterans, and the homefront / Daniel R. Green.
Description: Lanham : Rowman & Littlefield Publishing Group, 2021. | Includes bibliographical references and index. | Summary: "Daniel R. Green offers a unique and much-needed perspective on war veterans and the transitions they go through upon returning home, using his own experience following five military and civilian tours of Afghanistan and Iraq"— Provided by publisher.
Identifiers: LCCN 2021027501 (print) | LCCN 2021027502 (ebook) | ISBN 9781538142189 (paperback) | ISBN 9781538142196 (epub)
Subjects: LCSH: Green, Daniel R. | United States—Armed Forces—Biography. | Veterans—United States—Biography. | Veteran reintegration—United States. | War—Psychological aspects. | Afghan War, 2001– | Iraq War, 2003–2011.
Classification: LCC U53.G74 A3 2021 (print) | LCC U53.G74 (ebook) | DDC 355.0092 [B]—dc23
LC record available at https://lccn.loc.gov/2021027501
LC ebook record available at https://lccn.loc.gov/2021027502

Sergeant First Class Thomas Arnold Green

World War II Veteran

91st Signal Company
91st Infantry Division

Date of Entry into Service: November 4, 1942
Date of Discharge from the Service: November 30, 1945

"'Whom shall I send, and who will go for us?'
Then I said, 'Here am I. Send me.'"

"A man who has once been a soldier can never be quite a
civilian again. A military experience, especially in time of war,
leaves a mark upon a man. If we are to understand the veteran,
we must learn what he experiences as a soldier."

—WILLARD WALLER, *THE VETERAN COMES BACK*, 18

"A medal glitters, but it also casts a shadow."

—WINSTON CHURCHILL, "WAR DECORATIONS AND MEDALS,"
SPEECH TO THE HOUSE OF COMMONS, MARCH 22, 1944

How will you fare, sonny, how will you fare
In the far off winter night
When you sit by the fire in the old man's chair
And your neighbors talk of the fight?
Will you slink away, as it were from a blow,
Your old head shamed and bent?
Or say, "I was not the first to go,
But I went, Thank God, I went"?

—FROM THE SONG "FALL IN," BY HAROLD BEGBIE, 1914

Contents

Prologue

"I still had a long period of adjustment to go through simply to get used to being back home, back in America. Civilian life seemed so strange. People rushed around in a hurry about seemingly insignificant things. Few seemed to realize how blessed they were to be free and untouched by the horrors of war. To them, a veteran was a veteran—all were the same, whether one man had survived the deadliest combat or another had pounded a typewriter while in uniform."

—E. B. SLEDGE, *CHINA MARINE: AN INFANTRYMAN'S LIFE AFTER WORLD WAR II*, 130

A VERITABLE COTTAGE INDUSTRY OF BOOKS, reports, conferences, medical studies, and clinical efforts have erupted since the wars in Afghanistan and Iraq began focusing on helping veterans deal with the trauma of war service. Virtually all of these initiatives have revolved around the relationship of the veteran to violence, whether committed or experienced by him, and the field of psychology has dominated this landscape. Most of these studies center on the mental impact of trauma and are frequently written by specialists who are not war veterans, and their focus is principally on violence and its effects (e.g., posttraumatic stress disorder, posttraumatic stress, and traumatic brain injuries). Variations of this theme sometimes include the moral quandaries of violence in a counterinsurgency environment (e.g., accidentally killing civilians) and dealing with questionable indigenous partners.

These treatments miss the whole moral experience of these conflicts as well as the sociological, philosophical, societal, cultural, political, and literary contexts within which they take place. These other factors also shape how veterans process their war experiences and are often of greater consequence than the more violent aspects of their tours. Additionally, the story of the returning veteran has become so clichéd and misunderstood in American culture, especially in a time when so few have served, that the narrative of coming home dominates the veteran's return, and yet its true aspects (as it is discussed by veterans privately) must be hidden from polite civilian society. As much as the veteran is welcomed home, he must be seen to appreciate his return, which often leads to a less than accurate accounting of his service. A fuller account must be written that explores the experiences of the post-9/11 veteran from his perspective.

Front toward Enemy: War, Veterans, and the Homefront is a personal effort to use my experiences from five military and civilian tours to Afghanistan and Iraq, as well as the countless conversations I've had with my fellow veterans, to broaden the public discussion about veterans returning home from war. I intend to provide not just a war veteran's views but also the amplifying perspective of a political scientist as well as a reserve officer and a former defense official in order to rescue the issue of the "returning veteran" from the field of psychology. It is only from a firsthand, comprehensive, and multidisciplinary approach that we can hope to broaden the collective understanding of the experience of war and how veterans return from it and attempt to resume normal lives.

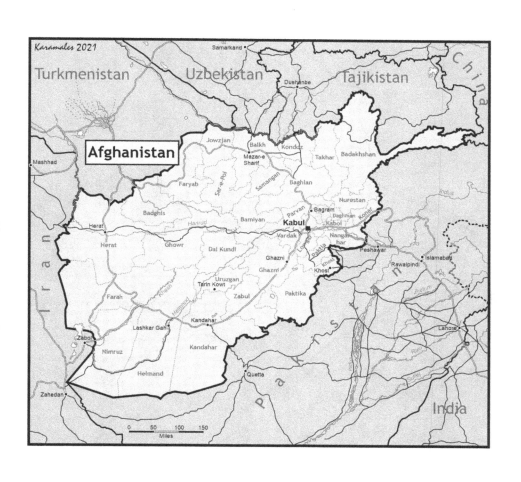

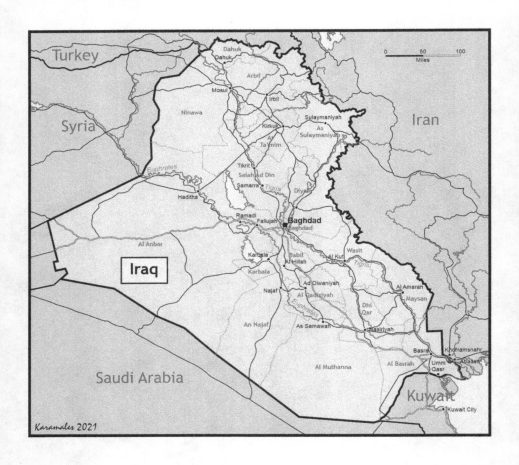

No Victory Parades 1

"*But many towns and cities would not be denied. Victory has always meant pageantry. And so nearly two hundred thousand doughboys, all told, marched in some four hundred and fifty parades.*"

—DIXON WECTER, *WHEN JOHNNY COMES MARCHING HOME*, 302

"*War does different things to different men. It disables one, unbalances the mind of a second, pauperizes a third, and makes a fourth write great literature to ease his tortured soul. Every type of veteran has his own characteristic problems of adjustment.*"

—WILLARD WALLER, *THE VETERAN COMES BACK*, 159

"*The symptoms caused by psychological injury that the American Psychiatric Association called PTSD . . . can be understood in one clear and simple concept: persistence of valid adaptations to danger into a time of safety afterward.*"

—JONATHAN SHAY, *ODYSSEUS IN AMERICA: COMBAT TRAUMA AND THE TRIALS OF HOMECOMING*, 149

IT IS A DIFFICULT TIME TO BE A VETERAN of a small war in the United States. After twenty years of combat and counterinsurgency, a generation of Afghan, Iraq, and global war on terror veterans struggle to integrate back into civilian society and lead productive lives. As the wars these men and women have participated in continue, while they simultaneously recede to the past, many feel a sense of estrangement from their country, friends, and prior lives. They often long to return to war but hope to never go again and are stuck in a nether world of war without end and peace that does not exist. When their experiences are talked about in civilian life, veterans are variously seen as heroes, victims, or psychopaths; yet they feel as if they do not fall into any one of these categories but have some sense of connection to all of them. They also don't understand why they feel the way they do, why being "thanked for their service" grates on their soul, and why the term *posttraumatic stress disorder* (PTSD) vaguely insults them, especially when wielded by civilians, even as its clinical certitude helps those who suffer. The veteran knows his service is valued, to a point, although there will be no victory parades for his generation, and the banal lives of the civilian population offer few enticements. Even as most Americans have moved on from the conflicts in Iraq and Afghanistan and the major headlines have receded, the mind of the veteran inevitably ranges back to his time overseas. It was when he was younger and full of life, where loss and victory were felt so intensely, sometimes for the very first time. It was a place where terms such as *loyalty, honor, conviction, morality, comradeship,* and *patriotism* were imbued with such visceral, tactile meaning that the pale paeans to them at home seem empty. Longing to understand his experiences, looking for meaning—for some context—to set his experiences the veteran is lost as he gropes in the dark for a return home that never fully takes place.

World War II

As approximately 16.5 million service members were discharged or separated from the Armed Forces of the United States after the defeat of the German and Japanese militaries in World War II, they were issued a small diamond-shaped patch, in either khaki or olive drab, with a golden eagle sewn into it with its wings outstretched against a gold circle.[1] It was issued to every service member upon their honorable discharge from the service, and military personnel were instructed to affix it to their uniform or a similar lapel button on civilian clothing.[2] Called, respectively, the "Honorable Discharge Emblem" and the "Honorable Service Lapel Button," the War and Navy Departments instructed the veterans to "[w]ear these symbols proudly. They signify to everyone that you have served honorably in the armed forces."[3] They were also told that "[t]he emblem will be worn as a badge of honor indicative of honest and faithful service while a member of the Armed Forces during World War II."[4] The eagle was sometimes referred to informally and irreverently as the "ruptured duck" by members of the military, such as, for example, when E. B. Sledge, the former Marine and author of the World War II memoirs *With the Old Breed* and *China Marine*, stated, "We all wore the 'ruptured duck,' a cloth insignia of an American eagle with outstretched wings that signified the wearer had been officially discharged from the armed forces."[5] In addition to the emblem, each service member received a small booklet titled "Going Back to Civilian Life," which had the same symbol of the "Honorable Discharge Emblem" on its cover.

The booklet contained necessary information for the service member on how to access his entitlements (such as those from the Veterans' Administration and his GI Bill of Rights) and on his duty to register with his local Selective Service (draft) board and share with them his discharge paperwork. It also instructed him on how to wear his uniform now that he had left the service and on the proper wearing of rank and medals/ribbons earned. In the foreword to the War Department's November 1944 version titled "Information for Soldiers: Going Back to Civilian Life," it reminds the service members:

> Our country was founded by men and women who were willing to fight for its freedom. It has remained free because, when the need arose, new generations were willing to fight and, if necessary, to die for what they loved. Our liberty is a precious thing. By your service in this war you have done your share to safeguard liberty for yourself, for your family, and for the Nation. You have helped to preserve it for those generations yet to come.[6]

A version issued jointly by the War and Navy Departments in February 1946 states, "When you return to the duties and responsibilities of civilian life, you take with you the good wishes of those who were in the service with you. You can always be proud that you were once a member of America's armed forces."[7] Elated to be home, ready to start a family, and anxious to find work, these men and women returned to the United States to families and communities also changed by war and having lived through the death of loved ones, unpredictability, austerity, and the hardships of life alone while the veteran was away. However, as these veterans came home by ship, rail, bus, and automobile, they were different men no matter how breezy the rhetoric and exhortations of the "Going Back to Civilian Life" pamphlets. What were these men bringing back home with them? How had they changed?

The men and women who returned home from World War II had been profoundly transformed by their experiences. Having engaged in a broadly conventional war against brutal nation-states, they had adapted to the exigencies of combat. Having become part of the large military force that had fought these wars, they had adapted to the demands of military hierarchy and rank, the communal living of shared sacrifice, and the uniformity of service. They had also adjusted to injury, death, and loss, and to chaos, privation, and uncertainty, and they had brought these adaptations and attitudes home with them. The veterans, like those of other conflicts, felt the changes acutely even if they could not define them precisely. The World War I Infantry officer and writer Siegfried Sassoon expresses these sentiments well in his novel *Memoirs of an Infantry Officer*, which was a thinly veiled memoir of his service in the war: "Emerging from my retrospective reverie, I felt that this had made the past seem very peculiar. People weren't the same as they used to be, or else I had changed. Was it because I had experienced something that they couldn't share or imagine?"[8] Vietnam War veteran William Jayne expresses similar views: "I had developed skills and personality traits that protected me both physically and mentally while in Vietnam: patience, an informed sense of night vision, doggedness, humorous bravado and cynicism."[9]

These changes were also seen by informed observers such as World War I veteran and sociologist Willard Waller and historian Dixon Wecter. Waller expresses these views about the returning war veteran:

> When war ends, the soldier, disillusioned and bitter, tries to find the road back, and does not always succeed. He knows the realities of war; he has adjusted his morality to the exigencies of war; he finds it hard to interest himself in the routine of civilian life; he misses the comradeship of the army; he had learned not to regard conventional sexual morality too seriously; all in all, the returned soldier is a disorganizing influence in society.[10]

Waller highlights the sense of disillusionment some veterans felt; he mentions how many missed the comradeship of service, how they found civilian life largely uninteresting, and how their morality had been altered by military and war service. He also mentions how they can have a "disorganizing influence in society" with the implications this can have on criminality, on personal morality and social life, and in politics, among other fields of endeavor. A key observation he makes is that the morality of the soldier had adapted to the exigencies of the war. These changes the veteran feels intensely are rooted in sensible adjustments to war to help him survive and win.[11]

Dixon Wecter, who wrote a study on returning war veterans drawn from the letters and diaries of participants in the Revolutionary War, Civil War, and First World War, observes the following: "So far as the soldier has borne the heat of battle, his training in stoicism and the shock of modern warfare have frozen his emotions, left him with a numbness that for a while sets him apart from volatile civilians, with their boastfulness, optimism, and vindictiveness."[12] This adoption of "stoicism" and "numbness" is another adjustment the veteran makes, partly due to self-selection, partly learned from training, but mostly strengthened through its necessity in combat in order to act calmly in the face of danger and in the presence of death and injury. Wecter further states:

> The man of smallest education, poorest development of mind, is apt to be most brutalized by war; the soldier deeply believing in what he is fighting for, most uplifted. Those who are spared take back from the battlefield certain convictions that help to shape their behavior in civil life. The best and worst in human nature, as everybody knows, appear under every mass ordeal from a sinking ship to a bitter war. A religious man comes home with new dependence upon the faith that has seen him through. But the skeptic often returns more fatalistic, the indifferent more callous.[13]

All of these adaptions to war and combat—such as aggression, numbness, and strong feelings of comradeship, among many others—were, as the psychologist Jonathan Shay states in his book *Odysseus in America: Combat Trauma and the Trials of Homecoming*, "the persistence into civilian life of adaptations that allowed the veteran to survive in battle."[14] More will be made of these combat adaptations later, but for the veteran, his process of adjusting to the relatively stable life of the civilian world takes place in a far larger context than what had happened to him on his deployment. Every veteran is a product of the social, historical, economic, personal, political, and literary context within which they grew up and served. These factors also impact how he processes his experiences, how he understands what he has gone through, and why he reacts as he does upon returning home.

A comprehensive series of large sample surveys of the attitudes of combat infantrymen during World War II by the U.S. Army provides additional insights into the views of these new war veterans. The research was eventually published in four volumes for public release in 1949 with the common title of *The American Soldier*. The books covered "Adjustment during Army Life" and "Combat and Its Aftermath," as well as "Experiments on Mass Communication" and "Measurement and Prediction." The research provided key insights into the thinking of U.S. service members and helped inform senior leader decision making within the U.S. Army. Many of the studies delved into "Combat Motivations among Ground Troops," "Problems Related to the Control of Fear," views on "The Aftermath of Hostilities," and "Attitudes before Combat and Behavior in Combat." The surveys indicated wide support for the goals of the United States with respect to defeating the Japanese Empire: "If we seek to define the area of consensus with regard to the war among Americans, both in and out of the Army, it lies simply in the undebatable assumptions that the Japanese attack on Pearl Harbor meant war, and that once in the war the United States had to win."[15] Broad acceptance of the need to win was shared by both soldiers and the American public. Having joined the armed forces to defeat Japan and Germany, Americans naturally disliked the restrictions of military life—from its chain of command and hierarchy to the limits on freedom it imposed and the general austerity of living conditions—but understood their necessity to achieve U.S. objectives. The study indicated that "[l]oving American freedom, they [the veterans] chafed under the authoritarianism and social customs of an institution [the U.S. military], which, though alien to democratic ways of life, was an agency for preserving those ways of life."[16]

These restrictions were felt acutely by members of the U.S. Army and were their greatest sources of grievance: "[M]uch of the dissatisfaction with the Army current among the men who comprised it could be traced to resentment of the deprivations—whether material comforts, symbols of status, or loss of freedom of action."[17] One way some soldiers compensated for these deprivations was to claim a higher distinction of social status if they were in the combat arms or served on the front line. Front-line soldiers "claimed higher status than those who were taking less punishment, and cherished feelings of fierce, often bitter, pride."[18] These attitudes paralleled other distinctions marking those who served in the rear compared to those who served in the front. This "status hierarchy" served a role in "channelizing the aggressive tensions felt between front and rear."[19] The surveys also revealed that the soldiers who had served in the war were more inclined to lead in their communities upon returning home: "At the same time, also in the American tradition, they were expecting to be 'joiners'—in fact, to be more active in local community organizations than before the war."[20] While most of the research focused on the problems faced by the U.S. Army during the war, these interesting insights into attitudes that manifested themselves toward the end of the war are instructive. There was clear agreement on the goals of the war; soldiers understood the need to subordinate individual interests to the broader good, they made distinctions between those who served in combat compared to those who hadn't, and they sought to become active in their communities even as they struggled with their experiences.

The men and women who served in World War II were part of a broad, national effort focused on total victory against the governments of Japan and Germany. They returned home in triumph and ticker-tape parades as well as to the accolades and good feelings of a triumphant nation. Most had been drafted, but many had volunteered, and they joined a small prewar active-duty force in the War and Navy Departments to wage the global campaign of victory. Approximately 70 percent served in the U.S. Army (including the U.S. Army Air Forces), 26 percent in the U.S. Navy, and 4 percent in the U.S. Marine Corps with roughly 73 percent of military personnel serving overseas.[21] Victory was clearly defined, although arduous to achieve; the veterans came from a broadly industrialized society with a large rural and farming population and were restricted in what they could communicate home through official censorship and then did so largely through letters. They also came from a society of relatively fixed gender roles, creating certain expectations of behavior, to which they were often held accountable when they returned. Unlike the veterans of World War I, they returned to a federal government ready to assist their transition to civilian life through robust assistance programs such as the GI Bill, loans for houses, and aid to start businesses, among other entitlements, which were administrated in large part by a greatly expanded Veterans Administration. Virtually all combat units were male, and the vast majority of combatants had European ancestry. They were also part of a U.S. military bureaucracy that had grown sharply during the war, and they also knew their tours would continue until the war was won or the United States had lost.

As they returned, the veterans began to have a direct and significant impact on American life, and the legacy of their service left an indelible imprint on U.S. culture. The number of American Legion and Veterans of Foreign Wars posts skyrocketed as did the number of military surplus stores. Literature began to reflect their war service as veteran authors published their first memoirs, fiction, and other works often based upon their wartime experiences. Others entered public office and, as the decades proceeded, were elected to every office in the land including the presidency. As time went on, the war eventually came to be captured in a few key reference points and in the names of certain leaders. Pearl Harbor endured, but so did the Battle of the Bulge, Midway, and Normandy. Names such as Eisenhower, Patton, Marshall, and McArthur were readily referenced. Books such as *The Naked and the Dead* by Norman Mailer, *Catch-22* by

Joseph Heller, *Slaughterhouse-Five* by Kurt Vonnegut, and *Battle Cry* by Leon Uris, all written by veterans, shaped the culture of remembering the conflict. Movies such as *The Longest Day*, *Patton*, *Midway*, and *The Great Escape* also influenced the collective memory of the war and, through the medium of film, privileged certain narratives over others. The totality of these changes crafted the myths and legends of the conflict and impacted how it was remembered. As firsthand participants in the war passed away, these reference points became the "history" of the conflict in the minds of most Americans and impacted future generations.

The Vietnam War

The roughly 2.7 million war veterans who returned home from fighting in the Vietnam War had expectations of what the war would be like, how the United States would support their efforts, and how they would be greeted upon returning home, which were based on the World War II era.[22] This "imagined war-in-his-head," as the author and World War II and Korean War Marine veteran Samuel Hynes puts it, was what the war veteran expected war to be like based on the movies, books, popular history, and collective memory of his country. These veterans quickly determined that the nature of the Vietnamese insurgency was entirely different from the German and Japanese militaries: "Philip Caputo writes in his prologue to *A Rumor of War*: 'I have found myself wishing that I had been the veteran of a conventional war, with dramatic campaigns and historic battles for subject matter instead of a monotonous succession of ambushes and fire-fights.'"[23] The veteran soon learned that however committed he was to the conflict, support on the home front for it was soft, and, eventually, the public came to oppose it altogether. Further, he was better able to communicate with the home front through recorded tape cassettes and phone calls, and his war was less of a mystery to his fellow Americans due to greater media coverage. The units he served in were now integrated and full of draftees, although now the U.S. military, and the army in particular, had large active-duty forces that could carry the burden. While he was away, society was going through profound changes, such as the civil rights movement and women's rights, causing long-held views on gender roles and race to be reimagined. Many of these veterans returned home from the war as part of regular rotations versus staying until the war was won, in part because the institutional capacity and careerism of the U.S. military required greater and broader participation in the war from the military as an institution, among other factors. The veteran also had to adapt to a hidden enemy who used an altogether different strategy than direct combat, did not generally wear a uniform, and used ambush tactics, assassination, and booby-traps to attack his forces. This strategy required a different set of skills for the veteran to develop to fight an enemy who avoided direct combat. Finally, the veterans of the war, even though they won the battles they had fought, had to resign themselves to defeat when the South Vietnamese government fell to North Vietnamese military forces in 1975.

As these veterans transitioned to civilian life, they too had a dramatic effect on American culture, politics, literature, history, and society. Defeat caused disillusionment and bitterness. Loss prompted a search for scapegoats as well as heroes. Debates raged over what should have been done, what strategies should have been pursued, and who was to blame for defeat. The veterans who returned participated in no victory parades and were often made to feel ashamed of their time in uniform and for their service to their country. Literature provided an outlet for many veterans to process their experiences, such as the memoirs *If I Die in a Combat Zone* by Tim O'Brien or *A Rumor of War* by Philip Caputo or in novels such as *Fields of Fire* by James Webb, *The 13th Valley* by John Del Vecchio, and *Paco's Story* by Larry Heinemann. Movies such as *Full Metal Jacket*, *Platoon*, *The Deer Hunter*, and *Rambo* channeled these ongoing debates about the war and what should have been done. Names such as McNamara, Westmoreland, Kerrey, Webb, and McCain became well known but so did Fonda and Calley. In politics, Vietnam veterans began to run for office, channeling their experiences on behalf of their country overseas in city council chambers, the halls of statehouses, Congress, and races for the presidency. The roles and expectations of women had started to change, and many veterans were uncertain how to navigate these new developments while others welcomed the new opportunities it provided.

They had likewise adapted to the insurgency itself not only with respect to how to fight its armed wing that hid within the civilian population but also regarding "the other war" of political action, propaganda, and assassination. In addition, they returned to an economy that was beginning to go through stagflation and an industrial base that was starting to shift to the southern and western portions of the United States while being reinvented and out-competed by the information and services revolution as well as foreign competition. As the United States grappled with defeat, nostalgia for World War II increased as the country sought a return to a sense of victory and hopefulness. As new generations came of age born at the end of the Vietnam War or after its conclusion, the debates about the war—how it was remembered and how it was represented in U.S. culture and in politics—influenced the thoughts of a new generation on the nature of war. Simultaneously, they were also influenced by how World War II was recalled, especially as it was remembered years later as the "Good War," which created this odd mix of loss and victory coexisting in U.S. culture. However much the Gulf War addressed the ability of the U.S. military to win wars, these two dominant strains of the legacies of World War II and Vietnam buffeted a new generation that confronted the attacks of 9/11 and participated in the invasion of Iraq.

The Afghan and Iraq War Generation

"But all was not right with the spirit of the men who came back. Something was wrong. They put on civilian clothes again, looked to their mothers and wives very much like the young men who had gone. . . . But they had not come back the same men. Something had altered in them. They were subject to queer moods, queer tempers, fits of profound depression alternating with a restless desire for pleasure. Many of them were easily moved to passion when they lost control of themselves. Many were bitter in their speech, violent in opinion, frightening. For some time while they drew their unemployment pensions, they did not make any effort to get work for the future. . . . Young soldiers who had been very skilled with machine-guns, trench-mortars, hand-grenades, found that they were classed with the ranks of unskilled labor in civil life."

—PHILIP GIBBS, *NOW IT CAN BE TOLD*, 547–48

The generation that answered the nation's call to serve after the attacks by al-Qaeda on the United States on September 11, 2001, and the decision to invade Iraq in 2003 were shaped by a number of social, historical, political, cultural, and institutional factors that influenced their return home. As of September 2019, approximately 775,000 members of the U.S. military had served in Afghanistan, and from 2003 to 2011, roughly one million had served in Iraq.[24] The veterans who returned had grown up on the legacies of the Vietnam War as well as those of World War II as these were the "wars in their head" they used to frame and contextualize their experiences. Their deployments to Afghanistan were motivated by the patriotism of having seen their country attacked, and their service in Iraq, a war started for different reasons, was considered honorable because their goal was to remove a dictator who had threatened the United States. The veterans served in multiple tours spread out over twenty years and were all volunteers. In Afghanistan alone, for example, approximately 28,267 veterans had served five or more tours by 2019.[25] They participated in combat as well as in counterinsurgency and adapted to the demands of fighting an insurgency, undertaking reconstruction and development activities, as well as good governance efforts, and helping train indigenous security forces. They mediated tribal disputes, drilled wells and built schools and clinics, performed countless meetings with local leaders, and helped administer villages, towns, and cities. As the U.S. military adapted to the unique demands of counterinsurgency warfare, the soldiers, sailors, airmen, and Marines who served there adapted as well. As they returned, a number of factors impacted and served to contextualize their process of adjusting back to civilian life, many of which they may have only vaguely been aware of at the time. Chief among these are five unifying themes that shape, define, and frame the returning veteran's experience: (1) the rise of the "professional" military state, (2) the shift to an all-volunteer military, (3) the development of a postmodern and postindustrial world, (4) the moral complexities of prolonged counter-insurgency wars in Muslim countries, and (5) the redefinition and de-legitimatization of masculinity.

The Rise of the "Professional" Military State

> *"I'd like . . . to have two armies: one for display with lovely guns, tanks, little soldiers, staffs, distinguished and doddering Generals, and dear little regimental officers who would be deeply concerned over their General's bowel movements or their Colonel's piles, an army that would be shown for a modest fee on every fairground in the country. The other would be the real one, composed entirely of young enthusiasts in camouflage battledress, who would not be put on display, but from whom impossible efforts would be demanded and to whom all sorts of tricks would be taught. That's the army in which I should like to fight."*

> —JEAN LARTÉGUY, *THE CENTURIONS*, 306

It is difficult to imagine a time in our country's history when the size of the U.S. military was modest, when its share of the federal budget was relatively small, and, when needed, a small active-duty component would be augmented by large numbers of volunteer units and conscripts. The rise of the modern U.S. military following the end of World War II grew out of the merger between the War and Navy Departments as part of the National Security Act of 1947. In 1939, for example, the U.S. Army and U.S. Navy had 189,839 soldiers and 125,202 sailors, respectively.[26] Just eight years later, U.S. Army numbers were at 990,000 soldiers and the U.S. Navy at 484,000 sailors.[27] In the fiscal year of 2019, there were approximately 478,000 soldiers and 335,400 sailors in the U.S. military.[28] These large standing active-duty forces stood in great contrast to the history of the U.S. military wherein forces were generated for a conflict and then, just as soon, demobilized and returned to civilian life. The practical effects of this were that careers and careerism became a central element of the modern military establishment. The need to recruit, train, promote, recognize, and provide upward mobility for uniformed personnel created institutional needs that have not always aligned with the requirements for success in the wars in Afghanistan and Iraq. The institutionalization of the U.S. military provided stability, expertise, and depth to U.S. forces, but it also created parochialism, risk aversion, a bias toward conventional warfare, and rampant careerism. These tendencies became readily apparent and were revealed most dramatically during wartime.

As the Vietnam veteran Edward L. King, author of *The Death of the Army: A Pre-Mortem*, puts it, "By the time the Vietnam situation came along, career objectives had largely superseded the desire for selfless service to the nation as a motivation for many career officers. . . . For the first time loyalty to the Army began to take on more importance in an officer's career than dedication to the country and the public good."[29] There is a reason many draftees in the Vietnam War referred to career army officers as "lifers" because so many of them appeared to be more focused on their careers and next assignments than the jobs and mission they had to perform while in country. Similarly, the dual missions of deterring nation-states and being prepared to fight them, such as the Soviet Union, while fighting an insurgency created conflicting institutional instincts within the U.S. Army, particularly as one was prioritized more over the other.[30] This careerist lens also led to short-termism in thinking when it came to strategy in Vietnam as well as a preference for combat as easily measured metrics, such as enemy killed in action and combat achievements, enhanced careers when more important counterinsurgency metrics were difficult to measure. This careerism made the wars in Afghanistan and Iraq that much more difficult as constant rotations of personnel, an inability and reluctance to adapt to the unique demands of insurgency, and an emphasis on "combat," which facilitated promotions, versus a balanced approach of "combat and building local forces," prolonged both wars unnecessarily.

A second aspect of the rise of the "professional" U.S. military was the shift to an all-volunteer force in 1973 and the development of, as Rutgers University professor of history Jennifer Mittelstadt puts it, the "military welfare state."[31] The challenge of constantly recruiting volunteers, especially in the U.S. Army, at the scale that was required and retaining currently serving personnel was especially difficult following the Vietnam War. Appeals to patriotism and selfless service yielded only so many recruits, and so U.S. Army leaders in particular sought to expand social welfare and other benefits beyond the small active-duty officer corps to include enlisted personnel as well as the families of all members.

> In all areas of army benefits, the most fulsome support represented the privilege of rank. But the army's chiefs of staff and their personnel deputies of the 1970s redefined that privilege, and extended these benefits and supports to the entire army. They undertook a sort of full "officerization" of the force that brought soldiers of every rank, and their families, into a universal system of support.[32]

Historically, social welfare programs had been "crafted for veterans as rewards for faithful service or compensation for loss. Their political success depended on differentiating the veteran from the civilian and elevating him as worthy of entitlement."[33] This was particularly the case in the conscript militaries of the Civil War, World War I, and World War II.[34] With large standing forces that had to be constantly replenished as members retired or left the service, the U.S. Army was "[n]o longer able to compel people to join and remain, it had to convince them."[35] This situation stands in contrast to the other services that rarely relied upon the draft, even during the worst years of the Vietnam War, and were able to attract recruits based on other factors: "The air force—perceived as modern and technology-driven—never relied on the draft, for example, and the navy and the marines only exceedingly rarely."[36] The practical effect of the development of this system, as well as the mentality that went with it, is that a sense of entitlement started to pervade the U.S. military. Mittelstadt states this situation well: "During the 1970s and 1980s, the army's senior officers and its civilian leaders drew sharp lines differentiating military social and economic supports from civilian ones."[37] However sharp these lines might have been, they had, cumulatively, a corrosive effect on the U.S. military. Constant rotations and the need to move up in one's career, along with a sense that the U.S. military owed the member certain entitlements, further inhibited the ability of the institution to readily adapt to the unique requirements of victory in Afghanistan and Iraq. These benefits also continued the process of the military feeling as if it was separate from civilian society, perhaps even better, and that entitlement meant more than sacrifice. It was another contributing factor to how the wars were fought, more so for the convenience of the bureaucracy versus the bureaucracy adapting to the needs of the war effort.

"Thank You for Your Service": The Understanding and the Death of Cowardice

> *"I was particularly impressed that night by Lieutenant Shenkel. A man who comes out of battle does not get over it for a long time afterward. I went with him that night to his billet, 'the billet of the feather bed.' While he turned in, I heard the story of the attack on Hill 204. A story of agony and pain, of death in the furnace. . . . A wonderful tale, told simply, but a story of mad adventure. Shenkel was still alive by a series of miracles. His face was flushed, and his eyes wide and brilliant with excitement. He was a different man. Something had come to him which had not yet come to us. It was the trial of battle. No one who passes through that is ever quite the same again."*
>
> —HERVEY ALLEN, *TOWARD THE FLAME*, 25

> *"It is easy to understand why the soldier hates the young man of his own age who manages somehow to escape military service."*
>
> —WILLARD WALLER, *THE VETERAN COMES BACK*, 98

The phrase "Thank you for your service" is a legacy of the Vietnam War, when many returning veterans were vilified by certain segments of our population for performing their duty to the country. In an era with conscription when many young men were susceptible to the draft, the concerted effort to delegitimize military service and to create shame within Vietnam veterans was a horrendous episode in our nation's recent history. The phrase itself was not used in any systematic manner until after the attacks of 9/11 and then only after a few years once multiple deployments became commonplace. It has now become a catchphrase for civilians whenever they see anyone in a military uniform, but for many war veterans, it is an expression that does not sit well with them. The ending of the draft severed a social contract of responsibility between the citizens of the United States and their duty to protect the Republic. While the vast majority of Americans would never be called upon to perform that duty, they were connected to the nation and each other through a shared sense of responsibility. Much like performing jury duty and voting, the obligation to be eligible to serve—to one day be expected to do so—crafted a sense of community obligation and identity. Having been freed from this obligation, many civilians who use the saying appear to want the best things for veterans, in a sense, but a veteran often hears something else.

The feelings of misgiving that many post-9/11 veterans have for the expression "thank you for your service" is an outgrowth of the attacks in 2001 that were against the whole United States, not just a subset of patriots who decided to do something about it. It was a patriotic war that all Americans had an obligation to do something about. The severing of this link between the obligation to serve as part of a society and wanting to serve was significantly strained as multiple tours became the norm in Afghanistan as well as in Iraq. These feelings were strongly felt by many veterans due to the somewhat closed nature of the military as those who volunteered for the armed forces and those who made it a career felt more apart from the civilian population than aligned with it. This was also the case because certain parts of the country and certain ethnic and racial groups joined the military at higher rates, making this sense of difference feel all the more pronounced. Some veterans, upon hearing "thank you for your service," would like to ask, "When are you joining up to do your part?" This feeling is felt very strongly whenever well-meaning civilians, including journalists, express sad misgivings about the death of a veteran in the wars by highlighting how many tours he had undertaken. This tone of victimhood exacerbates the veteran's frustration since he does not see himself as a victim, and the statement the civilian expresses seemingly exonerates them from not having served since they uttered words of concern for the veteran.

A secondary effect of the shift to an all-volunteer military is that increasingly large segments of the civilian population as well as the military began to see each other not as fellow Americans but as the "other." As the number of veterans in the civilian population dwindled over time, and as the number of military bases declined, concentrated in certain sections of the United States, and became more self-contained (e.g., shopping, housing, and medical support were plentiful), general knowledge of the military in civilian society was reduced. Similarly, as the U.S. military increasingly selected from narrower segments of the U.S. population and the sons and daughters of serving members also joined, the military became more inward focused as well, which was further buttressed by careerism. One example of this estrangement was in 2006 when an article was published in the *Los Angeles Times* titled "Warriors and Wusses" by Joel Stein.[38] Stein's principal argument is that the American people should not support "the troops" who were serving in Iraq because he did not support the war, referring to it as "American imperialism." The troops, as he sees it, are "[a]n army of people making individual moral choices . . . but an army of people ignoring their morality is horrifying." In his mind, support for the troops translated into support for imperialism, and since the troops had joined the military knowing they would serve in Iraq, they must also be supportive of imperialism. Setting aside his tortured logic, the language Stein used to describe the military was instructive. He says, "I don't support our troops," and "I'm sure I'd like the troops. They seem gutsy, young and up for anything," and "We know we're sending recruits to do our dirty work, and we want to seem grateful." The structure of his statements clearly indicates he does not see those serving their country as his fellow Americans but as members of some "other" tribe of people whom he appears to respect but fundamentally does not. They are "warriors," and he is, as he puts it, a member of the "wusses."

This sense of separateness and "other" is not confined to the civilian world but also exists in parts of the U.S. military. The book *On Combat* by Dave Grossman, who served as a lieutenant colonel in the U.S. Army, introduces a vignette that has been adopted by some portions of the military:

> If you have no capacity for violence then you are a healthy productive citizen: a sheep. If you have a capacity for violence and no empathy for your fellow citizens, then you have defined an aggressive sociopath—a wolf. But what if you have a capacity for violence, and a deep love for your fellow citizens? Then you are a sheepdog, a warrior, someone who is walking the hero's path.[39]

The three groups of sheep, wolves, and sheepdogs, and how the sheepdog is set apart from the sheep, reinforce the view that veterans are not like the sheep and, as a species, are more like the wolves since they are derived from the lineage of dogs; in other words, veterans are inherently different from the people they protect. This formulation speaks to the strong feeling some members of the military have that—through multiple deployments, the somewhat closed world of the U.S. military, and a feeling of a lack of shared risk among citizens for service in war—they are not only apart from but also superior to their fellow Americans. There is also a tone of resentment in this formulation that, already feeling like an outcast, the veteran "sheepdog" must out of a sense of duty protect his nation while the civilian "sheep" sit passively by waiting to be rescued. These phrases of "sheepdogs" and "wolves" have become a part of the post-military veteran subculture and frequently appear on T-shirts sold by veteran-owned companies.

The shift to an all-volunteer military in 1973 was an outgrowth of something I refer to as "the understanding" between the military and civilian society. In return for setting aside the draft, the U.S. military was allowed to attract those who wanted to serve in the armed forces versus compelling those who didn't. Civilian society, in return, would support the military in a general sense, and not attack it as some elements of it had done during the Vietnam War, and show respect for it as an institution. This arrangement endured largely because it was never fundamentally challenged by the relatively small wars that followed the end of the Vietnam War. The prolonged nature of the conflicts in Afghanistan and Iraq caused some members of the military to resent the fact they had had to deploy so many times and the burdens and risks of deployment were not being broadly shared by the public. As the post-9/11 U.S. military fought in Afghanistan and Iraq, they were regarded as heroes for having done so, but not many of their fellow citizens felt any compunction to do their part other than to offer general support and the occasional "thank you for your service." The cumulative effects of these shifts in attitude are that parts of the civilian population know little about the military and are unable or unwilling to hold it accountable for its shortfalls. They also often elevate members of the military into one of three categories: heroes, victims, or psychopaths. Additionally, some members of the military resent some civilians and aspects of civilian society that express support for the troops even though they never shouldered the burden of the wars as fellow Americans even as a small subset of their countrymen continue to do so.

"What Did You Do in the War?"

> *"It was difficult to sit with a group of friends and hear some 'Stateside commando' complain bitterly about how his corporal had made him carry out the garbage."*

—E. B. SLEDGE, *CHINA MARINE:*
AN INFANTRYMAN'S LIFE AFTER WORLD WAR II, 131

"When I was growing up on Air Force bases, I could read the story of a man's service in the hieroglyphics of his decorations."

—B. G. BURKETT AND GLENNA WHITLEY,
*STOLEN VALOR: HOW THE VIETNAM GENERATION
WAS ROBBED OF ITS HEROES AND ITS HISTORY*, 353

Whenever a military veteran encounters a fellow veteran in uniform, an unconscious eye-flutter takes place where they quickly scan the military ribbons/medals of the veteran to get a sense of their career. The man's personal decorations are at the top, and his campaign ribbons, if he has any, are toward the middle. The distinctive ribbons of Operation Enduring Freedom, Operation Iraqi Freedom, the Global War on Terror Service Ribbon, the Operation Inherent Resolve Ribbon, and the NATO Ribbons for service in Afghanistan and Iraq stand out to a war veteran's eyes. The number of stars attached to each ribbon, bronze or silver, are also quickly counted and indicate how many campaign phases the veteran served in. Having satisfied his initial curiosity, the veteran also glances at the personal decorations received by the veteran. Does he possess a Combat Infantryman's Badge, a Combat Action Ribbon, a Bronze Star with "V" for valor, for example, or perhaps a Purple Heart for wounds earned in combat? All these factors weigh on a veteran's mind as he meets his contemporaries, but it is the peer who has not served that garners most of his attention. "How is it that you have not served?" he quietly ponders. What is it that prevented you from serving all these twenty years? A veteran who has not served must also be asking these questions and be prepared with ready-made answers.

One of the fundamental distinctions made by members of the U.S. military is between those who have served in a war zone and those who haven't. It is a difference that means, as Vietnam War veteran and Navy Cross recipient Karl Marlantes coined, you are a member of "the club" of war veterans or you're not. Allowances are made for those who have just joined the service as well as those, while intending to go, are at the mercy of the rotational schedule of units into theater. However, in light of the war in Afghanistan going on for twenty years and in Iraq for eight years during Operation Iraqi Freedom and seven thus far during Operation Inherent Resolve, which is the campaign against the terrorist group ISIS, some do ponder why others haven't gone. The World War II and Korean War veteran Samuel Hynes expresses this sentiment well: "Wars sometime unite societies while they're being fought, but in the end they change and divide them. A generation that has lived through a war is different from one that hasn't; and within a war generation, those who fought stand apart from those who didn't."[40] This feeling is felt particularly strongly by many veterans in light of the attacks of 9/11 where there was no doubt that the obligation of service to the nation needed to be fulfilled.

> Friction often appeared between the silver stripe of home service and the gold of overseas. Privates at the ship's rail, seeing officers on the dock with three or four silver stripes, would give the Bronx cheer and shout "Yellow!" Some recalled the joke about the spurs on the boots of officers who had fought the Battle of Washington—spurs, it was said, whose purpose was to keep their feet from sliding off the desk. These officers in turn complained that in the street overseas men passed them without saluting.[41]

This anecdote highlights the differences between those who served in war and those who served stateside, but even in the midst of war, there are distinctions that are made between those who had "really served" and those who hadn't. World War I veteran and sociologist Willard Waller expresses this view well: "It is easy to understand why the soldiers hate the young man of his own age who manages somehow to escape military service. . . . Scarcely less violent is the soldier's hatred for that other soldier who managed to wrangle for himself a safe position behind the lines."[42] These feelings are felt particularly strongly by veterans with multiple tours who even sometimes look upon those with one tour with some suspicion.

These feelings are strong because war service changes a person in some fundamental ways, and repeated tours make these changes enduring: "Any man who had been on active service had an unfair advantage over those who hadn't. And the man who had really endured the War at its worst was everlastingly differentiated from everyone except his fellow soldiers."[43] This sense of having missed out on the war effort sometimes even leads those who haven't been to war to embellish their own records to approximate some of the affectations of the war veteran in order to fit in. It even leads to some veterans fabricating their records in cases of stolen valor (see chapter 8, "Stolen Valor and Fake Veterans"). Interestingly, there are also many members of the military who go out of their way not to deploy by feigning injuries; looking for safe, stateside assignments; and generally shirking from their responsibilities.

> The soldier who had not heard the shells scream was a somewhat different story. He was prone occasionally to imitate the veteran of the trenches, complaining of restlessness, boredom with war, jaded disillusion. But such phenomena were like a secondary rainbow. More often his brand of dissatisfaction came from having missed the big show, mixed with a dash of

envy as the men with gold stripes began to trickle home. To the latter belonged the glory, as no one could deny.[44]

This distinction between those who have gone to war and those who haven't endures after members of the military leave the service. In many veterans' organizations, a new social hierarchy often exists of those who had been to war and those who hadn't. Among those who had, there is a further distinction between those who had demonstrated valor and those who hadn't. This new rank structure replaces the formal one from their time in uniform when asserting one's rank in the service in civilian life would appear somewhat unsavory.

A second distinction veterans make is between those who have been to war and, among men of their age, civilians who haven't. If the feeling of national responsibility and service is felt strongly by many members of the military, especially after the nation was attacked, a veteran of multiple tours in such a war feels it even more strongly. No longer feeling a sense of obligation or even a connection to the country through the introduction of the all-volunteer military, many civilians are spectators to the protection of their own nation. They have missed out on the big calling of their generation and the profound shaping event of their era, and they have felt no sense of duty to play a part and contribute to the great effort.

General Patton, for example, drew on the familiar British recruiting poster to encourage his troops as they prepared for the Normandy invasion: "When it's all over and you're at home once more, you can thank God that twenty years from now, when you're sitting around the fireside with your grandson on your knee, and he asks you what you did in the war, you won't have to shift him to the other knee, cough, and say, 'I shoveled shit in Louisiana.'"[45]

Wecter puts this idea well: "[T]hese boys who grew into men in the army found that a strange barrier set them apart from civilians—from those who had never known the ways of camp and field, and ordeal by fire."[46] This feeling of estrangement can also lead to bitterness among some veterans who see the men of their age, who did not serve, move ahead in their civilian careers and lives when the veteran was sacrificing for his country. Sometimes these feelings can lead to a view that some civilians, especially military age males, were cowards for having avoided the fight. Sledge expresses this view upon returning home from the Pacific campaign in World War II: "We sat around and I caught up on local news—who was already home from the war and who had used political influence to stay safely in the United States. . . . [N]ever become embittered because many other men had safe, comfortable war assignments, all too often obtained through political influence. That's the way of cowards in this world."[47] These feelings are further buttressed by masculine gender expectations of protecting the weak and defeating threats. As this expectation changed following the development of women's rights, so, too, did the societal expectation that men had a responsibility to do their part in defending the nation. Although it was an ideal, while not always met, it did serve to anchor societal expectations that led to personal behavior consistent with its direction.

Postindustrial Society

> *"The boy who comes back from the wars is not the same boy who went away, and the society to which he returns is not the one he left behind."*

—WILLARD WALLER, *THE VETERAN COMES BACK*, 81

American society went through a profound shift starting in the late 1960s until the 2000s that impacted the economy, cultural and societal values, politics, and individual freedom and equality of its citizens. The move from a modern society to a postmodern society principally came about from a change in the economy from industrial to a postindustrial services economy, which also prompted a profound shift in the values of the country. The values of a modern or modernizing society are rooted in a world of uncertainty, whether it's security, health, nutrition, or employment, and it is often characterized as survivalist in orientation.

> Societies that emphasize survival values have relatively low levels of subjective well-being, report relatively poor health, and are low on interpersonal trust, relatively intolerant of outgroups, and low on support for gender equality. They emphasize materialist values, have relatively high levels of faith in science and technology, and are relatively low on environmental activism and relatively favorable to authoritarian government. Societies that rank high on self-expression values tend to have the opposite preferences on all of these topics. Overall, self-expression values reflect an emancipative and humanistic ethos, emphasizing human autonomy and choice.[48]

These values manifest themselves by zero-sum politics where disputes often revolve around the distribution of resources or "who gets what and when." The societies of Afghanistan and Iraq, one premodern and the other somewhat modern, had the values of survival societies. They were traditional societies where patron-clients relationships mattered more than individual freedom. They were also very tribal in their orientation with respect to organization, values, and behavior where group identity and solidarity mattered more than individual freedom. Similarly, the values of the U.S. military mimic aspects of survival values in terms of small unit action, zero-sum solutions against the enemy but non-zero sum within the group, and other basic survival behavior.

As with most Western societies, though, as the U.S. economy shifted away from industry and toward services many of its values shifted as well. Self-expression values were put in place of survival values although they coexisted as new generations, not having known privation, assumed stability was a normal feature of life. This created what the political scientist Ronald Inglehart calls "a second syndrome of cultural and institutional changes emerg[ing] in which economic growth becomes less central, and there is rising emphasis on the quality of life and democratic political institutions."[49] A simple way to express this change is that in survival societies securing a job was paramount whereas in postindustrial societies an employee wondered more often than not whether the job was personally satisfying. Postindustrial society values include "tolerance, trust, emphasis on subjective well-being, civic activism and self-expression" due to "high levels of existential security and individual autonomy."[50] Contrast these values with this statement by World War II Marine veteran and noted memoirist E. B. Sledge: "We had all become hardened. We were out there, human beings, the most highly developed form of life on earth, fighting each other like wild animals."[51] This view provides some perspective on the transition of veterans from war to a postindustrial society. As the economy shifted, "[w]hat counts is not raw muscle power, or energy, but information."[52] Due to a greater emphasis on information and less of an emphasis on strength, women play a much larger role in service economies, and it's no coincidence that modern women's rights principally developed as these shifts took place in many Western countries. As the sociologist Daniel Bell puts it, "The fact is that a service economy is very largely a female-centered economy."[53]

While war veterans have had to adapt to the conditions of war and fighting an insurgency as well as serving in the institution of the U.S. military, they have also had to adapt to the local cultures of Afghanistan and Iraq. The veterans who were often the most successful in these wars not only studied local culture but also learned how to influence it, to read the subtle signs of tribal politics, and to understand how communities operated and how power was created, wielded, and lost. In many respects, the counterinsurgency strategies pursued in Afghanistan and Iraq later in the wars adopted their strategies for stability from local communities and used them to fight the Taliban, al-Qaeda, and nationalist groups more effectively. Many of these veterans have adopted the survivalist and cultural values of the countries they have lived in, and local culture has made a sizable impression on these veterans since they have had to understand it deeply in order to practice counterinsurgency more effectively. Many war veterans from Iraq and Afghanistan, upon returning home, struggle with this profound difference in societal values, which is also influenced by the generation of the veteran; older veterans tend to have more survivalist values than younger ones. The values the veteran has learned in the military, which mimic hunter-gatherer societal values, are reinforced by his deep exposure and need to operate within local culture in Afghanistan and Iraq. While many Americans are accustomed to working through formal institutions, the counterinsurgency war veteran prefers informal influence networks. When many Americans accept direct causes and effects, the counterinsurgency veteran sees indirect influence and indirect links and has become highly intuitive. The need to save face in these cultures also leads to indirect thinking and indirect strategies as well as a formalism in interpersonal relations. For many veterans of the wars in Afghanistan and Iraq, the transition from survivalist societies that are modernizing to a postindustrial society can be quite profound and disorienting. It is a conditioning factor that is not often spoken about and may sometimes have more of an effect on the veteran than his combat experiences in country.

The Moral Landscape of Counterinsurgency (COIN)

> *"Here, on the borders of death, life follows an amazingly simple course, it is limited to what is most necessary, all else lies buried in gloomy sleep;—in that lies our primitiveness and our survival."*

—ERICH MARIA REMARQUE, *ALL QUIET ON THE WESTERN FRONT*, 270

> *"Our conception of right and wrong are in fact almost altogether dependent upon the customs of the group to which we belong. . . . These basic standards, the mores, are the sacred customs which it is wrong to violate and right to follow."*
>
> —WILLARD W. WALLER, *ON THE FAMILY, EDUCATION, AND WAR: SELECTED WRITINGS,* 321

There is a war going on in the mind of each Afghanistan and Iraq military veteran, and it is due to the competing demands of (1) defeating the enemy and (2) enlisting the support of the population. Defeating the enemy, which generally entails killing him, requires a mind-set that dehumanizes him, sums up and de-legitimizes his goals, and generally seeks to vanquish his supporters and their cause. In a counterinsurgency environment, killing the enemy is part of the effort, but gaining the support of the population and helping them turn against the insurgency are more important. These competing demands were not always acknowledged in the war, and as the conflicts persisted and the U.S. military adapted to the operating conditions of both conflicts, a shift took place as the second goal was embraced more frequently because it was more effective and enduring. But each goal had innumerable tasks that had to be accomplished, which required adjustments from a conventional warfare mind-set focused on nation-state competitors to irregular warfare opponents in predominantly Muslim countries. Cultural understanding, partnering with indigenous leaders, building governance, mediating tribal disputes, and developing countries became the ready repertoire of the Afghan/Iraq veteran. These contradictory impulses of dehumanization (coldness) and humanization (empathy) coexisted within countless veterans fostering a more robust moral universe for many of them.

A second moral adaptation is the need to compartmentalize moral quandaries and to use information asymmetrically. Within the need to humanize the local population and to partner with indigenous forces is the requirement to adapt to foreign cultures, build rapport with community and security leaders, and navigate the complexities of tribal and local politics. The nature of insurgency continually puts veterans in these moral dilemmas, which also impacts their behavior once they return home. There are aspects of morality that are clearly bad or good in a wartime environment, but in operating within the cultures of Afghanistan and Iraq, subtleties of morality and complexities of human interaction required a more adroit handling of situations. Instead of seeing morality as black and white, bad or good, and operating along a linear line, it was better to see it as a networked set of relationships or even in concentric circles. One way of looking at it is this passage from British general John Bagot Glubb, who served alongside Arab tribes in the Middle East for thirty-six years from 1920 to 1956:

> Another aspect of tribal law is that the same crime differs according to the circumstances and the identity of the victim. To murder or rob a member of an enemy tribe (in the days of tribal war) was, of course, no crime at all. To kill a man of another but friendly tribe cost the murderer only seven camels in compensation. To kill a man of his own tribe would cost fifty camels and many other expenses. In either case, if the victim were at the time a guest of the murderer, the compensation would be quadrupled.[54]

These differing moralities based upon the nature of the crime and the relationship of the victim to the tribe as well as their social status creates many coexisting moralities and not one. This is not to say the veteran agrees with this unconventional morality, but the fact his local partners do is a feature he must grapple with in order to exert influence with the population and its leaders. The counterinsurgency veteran has to navigate these dilemmas constantly while still achieving his objectives. Additionally, as a member of the developed world, the veteran has to navigate the morality of the developing countries of Afghanistan and Iraq, which has a greater focus on zero-sum relationships, tribal values, traditional/premodern values, and different views on freedom and equality.

Many veterans have had to set aside their deep moral misgivings about the indigenous leaders they have had to partner with as part of counterinsurgency work as they built security, facilitated reconstruction and development, and bolstered good governance. Veterans of the campaign in Iraq, for example, had to partner with many tribal leaders in the western part of the country during the Anbar Awakening (2006–2008) as part of an effort to work with them against al-Qaeda in Iraq (AQI). Many of these same leaders had clearly been behind operations attacking U.S. forces and had American blood on their hands but, due to changing alliances and politics, became "allies" as part of anti-AQI operations. In Afghanistan, for example, a young Afghan boy around eleven years of age planted an improvised explosive device (IED) at night outside Forward Operating Base Cobra in the summer of 2005 on a road the Special Operations Forces (SOF) there often used. The device exploded as he emplaced it, and he lost both of his legs and an arm. The SOF forces there saved the boy's life, but the question is this: How do you feel about the situation? The young child was trying to kill U.S. forces, but since he was a boy and from the Kuchi, who are poor nomads, it might have been because the Taliban were threatening his family. Was his intention to kill the Americans or to save his family? Did the answer to either question matter to the widow of a soldier who might have been killed by the device? One gets a sense of the moral complexities of the war.

One final example is the governor of Uruzgan Province in southern Afghanistan, Jan Mohammed Khan, who was appointed by President Karzai in 2002 and was a member of his tribe. Through his control of the militia, his political influence, and his access to information as the key political figure in the province, he often, although it was not proven, killed his political opponents, all of whom had "problems" with the Taliban, who were always targeting them. The governor never experienced such attacks, which is the key indicator of motivation and intent in Afghanistan. However, U.S. forces had to work with the governor on reconstruction, development, and good governance projects on a regular basis. How does one reconcile working to achieve one goal of improving the lives of local Afghans while partnering with a leader who was killing innocent locals who opposed him politically?

The Post-Masculine Male

> *"War is a test—of courage, of manhood, of self—that they are anxious to pass; and it is a romantic one, beyond anything else that life is likely to offer them."*
>
> —SAMUEL HYNES, *THE SOLDIERS' TALE: BEARING WITNESS TO MODERN WAR*, 137

Throughout history men have performed the lion's share of combat, and in an era where physical strength, aggression, and teamwork were vital in war, the attributes of masculinity were, out of necessity, consistently validated. This was also true in civilian life where agrarian societies and subsistence living privileged male attributes, which continued on through the Industrial Revolution. These habits of living and operating sometimes became "truisms" in society, and generally defined gender roles became the norm in society. These various attributes and ways of living began to loosen in the West; for the United States, this would take place in the 1960s, as our economy transitioned from an industrial to a postindustrial economy or from smokestacks to kilobytes. Societal conditions also changed along with this economic shift, and the great discriminator between men and women, physical strength, became less important as computers and similar innovations changed the nature of work. These changes were also reflected in how war was waged as it, too, became more technologically focused and less dependent upon the physicality of its force. The mores of gender roles that existed during the mid-twentieth century created a set of responsibilities and rights that bound each gender to certain behaviors, roles, and expectations. While exceptions did exist to this gender "system," it was based upon clearly defined categories that attributed roles, responsibilities, and rights to its members.

The generations that largely fought in Afghanistan and Iraq grew up in the midst of these shifting gender roles, but as with many social changes, adjustments took time. Cultural background, education levels, and the degree to which local economies had shifted to a postindustrial service economy affected some of this process. The experience of war, as it has been throughout history, was a rite of passage for many men even as gender roles were in flux. The World War II veteran writer Norman Mailer speaks to this directly:

> Like most of my generation, I was obsessed by a complex of terrors and longings connected with the idea "War." "War" in this purely neurotic sense, meant The Test. The test of your courage, your maturity, of your sexual prowess. "Are you really a Man?" Subconsciously, I believe, I longed to be subjected to this test; but I also dreaded failure. I dreaded failure so much—indeed, I was so certain that I *should* fail—that, consciously, I denied my longing to be tested altogether. I denied my all-consuming morbid interest in the idea of "war."[55]

Connected to this "test" was also a cultural view of men as protectors and heroes, and in a war where your country had been attacked, these perspectives gained new currency. For the Vietnam generation, this standard was the actor John Wayne, and for the generation that served in Afghanistan and Iraq, Captain America, Rambo, and Arnold Schwarzenegger resonated particularly strongly. The World War II veteran Roger Tuttrup expresses this view well: "I wanted to be a hero, let's face it. I was havin' trouble in school. I was havin' trouble with my mother. They didn't know what to do. The war'd been goin' on for two years. I didn't wanna miss it, for Chrissake. I was an American. I was seventeen."[56] One soldier, Sergeant First Class Dillard Johnson, who received the Silver Star and wrote a memoir about his service in Iraq titled *Carnivore*, states the following: "'When I was growing up, everyone wanted to be an astronaut, a cowboy, or a firefighter. I wanted to be Sgt. Rock,' he said, referring to DC Comics' gritty WWII hero."[57] This masculine standard that many men had in their minds when they joined the service was validated by service in war wherein many traditional male attributes and living in a world that was almost exclusively male reacquainted men with those characteristics that the modern society of America had sought to reinvent.

Part of this effort to reimagine what masculinity meant was in reaction to the end of the Vietnam War. If being a man meant going to war, those who opposed it needed to reinvent that standard. The fact that this process occurred while the economy shifted from industrial and agrarian to postindustrial and information based while gender roles were in flux reinforced this trend. The Vietnam War veteran, Navy Cross recipient, and noted author Karl Marlantes summarizes some of these changes well:

> I'm talking about a basic attitude about a traditional male role: protecting the community. I'm worried that somewhere between the women's movement and the nation's reaction to the Vietnam War, this traditional role came to be viewed as obsolete, even déclassé. Too many men abandoned it. Today we expect the police to do everything.[58]

Similarly, the hero became the antihero, the antihero became the hero, and Vietnam War veterans followed suit in these assessments as well.

> For the Vietnam generation, "John Wayne" was the Hollywood war-in-their-heads, exposed and mocked by the real, bitter thing. It's a sign of how completely the old values had faded that Wayne, the hero of the Westerns and war movies that the Vietnam War generation had grown up on, and the embodiment of what seemed a particularly American kind of independent courage, had become a soldier's joke, an anti-hero, everybody's example of how *not* to fight a war.[59]

Another facet to these changes is that war service confers a special status on men, and in the competition of life, it can give a decided leg up whether it's finding a companion, securing a job, or getting elected, among other things. The human emotion of envy is very powerful, and many men who didn't serve in war resent the prestige, attention, and influence of the returned war veteran. This is especially so in professions that are not particularly physical. The Vietnam veteran Sam Brown captures this view well:

> For other men, not joining the Army left them with the distinct feeling that they had missed a critical "rite of passage" in coming to terms with their manhood. Understanding the long-term consequences of missing that ritual passage is beyond my capacity. But the fact that this feeling came

at a time when the very idea of manhood was rightfully being challenged by the feminist movement has to be factored into any new conceptualization by our culture of what it means to be a man. This is a take that seems to me to be as profound as any we will face in the next ten years.[60]

The rise of the term *beta male* in military circles, compared to *alpha male*, reinforces the view that these differences were being felt acutely by veterans. Many so-called beta males build a counter-narrative of the returned war veteran, playing off of stereotypes of their allegedly being less intelligent and more prone to violence, and they even question whether what they did was that important or difficult. They define themselves in opposition to the values of the war veteran. They are trying to make themselves feel better and to delegitimize the prestige of the war veteran in order to compete with him more effectively in the civilian economy.

Conclusion

While much of the writing about returning war veterans naturally focuses on their wartime and combat experiences as well as some aspects of their service in the U.S. military, the contexts within which these veterans were reared and served also affects how they process their experiences upon returning home. Repeatedly serving in predominantly Muslim countries that were heavily influenced by tribal values where moral complexity and ambiguity were the norm altered how these veterans viewed right and wrong. As volunteers in a highly developed, "professional," and bureaucratic military, their views were often influenced by the needs of their respective services as institutions versus the requirements of success in the wars in Afghanistan and Iraq. Further, their views on patriotism, service, and the social compact of the responsibilities of citizens to their republic underwent great strain as tours multiplied over twenty years. The experiences of these veterans in war also reacquainted them with the values and necessity of masculinity as small-unit action in dusty villages, urban hothouses, and green valleys revalidated male attributes even as their home society sought to redefine and delegitimize many aspects of them. Finally, the world of the counterinsurgency veteran in Afghanistan and Iraq is to immerse yourself in a society based upon survival and uncertainty where brutality, tribes, and the power of the warlord and the faction leader impact how well you live during what might be a very short life. As these veterans of the wars in Afghanistan and Iraq returned home, what other adaptions did they bring with them?

The Mind of the War Veteran   **2**

> *"I realized close combat had changed those of us who endured it—we were just plain different from other people through no fault of our own. We saw life through a different lens and always would."*
>
> —E. B. SLEDGE, CHINA MARINE:
AN INFANTRYMAN'S LIFE AFTER WORLD WAR II, 132

"I was still mentally and nervously organized for War. Shells used to come bursting on my bed at midnight, even though Nancy shared it with me; strangers in daytime would assume the faces of friends who had been killed. When strong enough to climb the hill behind Harlech and revisit my favourite [sic] country, I could not help seeing it as a prospective battlefield. I would find myself working out tactical problems, planning how best to hold the Upper Artro valley against an attack from the sea, or where to place a Lewis gun if I were trying to rush Dolwreiddiog Farm from the brow of the hill, and what would be the best cover for my rifle-grenade section. I still had the Army habit of commandeering anything of uncertain ownership that I found lying about; also a difficulty in telling the truth—it was always easier for me now, when charged with any fault, to lie my way out in Army style. I applied the technique of taking over billets or trenches to a review of my present situation. Food, water supply, possible dangers, communication, sanitation,

protection against the weather, fuel and light—I ticked off each item as satisfactory.

"Other loose habits of wartime survived, such as stopping cars for a lift, talking without embarrassment to my fellow-travellers [sic] in railway carriages, and unbuttoning by the roadside without shame, whoever might be about. Also, I retained the technique of endurance; a brutal persistence in seeing things through, somehow, anyhow, without finesse, satisfied with the main points of any situation."

—ROBERT GRAVES, *GOOD-BYE TO ALL THAT*, 287

A S THE ABOVE QUOTE FROM WORLD WAR I infantry veteran, noted memoirist, and writer Robert Graves indicates, the individual veteran adapts to his experiences in war in ways that help him survive. Many of these adjustments persist into his civilian life once he returns home, but not all of them are counterproductive. While macro factors largely beyond his control shape how the veteran views his time in war, on a personal level though the veteran makes a series of adaptations to the unique circumstances of his conflict.[1] Many adjustments, upon coming home, give him an advantage in the various competitions of life such as an ability to focus on an objective, to think tactically in the service of a plan, and to be thorough and self-sufficient. Other adaptations and habits such as aggression, emotional deadening, and a general disdain for rules are not as constructive and can make the veteran's return that much more difficult. The generation of veterans who served in the wars in Afghanistan and Iraq also adapted to the unique conditions of the wars they fought in. In addition to fighting wars of counterinsurgency in predominantly Muslim countries, they served on multiple tours; many served in both conflicts, and they were all volunteers. These conditions, among many others, influenced the sorts of adaptations these veterans went through, but they adjusted to more than just combat conditions. They also adapted to the U.S. military as an institution, the nature and unique characteristics of insurgency warfare, and the local culture of the countries they served in.

While military veterans of the conflicts in Afghanistan and Iraq are war veterans, not all of their experiences were the same. Each campaign went through a series of phases: the Afghan war officially went through six (2001–present), the Iraq campaign (2003–2011) had seven, and the campaign against the Islamic State of Iraq and Syria (ISIS) (2014–present) has gone through four.[2] What phase a veteran served in impacts how he adjusted to the war effort. While a set of general characteristics can be seen in war veterans as a group, some are more pronounced depending upon when the veteran did his service. While there have been multiple phases to these campaigns, they can generally be summarized into four stages: (1) invasion, (2) endurance, (3) surge, and (4) withdrawal. Each stage had certain characteristics that influenced the behavior patterns of veterans upon their return. Five general conditions impacted these veterans: (1) risk tolerance, (2) rules and regulations, (3) different levels and types of violence, (4) knowledge of insurgency, and (5) understanding of local culture and relationships with locals. Other factors that impacted the veterans' experiences include the nature of their job (e.g., infantry, civil affairs, intelligence, etc.) and whether they served in Baghdad or Kabul, in a provincial capital or large city, on a large forward operating base or in a more austere location.

Veterans of the invasions of Afghanistan and Iraq had high risk tolerances, few rules and regulations, not a great deal of knowledge about insurgency or indigenous culture, and few (if any) relationships with locals. Their war experiences can generally be characterized as direct combat against the conventional forces of Iraq and the formally organized forces of the Taliban and al-Qaeda. Morale and esprit de corps were high. Veterans of the "endurance" phase witnessed a deterioration in security as the insurgencies began in earnest. Many of these veterans had started to undertake reconstruction, development, and good governance efforts but were now confronted with a full-blown insurgency. Additionally, the nature of the violence changed as improvised explosive devices (IEDs), suicide, and sniper attacks increased. Their knowledge of insurgency and local culture was increasing, and they had some relationships with indigenous leaders. In general, they were executing a series of approaches with respect to the local population that had not yet become a fully formed counterinsurgency strategy. Aspects of it were there, but it was not integrated or developed intellectually. There was great risk tolerance to fight the insurgency kinetically, but, due to mounting casualties, there was greater risk avoidance as well. Morale was starting to waver during this stage because it was becoming increasingly clear that a war-winning strategy had not yet been adopted.

War veterans who served in the "surge" phase had a much greater understanding of insurgency and local culture and developed deeper relationships with indigenous leaders. Morale was high, even as casualties were increasing, because there was a sense that the counterinsurgency strategies then being implemented were working. Risk tolerance had increased, but so had rules and regulations within the military (and within Iraq and

Afghanistan due to the increasing sovereignty of their respective governments). The "withdrawal" phase can generally be characterized as one of
high morale, at least in Iraq, as violence had subsided and local leaders and
security forces were better able to handle the much-degraded insurgency.
Rules and regulations were significantly advanced at this stage in the conflict, and risk avoidance was acute. Direct combat by U.S. forces was much
lower, and working by, with, and through local forces was the principal
method of operation. The "withdrawal" phase of the war in Afghanistan
was stopped due to the rise of ISIS in Syria and Iraq. Though withdrawal
was originally planned for 2014, the United States continued in its strategy
in Afghanistan. In some respects, this period, which goes to around 2021,
can be characterized as one of endurance and muddle. Rules and regulations
were high, and so was risk avoidance, as it became clear the United States
was not seeking to prevail. Relationships with local leaders were strong and
enduring, as working by, with, and through the Afghan government was
central to U.S. strategy. There was very little tolerance for risk in a general
sense; however, the unavoidable need to address a growing insurgency was
palpable, and so many risks were taken to address its worst aspects.

In order to better understand how the war veteran adapts to combat,
insurgency, serving in the U.S. military, and local culture, analysis focuses
on the view that veterans make reasonable, although sometimes unconscious, adaptations to their situation that allow them to survive, thrive, and
accomplish the mission. In the words of Dr. Jonathan Shay, formerly a staff
psychologist with the Veterans Administration who principally worked
with Vietnam War veterans, "The symptoms caused by psychological injury that the American Psychiatric Association called PTSD . . . can be understood in one clear and simple concept: persistence of valid adaptations
to danger into a time of safety afterward."[3] He further states, "The problem
of recovery from simple PTSD afterward in civilian life becomes a problem
of unlearning combat adaptations and particularly of educating those the
veteran lives with."[4] While most of Shay's work was with enlisted U.S.
Army veterans of the Vietnam War who served in the combat arms, other
adaptations take place, which he does not address in his two major books,
Achilles in Vietnam: Combat Trauma and the Undoing of Character and *Odysseus in America: Combat Trauma and the Trials of Homecoming*. In this respect,
adapting to local culture and the U.S. military, as well as other counterinsurgency tasks, are not addressed. In this regard, Dr. Willard Waller, a
World War I veteran and sociologist, provides a useful perspective: "We
must understand the veteran by imagining what it would be like to be in
his skin, borrow his eyes to see with, his heart to feel, his mind to recall

the present and to think about the future."[5] Waller elaborates further: "If we are to understand the veteran, we must learn what he experiences as a soldier."[6] What, then, can we learn from the experiences of Afghanistan and Iraq war veterans and how they changed the war veteran? How have these various adaptations manifested themselves on the home front, and how does the veteran behave?

Combat: Personality Adaptations

"In short, the soldier develops a mental system, complete with attitudes, behavior patterns, forms of logic, beliefs and philosophy, custom-tailored to the needs of his life."

—WILLARD WALLER, *THE VETERAN COMES BACK*, 63

The veteran goes through a series of profound adjustments to combat. This begins with his swearing an oath of allegiance to the U.S. Constitution when joining the U.S. military. Through self-selection, training, and the hard logic of combat, he thinks, acts, and behaves as a member of a small unit; the group is more important than the individual (see chapter 3, "Camaraderie, Love, and Humor"). This mind-set is focused on accomplishing specific missions where the individual veteran performs a vital function on behalf of the unit. As he participates in combat, as he kills the enemy, the abstract becomes real, and the veteran cultivates a calibrated aggression as well as emotional deadening. He knows when to go on the offensive and when to dominate his opponents; he cultivates a detachment to horrendous scenes such as the dead and injured enemy, and he is even hardened to the sight of his dead and injured friends. He does this because there is no time to dwell on such matters in a firefight but also because there is nothing to be done when someone is dead; his war is finished. This detachment is a function of another mind-set that develops, which I call "amoral instrumentalism." Waller provides a valuable perspective on this situation: "The values that the soldier has learned to respect in war are the values of war and not the values of peace. The hardness, obscenity, fatalism . . . cannot suddenly be dispelled."[7] This view of the ends justifying the means creates a mentality in the veteran that anything is possible and that everything can be done to secure the objective or achieve the mission. The famous World War II Marine E. B. Sledge also addresses this change: "The young man on the front line develops this insensitivity because it is the only way he can cope."[8] He is told to follow his orders and to "win" for his side, but the moral quandaries this situation can sometimes create are set aside in the service of achieving larger goals. In order to handle these complexities, the veteran detaches himself from them and never addresses them, burying them in his mind.

In combat, everything must serve a vital purpose, or it is not carried, used, or part of the patrol, convoy, or security operation. This mentality is focused on functionality and efficiency as well as redundancy. Camouflage exists in order to make it harder to be seen and thus harder to shoot. Buttons are used on military uniforms because they reduce the sound a soldier makes (when compared with using Velcro, for example) and are easy to replace if damaged or lost. Magazines are carried in chest rigs in order to get access to them quickly, and they are upside down with the bullets facing to the right so that when the magazine is grabbed by the soldier's left hand, they are already in the right position to load into the rifle. Further, in planning conveys, for example, every seat on a Humvee is scrutinized in order to determine the purpose of the passenger. Does he have the right training? What is his purpose if a firefight takes place? What is the value added of the individual to the objective of the mission? Another characteristic is "stick-to-itiveness," or seeing a process, a mission, an objective to its end. This focus or fixation is imperative because not doing so means that the objective was not met (which could endanger lives) and that the soldier did not give his everything to achieve it (which could mean that he let his fellow unit members down and could also lead to people losing their lives). Redundancy is also important because if a vital piece of gear isn't working, the mission could be a failure. One expression that is often heard is "two is one and one is none." This can include batteries, magazines, medical supplies, tourniquets, and similar items.

Military Life: Personality Adaptations

> "The military mentality is in part a result of the actual conditions of war, and in part a product of the army as a social environment."
>
> —WILLARD W. WALLER, ON THE FAMILY, EDUCATION, AND WAR: SELECTED WRITINGS, 337

The shift from a civilian life and outlook to a military one can be very dramatic because the volunteer must adjust to living in a chain of command, the formalism that comes with the military, and losing some of one's freedom to the service. Further, the U.S. military as an instrument of U.S. foreign policy is designed to deter our opponents, defeat our enemies, and protect the homeland; it delivers death to the nation's enemies and destruction to the things they hold dear while protecting the nation. Largely for these reasons, members of the military cultivate a calm and formal demeanor: he has a calm demeanor because a confident leader remains even-tempered in the face of adversity, which reverberates among his men into high morale, and he has a formal demeanor because a chain of command requires proper behavior, communication, and deference. This formal and impersonal decorum is also necessary in order to make difficult decisions that might cause the death and injury of fellow military members. An effective chain of command likewise confers benefits on military organizations because they fight more effectively, and calm leaders inspire confidence, which also turns into battlefield advantage.

In addition, the military has traditionally been a male institution, and the challenge of waging war frequently favors classic male attributes. Further, for an institution that rewards aggression and toughness, cultivating a calm demeanor in the execution of plans to fight the enemy is the epitome of the institution's preferences for behavior: "In the abnormal male world of war, the soldier schools himself to earthiness and toughness. These qualities show in his language, his humor, his obsession with food, as well as in his conduct under fire. His pleasures are simple."[9] The military likewise cultivates a sense of group identity, which is an essential feature of small unit combat: "In an army a great many men must live together in a semi-communal social order."[10] This "social order" also requires loyalty between its members and hostility to those outside its membership: "The most obvious change in the mores is the reversion to the tribal morality which commands solidarity within the group and enmity toward those outside."[11] As leaders, this often manifests itself in a teamwork mentality in which consideration is given to the benefit of the group. Additionally, the U.S. military insists its members have a high morality, which must exist within an institution like the military because it places great trust upon its members. Many members of the military adapt to the institution of the U.S. military by adopting a formal stoicism and behaving and cultivating traditional male attributes in a manner that asserts leadership but does so with a high morality and from a mentality of teamwork to accomplish a group objective.

One of the unique attributes of this generation of war veterans is the number of warzone tours they have served on in Afghanistan and Iraq as well as the opportunity to serve in two entirely different wars. While tours are variously defined, it is entirely possible for a war veteran to deploy frequently enough to span many years of a conflict and have time in between to contemplate the experience and apply this knowledge the next go-around. In the campaign in Afghanistan, for example, as of 2019, 384,836 veterans had served one tour, 222,630 served two, 99,046 served three, 40,698 served four, and approximately 28,267 served five or more tours.[12] As difficult as these numbers may seem to many readers, each and every one of these military veterans were volunteers. The World War II and Korean War veteran and writer Samuel Hynes puts it well: "I have never met a man who fought in the Second World War—actually *fought*—who regretted having been there."[13] The World War I infantry veteran Charles Edmonds expresses similar views: "I was hating the war and at the same time longing to be back with the regiment."[14] The effects of these constant deployments are multifaceted, including the opportunity to gain a certain wisdom about war that is rare, to defer life decisions due to service to the nation, and to never really have a reason to stop deploying due to the end of the conflict. Other aspects include the multi-memoir veteran (when most war memoirs are about one tour), the opportunity to compare and contrast two wars, and the chance to be promoted over time to apply wisdom in war at different levels.

A veteran friend of mine counseled me to remember to "make sure your deployed life doesn't become your home life and your home life doesn't become your deployed life." Many veterans welcomed the opportunity to deploy multiple times to war and found life exhilarating and fulfilling working in austere and violent places on behalf of the nation. This quote from a veteran of these contemporary wars captures this mentality well: "There are some 40-year-old sled dogs that Uncle Sam has been relying upon since 9/11. . . . They'll pull and they'll pull till their hearts explode."[15] This "patriotic addiction" means that some veterans of these wars welcome the multiple tours, meaning that the usual adjustments to war zones that veterans make may be harder to undo; in a sense, these types of veterans have transcended to a new dimension of resiliency. An article in the *New York Times* in 2016 about these phenomena states the following:

> The idea that these elite fighters can adapt solely by addressing emotional trauma, some experts said, is badly misplaced. Their primary difficulty is not necessarily one of healing emotional wounds; they thrived in combat. It is rather a matter of unlearning the very skills that have kept them alive: unceasing vigilance, snap decision making, intolerance for carelessness; the urge to act fast and decisively.[16]

These tendencies are especially strong among Special Operations Forces and other elite military units. The appeal of repeated tours is a function of a feeling that the job is not yet done, a feeling of freedom from life's demands back home, the exhilaration of combat and the joys of camaraderie, the fascination with foreign cultures, and the problem sets of insurgencies and counterterrorism. An Afghanistan war veteran states this view plainly:

> Yet, even in times of comfort, you find yourself missing the hardships of deployments. The tough times at least made you feel something. And that's what you miss the most—feeling truly alive. You say things like, "I was happier living in a plywood hooch in Afghanistan with my worldly possessions reduced to whatever fit into a backpack than I am now, living in this apartment, where everything I could ever want is within my grasp."[17]

There are plenty of stories of veterans from one war trying to join up again, whether it was General Joshua Chamberlain of Battle of Gettysburg fame who wanted to participate in the Spanish-American War or former president Theodore Roosevelt, who had served in the Spanish-American War, who sought service in World War I. Interestingly, four former Confederate general officers actually served with the U.S. Army in the Spanish-American War, principally with volunteer units, including Joseph Wheeler and Fitzhugh Lee, among others.[18] The appeal of combat is enduring to veterans who have served, and the opportunities for such service in Afghanistan and Iraq provided a meaningful outlet for these men that changed them well beyond their contemporary military peers.

Insurgency: Personality Adaptations

"My duties were simple; I was to encourage the local inhabitants to stand up for themselves."

—ALEC KIRKBRIDE, *AN AWAKENING: THE ARAB CAMPAIGN, 1917–1918*, 104

The nature of insurgency warfare, and successful counterinsurgency strategy, requires fighting skill as well as an ability to build rapport with local populations and their leaders while endeavoring to find the hidden presence of the insurgent. It also requires a bottom-up approach to security and a compelling political strategy to draw the population to the government and to marginalize the political message of the insurgency. All of these requirements necessitate a veteran who is not only knowledgeable of indigenous culture but also able to work with local populations and achieve shared objectives. These skill sets can generally be characterized as cross-cultural understanding and communication, but it requires the ability to build rapport; demonstrate empathy, patience, and doggedness; and understand intuitively what is sometimes lost in translation or misunderstanding. Many of the more successful veterans of the wars in Afghanistan and Iraq who worked with local tribal, political, civic, and security leaders in both countries demonstrated these abilities. Further, because most veterans could not speak Arabic, Pashto, or Dari, their other senses became more developed. This often meant that, in addition to hypervigilance brought about by being in a war zone, many veterans picked up on, for example, subtle clothing changes, the physicality of people, interpersonal relationships, and other nuances, which gave them better insights into people. When I was serving in Fallujah in 2007, I would often watch as the city council members entered the council chambers. I noted who walked in together (perhaps they were friends), where they sat (at the main table or against the wall), and who stood up when known leaders entered the room. I would also scrutinize the clothing they were wearing (was it clean, of high quality, or different each time?) and their overall health (was someone thin, robust, or injured?). These abilities facilitated the interactions of veterans with their local partners and were skills they brought back with them upon returning home.

A second key aspect of working against an insurgency is that all too often the signs of an insurgent's activities are evident—for example, an IED has been implanted, but one did not see the actual insurgent do it. The need to discern what has happened forces the veteran to consider how the enemy would approach the problem as well as second- and third-order effects. Further, the nature of Iraqi and Afghan society is one based on tribes, kinship groups, religious networks, and business coalitions that operate as informal influence systems. These networks are interlocking, dense, and complex, and traditional organizational charts in the Western model are not as useful in analyzing their behavior. As veterans in both countries worked against the insurgent threat and tried to exercise influence by, with, and through local partners, they had to develop an insatiable curiosity about these networks because they always influenced the decision-making calculus of both insurgents and the local population. Over time, many veterans developed a highly intuitive and deductive method of thinking that allowed for multidimensional types of analysis. The insurgent's preference for indirect violence required this sort of examination, as kinetic actions by the insurgency were not always focused on achieving the movement's military goals but may have had other political or tribal dimensions to them. Similarly, it was not uncommon for Afghans and Iraqis to use the cover of insurgent violence to settle scores and blood feuds and to achieve political power and influence by replicating the insurgents' use of violence. When veterans of these wars returned home, these highly advanced thinking skills honed on analyzing informal influence networks confronted a U.S. society that was based upon direct communication and formal networks of established institutions, where multiple layers of complexity and association were absent. These differences often gave veterans an advantage at analyzing the competitive strategies of people, companies, and institutions.

Local Culture: Personality Adaptations

> *"To enable one country to appreciate what another people really thinks and desires is both the most difficult and the most vital task which confronts us."*

> —JOHN BAGOT GLUBB, *BRITAIN AND THE ARABS:*
> *A STUDY OF FIFTY YEARS, 1908–1958*, 147

A significant factor, which does not often get the attention it deserves, in terms of its influence on how veterans return home from war is that many of them have spent years of their lives in developing countries working with local populations in a close and intimate manner. Both Afghanistan and Iraq are developing countries that are grappling with modernization but are still quite traditional, where rule of law is immature and informal justice systems are strong, where group identity (e.g., tribal, kinship networks) trumps individual rights and freedoms, and where life is difficult and violent. Navigating these shoals can be difficult because the vast majority of veterans have come from Western states that have first-world and postmodern problems. These profound differences between violent, traditional, and developing countries and first-world nations with first-world problems can cause some level of bitterness among veterans. The World War II Marine veteran E. B. Sledge captures this sentiment well: "In all the years since the war . . . I've never gotten accustomed to civilians complaining about trivial inconveniences."[19] In a simple sense, it is about navigating the return from societies based upon the values of scarcity versus one based upon the values of overabundance. One is more focused on their responsibilities and obligations versus one based upon their rights and entitlements. This attitude often manifests itself in a general disdain for the complaints of civilians in modern society. It also tends to lead to societal ennui among some veterans as the values of their home society seem so completely different from those they have developed abroad.

Conclusion

> *"The purgative force of danger which makes men coarser but perhaps more human will soon be lost and the first months of peace will make some of us yearn for the old days of conflict."*

—J. GLENN GRAY, *THE WARRIORS: REFLECTIONS ON MEN IN BATTLE*, 28

> *"This was a major crossroads for me—and I suspect for all of us coming home from overseas combat—closing down one world, opening a starkly contrasting new one with all its uncertainties."*

—E. B, SLEDGE, *CHINA MARINE:*
AN INFANTRYMAN'S LIFE AFTER WORLD WAR II, 125

> *"[T]he first way that combat soldiers lose their homecoming, having left the war zone physically—they may simply remain in combat mode, although not necessarily against the original enemy."*

—JONATHAN SHAY, *ODYSSEUS IN AMERICA:*
COMBAT TRAUMA AND THE TRIALS OF HOMECOMING, 20

The process of coming home on an individual level can be quite varied for war veterans and is dependent upon the nature of their tours, their support networks at home, and their success in starting their civilian lives. The veterans of the wars in Afghanistan and Iraq were all volunteers who often served multiple tours in both countries conducting both combat and counterinsurgency. They had adjusted not only to the brutal realities of combat but also to fighting insurgencies holistically, living in and influencing developing countries, as well as adapting to the exigencies of the U.S. military as an institution. The contrasting experiences of serving in both wars provided additional insights into how these factors impacted them and provided them with ready comparisons that offered further perspectives. The adjustments the veterans made to survive and thrive in war zones frequently manifested themselves upon returning home in aggressive behavior and emotional deadening, an emphasis on thinking and operating as a group, and a tendency to compartmentalize and set aside moral difficulties. They also tended to prioritize efficiency, functionality, and effectiveness and were quite formal in their interactions and respectful of authority. They valued toughness and assertiveness, as well as stoicism, and manifested and responded well to traditional male attributes. They also tended to be decisive and results oriented as well as teamwork focused. They likewise developed advanced abilities to build rapport, demonstrated empathy and patience, and had a determined doggedness to accomplish an objective. Their minds harnessed informal influence networks in a highly networked fashion to accomplish their objectives, and they often intuitively comprehended things when there was ambiguity in understanding. They also cultivated a set of values anchored in the complexities of developing countries as well as the U.S. military, so they frequently emphasized the most essential things of life and learned to ignore those that were marginal.

While many of these tendencies, ways of thinking, and methods of operating can be quite positive for the veteran upon returning home, there are many behaviors they can exhibit that can cause adjustment challenges. A dedication to accomplishing the mission can sometimes manifest itself in "fanaticism," and "for the sake of having a mission," it allows them to shut "everything else from their minds."[20] They are also sometimes "dissatisfied with the mere earning of our daily bread, bored with the conditions we once yearned for," and long to either return to war or think about it often.[21] Many of these veterans, upon returning home, find their morality a bit unsteady and uncertain.[22] Sometimes this situation manifests itself in criminal activity or going from one sexual relationship to another: "Speaking of his criminal activities he [the veteran] says, 'It's not the money, it's the *action*.' His skills, his cunning, his craft—a precise word, because it means both highly developed skill *and* cunning—all become valuable again in 'action' in a way that they never are in civilian life."[23] Waller provides a useful perspective here: "Some veterans report turning from one sex affair to another; trying, no doubt, to discover in the relationship of the sexes the meanings that war and army life had taken from their lives."[24] There is also a lack of patience for people, processes, and institutions as the tactical urgency of small-unit operations, which manifest immediate results, cannot wait for formal processes on a longer or uncertain time line to unfold.

They have also developed an intimate relationship with death: they have delivered it against the enemy, seen it among their friends, and avoided it throughout their tours: "Men who have faced death often and habitually can never again have the same attitude towards life. It is hard to be enthusiastic about things again. The fact that everybody is soon going to die is a little more patent than before. One sees behind the scenes, the flowers and the grave-blinds, the opiate of words read from the Good Book, and the prayers."[25] Even though many veterans have returned home, their experiences have left such an indelible mark upon them that it becomes the anchoring point of their lives. The World War I veteran and poet Edmund Blunden expresses this view well: "My experiences in the First World War have haunted me all my life and for many days I have, it seemed, lived in that world rather than this."[26] As these veterans return home, they turn to new pursuits—starting jobs, marrying and having children, founding businesses, and serving their community once again as volunteers or in politics. They begin to write about their experiences in memoir, fiction, and literature and see their exploits end up in cinema or in TV shows. Over time, they reconnect with their fellow veterans, seek out opportunities for comradeship and meaning, and endeavor to move on in their lives. In the end, as Afghan veteran Nolan Peterson puts it, "Combat veterans aren't damaged. They are enlightened, complicated souls forced to live life by a set of rules and expectations that can make pursuing true happiness feel like chasing the moon."[27]

Camaraderie, Love, and Humor **3**

> *"War, by making fates more shared, by manufacturing non-zero-sumness, accelerates the evolution of culture toward deeper and vaster social complexity. . . . That zero-sumness promotes non-zero-sumness should come as no surprise."*
>
> —ROBERT WRIGHT, *NON-ZERO: THE LOGIC OF HUMAN DESTINY*, 56–57

> *"[The veteran] is bitter over the denial of love, but does not know how to express love, or to elicit it in others. Lust, of course, he understands thoroughly, having explored its uttermost boundaries."*
>
> —WILLARD WALLER, *THE VETERAN COMES BACK*, 120

> *"But I'm afraid the jokes that made us reel with laughter would be flat to-day. One jumped at any excuse to be gay, and to laugh meant to forget that open door, facing the wrong way, through which a shell might come at any moment to burst in the midst of us."*
>
> —CHARLES EDMONDS, *A SUBALTERN'S WAR*, 174

PRIOR TO HER PASSING AWAY in December 2016, I asked my grandmother how the war had affected her husband, my grandfather, who had served in Europe in World War II as a U.S. Army communications sergeant in the 91st Infantry Division. She paused for a moment and mentioned how he would often yell out at night in his sleep and thrash around and how she would soothe him back to sleep. She next mentioned how most of his friends soon became other war veterans and how the friends of his who hadn't served quietly faded from his life. I often think about my grandfather's transition home, something I only know about second or third hand, and I wonder about my own. He had gone off to war as a twenty-two-year-old Iowan, captain of his high school's football team, and returned two years older with a Bronze Star, a few promotions, and a new baby boy (my father). The camaraderie he must have felt among these men, what Vietnam veteran and author Karl Marlantes calls a "member of the club" of combat veterans, must have been acute as he started work as an electrician in the small town of Ft. Dodge, Iowa.[1] I have also noticed a similar transition of my friends, most of whom have also served in Afghanistan and Iraq. We speak a special code to each other, easily slip into a jargon only we seem to know, and commiserate about society's unusual ways. Along these lines, the jokes and humorous observations we make to each other have a decidedly dark tone to them. There is often a gallows humor component, a love of the preposterous and ludicrous, and a collection of military-themed jokes. Similarly, as we navigate our returns home from war, the travails of finding a partner are often a topic of conversation. Themes such as, frankly speaking, adjusting back to a world of a balanced gender ratio, simply unlearning certain emotional adaptations to war, and relearning how to be a good companion are also common topics. The adjustments veterans make in war to survive and thrive confer many advantages on the veteran, but upon returning home, many veterans don't make the transition well, which can cause challenges for them.

The world of the war veteran is one of violence and death, and in this crucible he must navigate its dangers with strangers who have become his family through shared service, shared threats, and love of country. He must visit death on his enemies, protect his friends, operate in a group, and accomplish a common objective. By the time the veteran is involved in combat, when he exposes himself to enemy fire on behalf of his teammates or leaps from cover to grab a colleague who has been injured to drag him to safety, it represents the culminating point of a long, drawn-out process of fashioning strangers into a team. The U.S. military emphasizes what it calls "selfless service," which is about putting others above oneself, and the process of military training reinforces these values. However, selfless service is not just about service to one's nation and community; it also serves a vital function of survival as individuals are forged into a group.

In the words of Alexis de Tocqueville, the French commentator on early America and author of the book *Democracy in America* (1835, 1840), it is about "self-interest rightly understood," wherein furthering the interests of others eventually serves one's self-interest. But there is more than a simple logical calculation of balancing short-term versus long-term gain and self-interest properly understood. There are bonds of loyalty and responsibility, of rights and obligations, which intertwine members of military units to each other that transcend any logical calculation.

The selfless service, sense of sacrifice, and camaraderie among veterans begins with the simple act of joining the military. This choice already suggests that some commonalities of outlook already exist among those who join the armed services, even among strangers, but soon thereafter other factors come to bear on these recruits. In addition to the individual being sublimated within the group and unit, differences of class, race, ethnicity, and such are broken down in the training process.

> I confess that a large number of Americans I met in the Army amazed me by their differences. I had not known their like before, nor have I met them since. Nothing else could have made me realize how narrow the circle in which we move in peacetime is. Most of us hardly get an inkling of how ninety per cent of our fellows live or think. Naively we assume that they must be like us or not very different.[2]

This is not to say these distinctions are completely done away with, but the shared experiences of difficult training, common living, and similar material conditions, among other factors, inculcate the beginnings of group identity and demonstrate the many things veterans share in common despite their differences. Shared living conditions in particular facilitate the breaking down of barriers between individuals even of starkly different backgrounds: "In an army a great many men must live together in a semi-communal social order."[3] It starts with simply sharing a common living space such as a barracks when you ask someone, probably your bunk mate, to keep an eye on your gear while you step away to take care of something. This is a very modest but illustrative example of how bonds of trust are fashioned by these small acts, which are only amplified by dozens of others.

> As a consequence, an individual was dependent on others, on people who could not formerly have entered the periphery of his consciousness. For them in turn, he was of interest only as a center of force, a wielder of weapons, a means of security and survival. This confraternity of danger and exposure is unequaled in forging links among people of unlike desire and

temperament, links that are utilitarian and narrow but no less passionate because of their accidental and general nature.[4]

As the idiosyncrasies of your training group become known—who snores, who has a girlfriend, who is going through a divorce, who shows up late for training, who excels at the rifle range, for example—these strangers begin to assume the status of friends.

The physicality of basic training—where you help colleagues overcome obstacles and drag them behind cover under simulated fighting conditions, among other tasks—also breaks down individuality. This tendency is sometimes directly compelled by the training environment itself when instructors direct new recruits to find a battle buddy and then further require them to always be with that person when they are doing anything. This can mean such simple things as going to the bathroom, eating chow, and running errands.

> Friendship, for example, is different there—different enough to need another name: *comradeship*. . . . But though comradeship is accidental, it is intense beyond the likelihood of back-home life. A soldier spends virtually all his time, awake and asleep, with his mates; he is with them more continuously than most men are with their wives. And at critical moments his life may depend on their fidelity and courage.[5]

However, as the training continues, these burgeoning bonds of friendship are further strengthened as individuals are assigned roles in their unit. In combat units in particular, such as the infantry, these positions serve vital functions of survival as the logic of small-unit action in combat is applied to these men. Having been fashioned to think as a group, these roles differentiate the men into the important functions they will play in combat. An infantryman has distinct responsibilities to his unit, as does a machine-gunner and a mortar man, among others. These roles must be executed superbly because survival in combat depends upon it. When suppressive fire is required, it must be delivered; when indirect fire is called for, it must arrive on time and on target; and, when pulling your friend from a burning Humvee due to an improvised explosive device blowing up, the sense of obligation must not hesitate. It is only by working together as a unit that the chances of survival of the individual soldier, sailor, airman, and Marine are improved.

Any member of the group who operates as an individual versus as a teammate with a vital function to perform puts the group's survival into jeopardy as much as putting themselves at great risk. The interlocking strands of obligation that military training and service forge create expectations of performance that, if not met in combat, incur the wrath of one's colleagues.

> For them in turn, he was of interest only as a center of force, a wielder of weapons, a means of security and survival. This confraternity of danger and exposure is unequaled in forging links among people of unlike desire and temperament.[6]

The famous World War II Marine veteran E. B. Sledge also puts it well: "The only thing that kept you going was your faith in your buddies. It wasn't just a case of friendship. . . . What was worse than death was the indignation of your buddies. You couldn't let 'em down. It was stronger than flag and country."[7] The experience of combat, of taking life, of losing friends, and of operating in incredibly harsh and unforgiving circumstances reinforces these connections of comradeship. As the well-known war correspondent Ernie Pyle puts it, "[T]he ties that grow up between men who live savagely and die relentlessly. . . . There is a sense of fidelity to each other among little corps of men who have endured so long and whose hope in the end can be but so small."[8] In many respects, the more brutal the war experience in terms of loss of life, combat service, and harshness of living circumstances the greater the identification of the service member to the group. This group identity is further reinforced by distinctive badges and patches, uniforms, gear, and such, which foster an even greater sense of identity and of interlocking networks of mutual obligation. As the unit's actions are made part of the historical record, as their accomplishments are shown to have played an important role in a battle or even a war, this sense of group identity is further reinforced and elevated.

Science and Solidarity

> *"When people interact with each other in mutually profitable fashion, they don't necessarily realize exactly what they're doing. Evolutionary psychologists have made a strong—in my view, compelling—case that this unconscious savviness is a part of human-nature, rooted ultimately in the genes; that natural selection, via the evolution of 'reciprocal altruism,' has built*

*into us various impulses which, however warm and mushy they
may feel, are designed for the cool, practical purpose of bringing
beneficial exchange.*"

—ROBERT WRIGHT, *NON-ZERO: THE LOGIC OF HUMAN DESTINY*, 22–23

The conditions that facilitate this sense of group identity, which fashion strangers into coherent units of obligation and action within the military, are successful, in part, due to our hard-wiring as humans after years of evolution in hunter-gatherer societies. Modern evolutionary psychology, informed by advances in genetic understanding, modern computing, and simulations and modeling, demonstrate that habits of reciprocity, or enlightened self-interest, provide long-standing benefits to both individuals and communities.[9] Military training and war service, especially in combat, reacquaints veterans with these instincts that resided in their genetic makeup but had lain dormant or unused due to modern society's stability and safety. In many respects, military training helps first-world members of the military return to their hunter-gather selves with its attendant mores, obligations, and behavioral patterns. The evolutionary psychologist writer Robert Wright summarizes this perspective succinctly: "[H]uman nature itself, unadorned by technology, carries mutual benefit, and thus social structure, beyond the confines of family. . . . A universal feature of hunter-gatherer societies, some anthropologists say, is 'generalized reciprocity'— not just within families but between them."[10] This "reciprocal altruism" or "non-zero sumness," wherein both parties benefit from the exchange, operates beyond the level of the individual; as social groups increase in size and complexity, similar behavior accrues to the benefit of the group, which confers additional advantages.

These cooperative instincts confer evolutionary benefits since the group itself is better positioned through cooperation, specialization, and complexity to perpetuate itself: "This superficially selfless gene will do much better over the ages than a superficially selfish gene."[11] Computer modeling of societies that behave in a non-zero-sum manner compared to those that exhibit zero-sum behavior demonstrate that reciprocal altruism confers long-term benefits of growth and complexity.[12] Non-zero-sum behavior facilitates "[f]riendship, affection, [and] trust—these are the things that, long before people signed contracts, long before they wrote down laws, held human societies together."[13] Other benefits include improved coordination across increasingly larger groups of individuals and the specialization of functions and division of labor, which accrues to the benefit of the broader group.

> The successful playing of a non-zero-sum game typically *amounts to* a growth of social complexity. The players must coordinate their behavior, so people who might otherwise be off in their own orbits come together and form a single solar system, a larger synchronized whole. And typically there is division of labor within the whole. . . . One minute you're a bunch of independent foragers, and the next minute you're a single, integrated rabbit-catching team, differentiated yet united. Complex coherence has materialized.[14]

The behavioral patterns honed by reciprocal altruism in generally peaceful hunter-gatherer societies are significantly deepened by war conditions. External competitors for resources such as arable land, wild game, and markets, among other considerations, further hone these tendencies. The rise of challengers focused on zero-sum relationships, wherein one party definitively loses from an exchange with another, conditions these factors in key ways.

> One could describe the congealing effect of war by saying it *pushes* people together into organic solidarity; it poses an external threat that impels them into closer cooperation. And one could describe the causes of solidarity . . . as *pulling* people together; opportunities for gain originate within the society and draw people into closer cooperation.[15]

The external competitor pushes the group together, prompting it to pull closer in order to rise to the challenge. It also reinforces community resiliency and adaptation as the loss of life, prestige, and resources prompts change. It further "accelerates the evolution of culture toward deeper and vaster social complexity. . . . That zero-sumness promotes non-zero-sumness should come as no surprise."[16] The insights of this research, however, are largely confined to how small, hunter-gatherer societies operate, and it also tends to assume individuals have some degree of perfect information, a hierarchical ordering of their preferences, and relatively easy communications, among other factors. As societies grow in complexity, moving away from hunter-gather communities to agrarian, industrial, and postindustrial economies and societies, these behavioral patterns are forced to change, but the roots of human behavior are largely fixed, at least in the near term: "We live in cities and suburbs and watch TV and drink beer, all the while being pushed and pulled by feelings designed to propagate our genes in a small hunter-gather population."[17]

The Home Front

> *"The ultimate aim of all this [training], it should be said, is to weld the men together into a social machine which will not disintegrate in a crisis situation."*
>
> —WILLARD W. WALLER, *ON THE FAMILY, EDUCATION, AND WAR: SELECTED WRITINGS,* 336

The world of the war veteran, which is very similar to the moral universe of hunter-gatherer societies, is a life of small-unit action, of using non-zero-sum solutions to impose zero-sum outcomes on the enemy. These insights from evolutionary psychology help to better understand the behavioral patterns of men in units of this size and why they often use such familial phrases such as "brother" to address each other (e.g., the World War II miniseries *Band of Brothers* is an example of this tendency). It also helps explain why they will instinctively sacrifice for each other in civilian life when they return home; combat adaptations persist into civilian life. These instincts are likely reinforced even further for many counterinsurgency veterans since, in addition to combat, they are often arrayed in a dispersed manner in isolated locations to provide protection to local Afghan and Iraqi populations through persistent presence. Their lives, which are largely about living in a small-unit environment for a prolonged period of time working with partnered tribal groups, significantly reinforce the logic of group action and solidarity. In conducting counterinsurgency operations by, with, and through the local government and security forces, these small military detachments have approximated as closely as they can the behavioral patterns of tribal groups with all of their modalities; group identity is more important than the individual, group solidarity is paramount, and interlocking linkages of obligations and rights exist within the group. Similarly, repeated deployments, a key feature of the wars following 9/11, mean that group solidarity is constantly reinforced in a war zone environment. The adaptations of individuals to group action are frequently replenished likely causing greater difficulties for veterans when they return home and, eventually, to civilian life. The challenge for many veterans is, after having made these crucial adjustments to group solidarity in order to survive, the reality of the homeland they are returning to is organized fundamentally differently with correspondingly different mores.

Upon returning home from war and demobilizing back to civilian life, the veteran quickly sheds this sense of group identity, at least in the short term, and he almost rebels against it, setting aside the requirements of communal living to enjoy, once again, individuality, safety, and freedom. This is not surprising since none of his fellow unit members are related to him (shared genetic heritage builds stronger bonds of fidelity), and he has family and nonmilitary friends who want to see him, as well as the benefits of civilian life to enjoy. But the old bonds of camaraderie draw him back as he navigates the travails of relationships, employment, and life: "In short, the soldier develops a mental system, complete with attitudes, behavior patterns, forms of logic, beliefs and philosophy, custom-tailored to the needs of his life."[18] For some, the stability of being a member of a group, whether it's his old unit or the men he served with or even the military service he was a part of, is comforting and is a part of his life when his obligations were simple. It is also where life seemed richer, although the consequences could be severe, and he was buffered by a support system of friends, comrades, and networks of obligation that made life easier. In some respects, he was free of many of life's responsibilities but, at the same time, playing a small part in great historical events. He has become, in some respects, a member of a tribe and has returned to a society that is not organized as such.[19] This feeling is particularly acute among service members who are single and those who lack robust family support networks; the draw of group solidarity is strong.

As some veterans feel frustrated by society and by life outside the military and find they are unable to or don't want to rejoin the military, they look for some sense of group membership elsewhere. They search for it in many forms, looking for organizations they can attach to that echo the sense of comradeship they had had in the service. Many of these veterans join fraternal veterans groups such as the American Legion and the Veterans of Foreign Wars while others join civic organizations such as Rotary and the Exchange Clubs. Family obligations also substitute for the group solidarity of military life, and veterans return to the origins of group feeling in humans, the family. Some veterans, in their search for group membership, turn to less than savory groups, some of which may be criminal: "Sometimes the veteran has been so completely alienated from the attitudes and controls of civilian life that he becomes a criminal."[20] Attitudes, mores, and organizational adaptations learned in war, as well as networks forged overseas, facilitate success for many veterans on the home front as they start companies, launch political campaigns, and begin public-service ventures, among many other efforts: "When the civilian-turned-soldier has adjusted his personality to the demands of the military machine, he has thereby lost some part of his ability to adjust to the demands of civilian society."[21] It's not surprising that so many veteran-owned companies are created from networks of veterans who served with each other. The values of the group, the common reference points, and the shared journey of navigating civilian life bring these veterans together. Similarly, civilian attitudes that are more zero-sum quickly disabuse many returned war veterans of a sense of solidarity with their fellow Americans. This also prompts him to return to the military camaraderie he knows and misses, even a civilianized version that mimics what he used to experience in the service. For some veterans, these quasi-military organizations allow him to never fully return from the war experience and to persist in this nether world of war with peace and peace with war.

The mental reference points of many returned war veterans also reflect these lingering adaptations to war zone solidarity and group action and identity. The strength of the group was its reciprocal altruism that was constantly reinforced by the operating environment of combat. This leaves a mental outlook for the returned veteran of seeking group advantage in civilian settings that leads to a "win–win" mentality, which runs counter to a prevailing view of most of competitive civilian society, even on teams, of "win–lose." There are certainly many "win–win" situations that take place every day in civilian society, but the veteran's perspective is imbued with emotional and psychological energy. He is "taking care" of his team when he looks out for a colleague's long-term career interests versus undermining him as part of a short-term competitive strategy. He is "thinking like a teammate" when he seeks harmony within the group because, by doing so, the group benefits. The veteran also thinks of his group as an integrated team, all of whom serve vital and important functions, which shows his consideration of others. This perspective is partly forged from the communal living conditions of his war service as well as the small-unit action he was involved in. Similarly, there also resides in the veteran's outlook a competitive instinct, sometimes bordering on the aggressive, against those outside the group. This perspective can certainly prompt great creativity within a group and a sense of mission, but the determination of the veteran to prevail, forged in combat conditions, can sometimes cause complications. There is often an intensity and drive to his purpose as well as a harshness that can be off-putting. The veteran's perspective on "zero-sum" is likely beyond the stakes of the issue at hand in a civilian setting; it is not likely about a life-or-death situation, but he unconsciously operates as such. While the returned war veteran navigates the civilian world of employment, civic groups, politics, and the like, his most impactful transition is returning home to a wife, girlfriend, or loved one or navigating the challenges of finding love.

The War Veteran and Love

> *"I have observed three distinct kinds of love operating during war. They are erotic love between the sexes, preservative love, which is independent of sex distinctions, and the love called friendship. . . . For many soldiers of World War II, love between the sexes appeared to be nothing else than an outlet in the purely physical sense, which physiologists of love are fond of describing."*

> —J. GLENN GRAY, *THE WARRIORS:
> ON MEN IN BATTLE*, 64–65

The camaraderie and brotherly love that is forged in wartime military service is an example of how self-selection, training, certain genetic predispositions, and the crucible of combat cause individuals who are strangers to become colleagues, friends, and then brothers. This process involves a series of adaptations—moral, physical, intellectual, and psychological—to the exigencies of war zone survival. The morality and ethical logic of a largely peaceful, first-world civilian society gives way to the demands of war and death. For veterans of the Afghanistan and Iraq wars, this means adapting to the moral universe of counterinsurgency in developing countries with largely premodern values. As the World War I veteran and sociologist Willard Waller puts it, "New situations arise which call for new folkways, and, ultimately, for new moral codes."[22] These moral codes adapt to the conditions of war as well as to the operating conditions of the conflict. However, as the veteran occupies this new moral universe the values of his prewar, civilian life continue on the home front, even as they undergo their own stresses due to wartime conditions (e.g., scarcity, imbalanced gender ratios, etc.).[23] Upon his return, the veteran feels the differences between these moralities acutely although he may not be completely conscious of it. For many civilians, the returned veteran's mores and behavior shock polite society. As Waller puts it further, "All of the mores, naturally, change in somewhat different ways in war time, but it seems accurate enough to say that they are, in general, weakened."[24] The returned war veteran has a morality adapted to war, and all that goes with it that, in many respects, is in opposition to civilian morality. The greatest differences he must navigate between these moralities revolves around love, partnership, and companionship.

The morality of stable, developed societies, and especially that of the United States, is largely about self-denial and self-control (e.g., thrift, hard work) for long-term success. The lived experience of Americans has largely borne out this expectation of eventual long-term reward as each generation has generally improved its living circumstances. The anchoring concept for this morality in the United States is largely individualism, and society has created economic, political, and cultural institutions that incentivize individuals to invest in long-term stability. This can mean, for example, favorable tax incentives for house mortgages to encourage stable families, incentives to marry, or community efforts to buttress fidelity.

When it comes to love, this can often mean efforts to sanction personal behavior that is considered destructive of long-term success and an ordered community. This can mean the outlawing of prostitution, emphasizing family values, prioritizing the needs of children over short-term personal interests, and the moral shaming of activities such as gambling that weaken families. All of these efforts also take place in a society with a largely balanced sex ratio where the numbers of men and women are fairly equal. Further, the men of this society have, by and large, been acculturated into the mores of a culture that prioritizes and incentivizes long-term success based upon hard work, self-denial, and self-control. As the civilian joins the military and then serves in a war zone, these moral traditions undergo significant strain and are slowly adjusted to the realities of war service, while others are reinforced and given new meaning, and some are created anew.

One of the most significant adjustments for most men joining the service is contending with the profoundly imbalanced sex ratio of the military. This is especially the case in many combat arms (e.g., infantry) and Special Operations units (e.g., SEALS, Special Forces), which, until recently, barred women from serving. This new reality is further influenced by the fact that the service member has left his home and community, which provided some moral anchoring for long-term success, and is now adjusting not only to the new morality of the military but also to those of his peers who come from disparate communities with sometimes conflicting moralities.

War takes large sections of the population away from their homes and their local communities; it stirs up populations as one stirs soup; people are thrown together who have never seen one another before and will never see one another again; regions, culture groups, religious groups, and classes are all mixed as they are at no other period in life. At the same time, people are unable to satisfy their primal needs in the usual way. Millions of men are pulled out of the family and compelled to live with other men; millions of women are similarly taken out of their customary places; there could be no other result than unconventional behavior.[25]

The veteran must adjust his behavior to this new reality where his normal pursuit of companionship is truncated by the rules and regulations that govern his life in the military, as well as the lack of opportunities to meet a possible partner. The communal living of the military, especially in the barracks, also reduces the reality of privacy, and living with the people you work with on a daily basis creates further complications. It is no surprise that off-base opportunities are actively sought after by military members. Additionally, most members of the military are between the ages of eighteen and twenty-four, which generally means they are less inclined to settle down and are focused on more short-term interests with respect to the opposite sex. This reality naturally creates certain behavior patterns, which are further reinforced by the competitive nature of many men: "Anyone entering military service for the first time can only be astonished by soldiers' concentration upon the subject of women and, more especially, upon the sexual act. The most common word in the mouths of American soldiers has been the vulgar expression for sexual intercourse."[26] However, the stability of a regular paycheck and a steady job also incentivize many members of the military to settle down and establish families. However much an imbalanced sex ratio in the military can create complications, the military member is still serving stateside in a society that has a largely balanced male-to-female ratio. If he so desires, he can find a partner who is willing to join him for the long term.

When the veteran deploys to war, the military morality he has adjusted to, albeit in a civilian society, is further strained by war service, including the conditions within which he is serving. The first adjustment is that the sex ratio becomes even more highly skewed as the veteran departs the homeland. However, this may be mitigated somewhat depending upon the nature of the operations the veteran is involved in and the country he serves in. If the barriers (e.g., physical, cultural, or legal/regulatory) between the deployed military unit and the civilian population are low, then opportunities exist for the veteran to find companionship. Even then, though, the introduction of a large number of military-aged males to a society that has a relatively equal gender ratio can cause complications as it makes the ratio unbalanced. If the veteran arrives in a society where its males are away fighting or have been killed, the arrival of the unit might help balance out a skewed local ratio. In environments where there are fewer cultural barriers between the deployed service member and the local population, liaisons are much more common: "War seriously disturbs the sex ratio. Ordinarily the mores work because most of the population can satisfy its wishes within the framework of the mores. When the sex ratio is seriously unbalanced . . . [it] furnish[es] the dynamic for many new and strange moralities."[27]

One of these "strange moralities" is the growth of prostitution and its general acceptance by a large number of military members: "In places other than ports of debarkation, houses of prostitution were tolerated by our officers, and our soldiers were permitted free access."[28] While many military members disapprove of this practice, the general moral attitudes of war, which already weaken traditional morality, create an atmosphere of tolerance or, more likely, indifference. Privation in the local economy and the steady pay of soldiers also facilitates arrangements between the sexes. However, the unregulated nature of these relationships, and their some-time deleterious effect on the fighting effectiveness of some soldiers (e.g., due to sexually transmitted diseases), occasionally prompts the military authorities to get involved. A famous public health poster issued by the U.S. military during World War I in Europe makes this point fairly explicitly: "A German bullet is cleaner than a whore!"[29]

> About 75,000 prostitutes were in Paris during the war [World War I], and the overwhelming majority were street-walkers. Only about 5,000 were licensed and inspected, the remaining 70,000 being without supervision or control. Solicitation was the rule. Paris provost marshals and plainclothes members of the intelligence force were ordered to report those associating with prostitutes and women of questionable character.[30]

Due to the cultural and security barriers between U.S. military personnel and the local populations in Afghanistan and Iraq, there were few opportunities for local relationships to develop. There are some reports of Iraqi "war brides" but not many from Afghanistan. However, prostitution did take place in brothels in Baghdad and in Kabul. None were officially sanctioned, but some service members did partake in their services.[31] Some prostitution also took place within the forward operating bases of deployed personnel by third-country nationals, among other arrangements. A new feature, which largely did not exist in earlier wars, or at least not to the degree of these wars, was the increasing number of females serving in the military. The gender ratio was not as skewed as it had been in the past, and there are more examples today, compared to past wars, of soldiers meeting their wives and husbands on deployment from among other service members.

The experiences of war, combat, and having the power of life and death that soldiers possess further complicate an already pressurized environment of sexual relations. Taking life, living in privation, and the constant exposure to death, injury, and pain foster a short-term mind-set: "In wartime, many of the group mores are shelved, their place taken by the touchstone of pleasure versus pain. To eat, drink, and be merry today anticipates the rendezvous with death tomorrow."[32] Waller provides additional perspective:

> Because [the soldier] can make no plans, because he is deprived of many of the comforts of life, because a great deal of his time is spent in just waiting and those empty hours must be filled somehow, because life is uncertain, the soldier adopts a philosophy of life on a short-term hedonistic basis— hence his vices.[33]

It is challenging to live in an environment where death is constant, takes place for the most profound but often banal reasons, and seems, at times, unpredictable and capricious. Having adjusted to the exigencies of war, the veteran has now taken life, lived in a world of destruction and death, seen friends die, dealt with the unpredictability of war, and has a moral horizon of the next day. When it comes to love and relationships, the veteran is ill suited to pursue them. As the war journalist Chris Hedges puts it:

> There is in wartime a nearly universal preoccupation with sexual liaisons. There is a kind of breathless abandon in wartime, and those who in peacetime would lead conservative and sheltered lives give themselves over to wanton carnal relationships. Men, and especially soldiers, are preoccupied with little else. With power reduced to such a raw level and the currency of life and death cheap, eroticism races through all relationships. There is in these encounters a frenetic lust that seeks, on some level, to replicate or augment the drug of war. It is certainly not about love, indeed love itself in wartime is hard to sustain or establish.[34]

However, the drive for companionship is not just for short-term physical reasons; it is also sought for less prurient reasons, as an antidote to "gloom, irony and disgust."[35] It is a form of restorative love that helps veterans cope with hardship, which allows them to drop the veil of harshness they have cultivated to be vulnerable once again, to be what they had once been before the war. It is also a moment for privacy away from their unit and colleagues and to be safe, even for a brief moment. But the violence of the veteran's experience isn't confined to what he does to the enemy; it sometimes crosses into his personal relations: "The widespread casual and frenetic sex in wartime often crosses the line into perversion and violence. It exposes the vast moral void. When life becomes worth nothing, when one is not sure of survival, when a society is ruled by fear, there often seems only death or fleeting, carnal pleasure."[36] In these situations, the violence of war is visited on the population or on relationships the veteran has in his life, and the casual nature of companionship changes into abuse, assault, rape, or worse.

Returning Home

> *"In seeking to explain the peculiar morality of the soldier, we must take cognizance of the following facts: The soldier lives in a one-sex group, away from his own community and out of touch with the women whom he knows and who know him. The soldier has given up, or had taken from him, all responsibility for the conduct of his own life; he is under orders; it is not up to him to plan his life or to reason why, he must merely obey orders and live or die in accordance with the destiny that does or does not bring a bullet in his direction. . . . [T]he strict regimentation of life in the army necessitates release in some other department of life, and that release is found in the relaxation of conventional morality, particularly in the field of sex. Finally, the soldier develops a sort of last-fling psychology which characterizes his behavior when off duty. Any day may be his last; he may soon be an inanimate object incapable of enjoying wine, women, or song, and he feels that he must make the most of all his opportunities."*
>
> —WILLARD WALLER, *WAR AND THE FAMILY*, 14–15

The veteran who returns home from war has a set of conflicting moralities that exist simultaneously in his mind, and the morality he returns with has adapted to war, the institution of the U.S. military, and the unique conditions of his particular conflict.

Gradually new, wartime mores arise to cover novel situations; also adaptations of the old mores. There are many violations of the prewar mores, some of which are condoned by the mores of war time. Still the former mores persist and one cannot violate them even under the urge of imperative necessity without paying some penalty.[37]

His moral horizons are short term, and he is quick to aggression, has little patience, and is emotionally dead or underreacts. He has adapted to the formalism of the service (which has its own rigid codes and mores) and the imbalanced sex ratio of the military and of wartime, and he has developed a harshness to endure the conditions of his service. These tendencies are reinforced for many Afghan and Iraq War military veterans due to the repeated nature of their deployments and the cultural and security barriers between them and the local population. Similarly, many counterinsurgency veterans have developed an indirect manner of thinking and communicating, honed, in part, by the face-saving characteristics of Afghan and Iraqi culture as well as the manner in which the insurgency fights. The veteran has also become highly intuitive and thinks of second- and third-order effects all the time. He has begun to think and operate like an insurgent. Further, released from his small unit and his comrades, he now lacks the temporizing effects of group identity and its ability to moderate his tendencies. Waller captures this process well: "The confusion of morality produced by war probably reaches its height in the post-war period. The old mores persist, along with new mores produced by the war and nascent attempts at adjustment of the mores to the changed conditions produced by war."[38]

Having returned home, the veteran now seeks companionship but finds he is not well suited for long-term partnership. Unshackled from the rigidities of military life, free from the stress of war service, and accustomed to aggression and short-term liaisons, the veteran is unleashed on a society with a balanced sex ratio that has a generally relaxed civilian morality. The veteran is almost euphoric from the lack of regimentation and stress, and he now has ready access to all the things that were prohibited to him in military life or due to austere living conditions.

In war time there is a decay of all the established moralities, which tend to be replaced by hedonistic life adjustments on a short-term basis. In a word, the mores decline, and vices spread and become respectable. . . . If we study the impact of war upon the mores more soberly and in more detail, we discover a long series of moral dislocations comparable to the dislocations of economic life which war entails.[39]

Additionally, because his family, friends, and community are accustomed to him being away, the veteran exists in this transitional phase where the moral anchoring of his prior life has not yet incorporated him back. Similarly, the veteran has money from his deployment (and perhaps even a pension or disability check), the prestige of war service, and time on his hands to indulge his proclivities. As a reaction to the rigidity of military life and communal living, the veteran adopts an almost rebellious mood: "During the war years, a rigid military control pervades the whole life of the nation, but after the war this is relaxed. One effect of military control is to engender widespread rebellion, so that when the control is removed there is a tendency to react violently in defiance of previously accepted standards."[40] In this environment, such short-term hedonism augmented by "moral dislocation" causes all sorts of problems for the returned war veteran as he simultaneously gropes for love and lust.

Many war veterans move from one "relationship" to another in a frantic manner, seeking companionship wherever they can get it. They juggle multiple partners and are not limited (or not as influenced) by the moral dictates of civilian life. They use their war and military adaptations in the dating world and compartmentalize each relationship, plan dates as if they are missions, scrutinize possible partners as if they are assembling a target package, are aggressive and assertive, and have the moral horizon of the next mission: "Some veterans report turning from one sex affair to another; trying, no doubt, to discover in the relationship of the sexes the meanings that war and army life had taken from their lives."[41] Unconstrained by civilian morality, or a civilian morality ill suited to the veteran at that time in his life, and infused by the amoral utilitarianism of war, many war veterans become sources of moral anarchy: "In war all this is changed; the habit systems of individuals are shattered and their morality is dissolved; institutions lose their power to keep human beings in line."[42]

> Almost inevitably, the soldier falls into a short-term hedonism. In the place of the accepted morality of civilian society, the soldier regulates his life by individualistic, hedonistic adjustments on a short-term basis. Morality is a matter of the long pull; it involves long-term rewards and punishments.[43]

However, as the veteran's support networks reintegrate him back into civilian life, and as he overreaches in his hedonism, he begins to reach his thermidor wherein he takes stock of his destruction and seeks balance. This process also takes place because other responsibilities or relationships in the veteran's life, such as employment and friendships, have not gone well or his behavior has been corrected (e.g., by workplace rules and mores if he has found a job). The veteran has hit the wall of proper behavior and now seeks some return to normalcy.

At this point in the veteran's integration home, the object of his short-term horizons becomes the means by which he can refocus on long-term stability. The sharp aggression of his war zone mentality begins to recede, the war adaptations don't serve as vital a function as they used to, although his morality is still some combination of his war and prewar morality: "[The veteran] is bitter over the denial of love, but does not know how to express love, or to elicit it in others. Lust, of course, he understands thoroughly, having explored its uttermost boundaries."[44] The veteran now begins a process of seeking long-term stability and happiness with a partner, and it is here that women help many veterans navigate this journey: "It is primarily women who reintegrate the warrior back into society, the energy of the queen, not the king. Women carry this queen for most young men."[45] This doesn't necessarily mean only women he has a personal interest in but also includes his mother, sisters, and female friends who, through their examples, patience, and counsel, redirect the veteran to a calmer life. In many respects, the veteran welcomes this shift, this change to normalcy, as the costs of his moral instability become evident and he loses the war zone adaptations of short-term behaviors. Further, this process of regularizing his behavior also allows him to work through his war experience, and having a companion invested in long-term stability increases the likelihood of deep understanding between partners. Sometimes, though, the veteran rushes too quickly into this normalcy of marriage; he still has the short-term impulsiveness of the war veteran and finds his choice for partnership was not the best.

> During a war-time period and especially when there is more or less universal conscription among certain age ranges, many young men and women who would normally contract marriage are forced to delay this act. Such a delay period, spent in partial segregation between the sexes, serves to intensify the normal desire to participate in matrimony and this intensified desire has the effect of reducing even the customary rationality which men and women display when they agree to contract marriage. . . . Thus heightened desire, post-war hysteria, and personality or physical changes, operating singly or together, can account for the instability of post-war marriages.[46]

Similarly, many women accustomed to too few men in society due to war service also rush into matrimony, causing further instability. However it works out, the war veteran navigates this transition home and the search for love in various ways. Some veterans never truly make a successful transition home with respect to finding a long-term partner or, only much later, arrive at a new balance in life when they find someone. For these veterans, the short-term hedonistic culture of war almost becomes an elevated form of human existence that is primal and free from obligation. They have created some new version of morality that works for their disposition: "War creates a great number of new social situations and forms of human association which are not regulated by a pre-existing custom."[47] For many of these male veterans, they craft their lives around this tendency and are drawn to various pursuits that facilitate it.

The war veteran makes a series of moral, physical, intellectual, and psychological adaptions to survive in war. He also adjusts to service in the U.S. military and living in an environment of austerity and hardship and, depending on the nature of the country, in cultures that may not be as compatible with his own. In this world of combat, death, and injury, he has crafted a personality that includes a quickness to aggression, emotional deadening, and high tolerance of risk, as well as short-term moral adjustments that are often quite hedonistic. Upon his return, the war veteran navigates the transition from these moralities to those of his home front while he seeks companionship. He has seen his life delayed while he has been away fighting for his country and simultaneously seeks to make up for lost time while sometimes seeking other short-term arrangements. As the veteran balances these impulses, which are in tension with each other, he slowly reintegrates into the moral universe of his country, with friends and family helping him regain balance in his personal life. While most veterans navigate these various transitions relatively successfully, some veterans continue to struggle to find love, companionship, and long-term love.

Military Humor

> "But I'm afraid the jokes that made us reel with laughter would be flat to-day. One jumped at any excuse to be gay, and to laugh meant to forget that open door, facing the wrong way, through which a shell might come at any moment to burst in the midst of us."
>
> —CHARLES EDMONDS, *A SUBALTERN'S WAR*, 174

As the grandson of a World War II veteran and the son of a former U.S. Army officer, I grew up watching military movies and TV shows and reading the comic strips *Up Front* by Bill Mauldin and *Beetle Bailey* by Mort Walker. I frequently didn't understand many of the references to military life or the nuances the comic strips portrayed, but I appreciated the humorous situations the characters often found themselves in. The TV show *M*A*S*H* was a staple in my household, and it made military life a real thing for me, with my father sometimes referencing his own time in the service as we watched it together. As I got older and then started to deploy overseas, I gained a new appreciation for these types of shows and comic strips, seeing the sometimes caustic, sometimes ludicrous humor as good people adapting to difficult and unusual situations. I noted more and more the themes of living with death, confronting the inane procedures of the military bureaucracy, the fear of combat, the challenges of love and companionship, and all the complexities of people thrown together to achieve a common purpose under stressful conditions. The humor of veterans is often profane, ironic, dark, and morbid, but it is also childish, sophomoric, and frequently ridiculous, and it involves numerous pranks. As with most people, veterans use humor to deal with life's travails, to build camaraderie, and to make sense of often demanding and difficult circumstances.

One of the most challenging adjustments for veterans when they serve in war is dealing with the violence and reality of death. Similarly, they are also called upon to visit violence on our nation's enemies as part of a group (e.g., small unit) while navigating the complexities of the U.S. military and its bureaucracy. War veterans usually operate in an almost completely male environment in war, more so in combat units, and the men are young and share many common life experiences that come with their youth. These young men grapple with significant challenges in war such as coping with injury, death, and hardship: "Soldier's language is profane and vigorous, symbolic of his world without women. It was often otherwise with him as a civilian."[48] The most prominent type of humor for war veterans is usually referred to as "gallows humor," which, invariably, revolves around the subject of death: "The cynicism of slang helps to make bearable the grim realities of maiming and death—of 'pushing daisies in Skeleton Park' and the macabre jokes about well-ripened cadavers that soldiers on the firing-line have always favored."[49] This type of humor is typically used to relieve stress and build camaraderie, but it also serves other purposes as well and functions as an almost oral history of war knowledge passed on to other combatants.[50] It conveys the best practices and lessons learned of combat, acquaints the veteran with the themes of bad luck and preparedness, and teaches him how to navigate the hierarchy of the military and how to think of the enemy. In 2005, when

I served with the U.S. Department of State at the Tarin Kowt Provincial Reconstruction Team in Uruzgan Province, Afghanistan, I was first introduced to something called Murphy's Laws of Combat.[51] These "laws" are patterned after Murphy's famous "law" that "anything that can go wrong will go wrong" but adapted to war zones.

Many of its maxims focus exclusively on lessons learned from combat and making do with adversity. Its central theme is how to survive in a war zone, emphasizing how to avoid danger as well as how to successfully operate as part of a military unit. It is done in a somewhat humorous and somewhat cynical manner befitting war veterans. Chief among these is "Teamwork is essential, it gives them someone else to shoot at" as well as "Don't look conspicuous, it draws fire" and, relatedly, "Never draw fire, it irritates everyone around you." The lessons here are to operate as a member of a team and, as you do so, be mindful of how your individual choices can impact the group. As a member of a small unit involved in combat, there are several maxims that provide guidance to the veteran to shape his behavior. These include "When in doubt, empty your magazine" (a good way to handle uncertainty); "If at first you don't succeed, call in an air strike" (no need to put yourself in danger if a better option is available); and "Anything you do can get you shot, including nothing" (which suggests not thinking of inaction as an option because the enemy always gets a vote). Additionally, "The easy way is always mined" reminds the veteran that the enemy counts on him to be lazy or less tactically aware, and so this truism pushes the veteran to think like his opponent. Some dictums pertain to gear and operating in a joint (multiservice) environment, such as "Air strikes always overshoot the target; artillery always falls short" and "A grenade with a seven-second fuse will always burn down in four seconds." Further, in order to survive combat, it is good to remember that "incoming fire has the right of way," which is to say, don't be a hero when bullets are flying; your safety is more important.

The second major theme of these rules is how the enemy operates and their strategy, as well as how to handle them in combat. The key theme is the need to be ever vigilant in a war zone environment, such as "The enemy never watches until you make a mistake," "The enemy never monitors your radio frequency until you broadcast on an insecure channel," and "The enemy *always* times his attack to the second you drop your pants in the latrine!" Another theme is to remember that what you think the enemy is doing may not actually be what he is doing, and so the veteran must be skeptical about what he "thinks" is going on in combat. Chief among these are "If the enemy is in range, so are you," and "Whenever you lose contact with the enemy, look behind you," as well as "Remember, a retreating enemy is probably just regrouping for a counterattack." Related themes include "The enemy diversion you have been ignoring will be the main attack" and "If your attack is going well, you have walked into an ambush," as well as "When you have secured an area, don't forget to tell the enemy." These maxims remind the veteran that the enemy is a dynamic opponent who is constantly adapting his strategy as well as using deception to achieve his objectives.

The world of the war veteran is also one where serendipity, luck (good and bad), and fatalism exist unevenly with his natural urge to project order and logic on the world around him. Many humorous maxims try to narrow this gap between logic and unpredictability as well as help the veteran make do with the fact that he may be unable to do anything about aspects of it. Chief among these are "Radios will fail as soon as you need fire support," "The Cavalry doesn't always come to the rescue," "Whenever you drop your equipment in a firefight, your ammo and grenades always fall the farthest away (and your canteen always lands at your feet)," and "The one item you need is always in short supply." Some are more philosophical, such as "The important things are always simple; the simple are always hard," "If you are short of everything but the enemy, you are in the combat zone," and "Whenever you have plenty of ammo, you never miss. Whenever you are low on ammo, you can't hit the broad side of a barn." Others are just good common sense wrapped in humorous language, although often cynical, such as "Interchangeable parts aren't," "Combat will occur on the ground between two adjoining maps," and "The only thing more accurate than incoming enemy fire is incoming friendly fire." Some maxims also help the veteran put his injuries in their proper context as well as help him process, in a humorous manner, his injuries, such as "A Purple Heart just goes to prove that were you smart enough to think of a plan, stupid enough to try it, and lucky enough to survive" and "A 'sucking chest wound' is nature's way of telling you to slow down." These efforts to help the veteran make peace with the unpredictability of war are part of the informal oral tradition of veterans in war helping other veterans improve their odds of survival.

However challenging it is to successfully operate in a war zone, there is the added challenge of navigating the complexities of the military bureaucracy and its hierarchy, as well as living with the people you work with overseas. Since the world of the deployed military is largely one of enlisted men, many of these aphorisms are focused on officers and how they think and lead. One of the more famous is this observation about second lieutenants: "The most dangerous thing in the world is a second lieutenant with a map and a compass." Others include "If you really need an officer in a hurry, take a nap" and "The tough part about being an officer is that the troops don't know what they want, but they know for certain what they *don't* want." The second area of focus is on non–commissioned officers and includes "If the platoon sergeant can see you, so can the enemy" and "Never tell the platoon sergeant you have nothing to do." Others are simply reflections on the nature of the military personnel system and life in a hierarchical organization, such as "The perfect officer for the job will transfer in the day after that billet is filled by someone else" and "Why is it the commanding officer sticks his head in your radio hooch to see if anything has come down from Division when you are listening to Voice of America broadcasting the baseball games?" Some humorous observations are about the nature of working in a military bureaucracy, such as "Things that must work together can't be carried to the field that way," "Things that must be shipped together as a set, aren't," and "The quartermaster has only two sizes, too large and too small."

Most of Murphy's Laws of Combat focus on combat and war in a largely conventional warfare setting. Counterinsurgency veterans would likely take issue with the maxims of "When in doubt, empty your magazine" and "If at first you don't succeed, call in an air strike" when clearing homes, villages, and city blocks, where discretion in the use of violence and the need to minimize civilian casualties and damage to civilian property is paramount. However, due to how closely U.S. military personnel worked with indigenous military units in Afghanistan and Iraq as well as local leaders in both countries, another strand of humor is focused on local culture as well as on how insurgents fought in that context. One of the more common is how attractive Afghan "T&A" was among the soldiers, which meant, in this context, "toes and ankles" of women ostensibly covered head to toe in burkas, rather than another, more popular meaning. Other humorous stories included asking the question "What would you do with a million dollars?" which is taken from the 1999 movie *Office Space*, where the character responds with "Two chicks at the same time." In the Afghan context, one such response was "Two shuras [meetings with Afghan elders] at the same time." This was a reference to the interminable meetings U.S. personnel had with village elders and the frustration some military personnel had with balancing U.S. development needs and the seemingly unquenchable thirst of the Afghans for projects. It's probably not the funniest statement in the U.S. civilian context, but it was quite humorous overseas. Another story comes from a civilian advisor working at a provincial reconstruction team in Ghazni Province who had a meeting with the provincial chief of police. The advisor thrust his hand out to greet the man but, upon a close inspection of the officer's fingers, noticed he had two thumbs on both hands. He could not withdraw his hand since this would have been disrespectful, so he clenched the man's hand tightly and gave it a good shaking even as the extra thumb bounced around all the while never breaking contact with his eyes. He later wrote a report titled "Security in Ghazni Province: Two Thumbs Up."

Other humorous stories focus on locals and the role of violence in their lives. Another advisor witnessed one rocket fly over his base in Farah Province in western Afghanistan only to see a second follow soon thereafter. Roughly twenty minutes later an injured Afghan man with burns on large parts of his body came to the gate of the base asking for help. The Americans there thought he had been injured by the rockets, but, upon further discussion, it turns out the man had fired both rockets at the base. He had set the first rocket up against a rock, attached two wires to it, and then connected them to a battery. He then balanced a second rocket against the rock and, using the same wires, connected them to the rocket. Since he was standing right next to the rocket when it went off, because the wires were still connected to the battery, it severely burned him. The moxy of the Afghan villager to launch an attack against the base and then request medical assistance from the same U.S. personnel he was targeting was shocking but not surprising. In Iraq, a story circulated that might have been apocryphal, but it always brought a chuckle to veterans. It was very brief, and it essentially was about a suicide bomber who was on his way to a mission but fell down the stairs of his house and blew himself up. Most veterans got a laugh from that since it showed amazing ineptitude on the part of the attacker and signified one less insurgent to kill. Sometimes veterans would mock the insurgents, such as when a group of Marines filmed themselves standing around a large fish placed on a table. The five Marines were standing together, wearing masks as the insurgents tended to do, and then made threatening gestures and read a speech condemning U.S. forces in Iraq (as insurgents would do) whereupon one of the Marines took a large knife out of his blouse and quickly beheaded the fish much like al-Qaeda in Iraq did against several of its prisoners. This humor was decidedly dark but also mocked the brutality of the insurgents.

Some humor also made fun of other Coalition partners, such as the humorous reinterpretation of the ISAF acronym in Afghanistan, which stood for "International Security Assistance Force." Some U.S. soldiers said it meant "I suck at fighting," "I saw Americans Fight," or "I sun at the FOB [forward operating base]." All of these observations are criticisms of the abilities of international partners to fight the war in Afghanistan effectively. Other humor touched on companionship in war, such as "Never go to bed with anyone crazier than yourself" from Murphy's Laws of Combat. One set of rules that was shared pertaining to sex in war zones included the following: "Always sleep up the chain of command, never sleep with crazy, and, if you can't sleep with an American, sleep 'ABC'—Australians, the British, or the Canadians." Other humorous expressions that are also tragic include using the word *Jody* to describe U.S.-based men who sleep with the wives and girlfriends of deployed military personnel. Related is the use of the term *Dependapotamus*, which is a military dependent, typically a local who lives near a base and who seems largely to be in a relationship with a member of the military in order to derive benefits (e.g., housing, health care, etc.) from the service member. It's a play on the words *dependent* and *hippopotamus* and was made popular by the comic strip and graphic novels of former U.S. Marine and Iraq veteran Maximilian Uriarte.

A lot of deployed humor focuses on military personnel playing pranks on each other, which is not that surprising since most veterans are young men. Pranks have included removing the slats of a bunk bed, causing the person to crash through it, or locking a sex doll in someone's Humvee. Others include hiding a mechanism that makes the sound of a cricket in someone's room and having them go crazy trying to find it. Some humor I've witnessed included the diligent collecting of body-building photos over a number of months and then putting them throughout a master chief's hooch when he was on a mission. Another humorous episode included having four SEALs dress in body suits from head to toe and then pose (such as in a human pyramid) for various photos in the same master chief's room when he was on a mission only to slowly post each photo in a nightly brief over the next two weeks. Most of these episodes are silly and not particularly hilarious but make for great levity on deployment.

A final aspect of humor in war zones concerns the use of morale patches, which veterans put on their uniforms while on deployment (see also chapter 7, "Militaria"). Many of these patches are lines from popular movies such as "Get to the Choppa," which is from the movie *Predator* and is said by the actor Arnold Schwarzenegger, and "Stay Classy," which is from the movie *Ron Burgundy* and said by the actor Will Ferrell. Others include the usual references to zombies, such as "Zombie Outbreak Response Team" and "Running on Hulk Mode," and a rich variety of others that bring a smile to deployed personnel: "Raining Freedom (C-130 gunship)," "Special Snowflake," "We Do Bad Things to Bad People," "Shut

Up, Listen, Perform," "Mama Says I'm Special," "Embrace the Suck," "Don't Tread on Me," and "Like a Boss," among many others.

Conclusion

The civilian who joins the military and then deploys to war undergoes a series of transformations in how he thinks, organizes, and behaves. He necessarily adjusts psychologically, morally, physically, and intellectually to a world of violence and death as a member of a small unit fighting the enemies of his nation. He exists in a largely all-male environment where, out of necessity, he thinks as a member of a group and, depending upon cultural and security conditions, is largely walled off from the indigenous population. As he grapples with the implications of a violent death, his behavior and horizons narrow to the next minute, the next hour, and the next day; he cannot think of the future. His fatalistic short-termism is augmented by the jocularity of the brotherhood of his fellow veterans, and their reversion to child-like or immature humor helps him cope with stress, build camaraderie, and learn how to successfully operate in a war zone. His cynicism, sense of humor, preference for action, and narrow time horizons are all adapted behaviors that he must adjust upon returning home and leaving the service. Many of these give the returned war veteran decided advantages in life, but others cause him complications that affect how he copes with the new challenges of life on the home front.

Zombies, Movies, and Video Games   **4**

"The hardest part about a zombie apocalypse will be pretending I'm not excited."

—POPULAR VETERAN T-SHIRT

"Cardio. To escape a pursuing zombie you will need to out-run it, and this means being in good shape."

—*ZOMBIELAND* (FILM), 2009

W HEN I WAS GROWING UP IN FLORIDA toward the end of the Cold War, one of the perennial topics I used to think about was how to survive a nuclear war and the apocalyptic world it would create. However dark this may seem in retrospect, discussions of this kind took place in the 1980s but were more of a thought exercise for impressionable boys than any practical, actionable plan. While the odds of nuclear war were incredibly remote during this time, the challenge of thinking through its implications was enticing for me. In this vein, one book that influenced me greatly was Pat Frank's 1959 classic *Alas, Babylon*, which is a postapocalyptic novel set in a small town in Florida following a nuclear war. As a thirteen-year-old attending Vero Beach Junior High School, I devoured the book and remember to this day some of its lessons about survival and its observations of those who survived, and those who did not, in this new world of radiation, devastation, scarcity, and a non-functioning government. The harsh reality that those who relied upon refrigerated medicines to survive were the first to perish due to a lack of electricity, for example, was disturbingly instructive. The observation of the protagonist, Randy Bragg, that his old southern home, raised off the ground and designed to facilitate airflow in an era before electricity and air-conditioning, was ideally suited to this new reality was a revelation. The need to organize the community to reestablish law and order as stability broke down was also informative. Over the years, my friends and I used to talk about what we would do in such a situation, what skills we would need to acquire, where we would hole up during the apocalypse, and what supplies we would need. As the Soviet Union collapsed and the reality of nuclear war diminished, my friends and I still thought about survival scenarios to include, increasingly, how we would deal with zombies.

One of the many pastimes of war veterans is thinking about what can only be characterized as survival scenarios. It comes naturally to a veteran in war because its ideation helps him think through how he would perform in combat, how he would undertake his vital role in his unit, and what tactics, techniques, and procedures he would use to prevail. The survival instinct is natural for a war veteran and explains such idiosyncrasies as sitting with your back against a wall with a good view of the front door, planning for redundancy, having a healthy skepticism of people's motives, and thinking through secondary and tertiary steps: "In short, the soldier develops a mental system, complete with attitudes, behavior patterns, forms of logic, beliefs and philosophy, custom-tailored to the needs of his life."[1] Aspects of this mentality usually include extensive discussions about gear, weapons, fighting strategies, locations to escape to, conversations of who to include in your group, and various scenarios of how people would react. Many veterans have thought through these varied aspects of survival, and it is commonplace for them to discuss the finer points of their strategies with each other. These kinds of conversations are often more prevalent on the home front as the distance between the adapted responses of veterans to war (which help veterans survive) confront the practicalities of a largely peaceful and stable society upon return. It is quite common for many veterans to privately judge the survival strategies of civilians, to marvel at the trust they have in people and institutions, and to comment on how generally ill prepared they are for adversity. Into this mental framework steps the world of zombies.

Whether it's from an asteroid, a virus, or some experiment that escaped a government lab, the world of the zombie is a world with which most war veterans are familiar. It is a war zone, and the veteran knows its rules inherently. He understands the motivations and abilities of the enemy, both human and zombie, and has already thought through his strategy and gear and feels confident in his abilities. The old habits from deployment are dusted off; he can set aside the responsibilities of his peacetime life—the job that does not excite him but pays the bills—and focus anew on what he is good at and what he knows: "When the civilian-turned-soldier has adjusted his personality to the demands of the military machine, he has thereby lost some part of his ability to adjust to the demands of civilian society."[2] He can crack open that trunk with his old deployment gear sitting in the attic; it is ready for use again. His obligations are greater now; he likely has a family, but the habits that his family consider endearing quirks or his civilian colleagues regard as peculiar habits are vindicated. There is a reason he insisted on a four-wheel-drive truck, why he has a family medical bag ready, why he retains so many weapons, and why his house is on higher ground and has a clear line of fire. These are all war zone adaptations that have been repurposed for civilian life and regain their meaning in the zombie apocalypse. That is, at least, how this type of survival scenario would work in his mind if zombies were real. For the war veteran, zombie movies and conversations about how to survive a zombie apocalypse fulfill a need that war veterans have, which they might not be aware of in its totality.

Most zombie movies take place in a peaceful civilian setting that quickly devolves into a postapocalyptic world of flesh-eating undead and humans willing to do anything to survive. For the war veteran who has returned home, this abrupt shift is the reverse of his adjustment to home; civilians must now adapt to the world of war he had adjusted to overseas: "One's attitudes are the function of one's life situation. The soldier revaluates the civilian attitudes of his former self, because his new life situation as a warrior forces him to reevaluate them. . . . The values that the soldier has learned to respect in war are the values of war and not the values of peace. The hardness, obscenity, fatalism . . . cannot suddenly be dispelled."[3] Many civilians grasp for the rules of this new reality, and many do adapt quite readily, but the war veteran already has a leg up. His mind is infused with the framework of war and the mathematics of violence. To illustrate the overlap in this war mentality and the requirements of survival in a zombie world, here is a selection of the more relevant rules of survival from the 2009 movie *Zombieland*.

> #1: Cardio: When the virus struck, for obvious reasons, the first ones to go were the fatties.
> #2: Double tap: In those moments when you're not sure the undead are really dead dead, don't get all stingy with your bullets.

#3: Beware of bathrooms: Don't let them catch you with your pants down.

#4: Seat belts: Fasten your seat belts. It's gonna be a bumpy ride.

#7: Travel light: And I don't mean just luggage.

#17: Don't be a hero: Why don't you take this one?

#17: Be a hero: Some rules are made to be broken. (Rule updated.)

#18: Limber up: Going down that hill, it is very important.

#22: When in doubt, know your way out.

#23: Ziploc bags: You got enough problems; moisture shouldn't be one of them.

#31: Check the back seat: No one back there but my duffel bag.

#32: Enjoy the little things: I hate to give credit to anyone who looks like Yosemite Sam, but I'm writing it down.

#52: Don't be afraid to ask for help: Yeah, and they ignored rule 52: don't be afraid to ask for help.

The essence of these rules is to be physically fit and ready for action, be aggressive with the enemy, plan for resiliency in your strategy, maintain tactical awareness, work as a team, don't get tunnel vision in a firefight, and keep your head on a swivel. The war veteran understands these and other rules completely. However useful and entertaining it is for the war veteran to think through various survival strategies in a zombie world, these types of movies, books, and games resonate with him on many deeper levels.

The adjustment to civilian life or simply returning home from war can be difficult for many veterans. Zombie postapocalyptic scenarios resonate with veterans because they are a way for them to still use their training in a manner that is entertaining for them, as well as a way to maintain connections with other veterans and deployment friends. However, there is also an underlying critique of civilians by veterans in these situations. Some veterans experience a less than positive integration experience when they come home and are sometimes resentful of civilian life and its perceived "softness." For these veterans, there is some satisfaction at seeing the "softness" of society exposed by the ruthless violence and logic of the zombie apocalypse. Seeing poorly thought-out strategies defeated by the zombies is somewhat soul satisfying for some war veterans and serves as a sort of vindication for their war zone adaptations and general way of living life. Another dimension to this situation is that the veteran, conversely, rises to the occasion; he is once again in the arena, and his knowledge, training, and gear elevates him to a position of prominence. For many veterans, the authority and, frankly, power they had in war is difficult to replicate on the home front once they demobilize. Zombie movies allow veterans to vicariously experience this sort of importance once more and to be central again in the world of war.

Zombie scenarios in particular resonate with veterans of the wars in Afghanistan and Iraq because, in an era of protracted and relatively inconclusive wars of counterinsurgency, they provide what I term "attrition escapism." The only solution in a zombie apocalypse is attrition: the systematic destruction and killing of zombies. The zombies wear a uniform of sorts—they are the undead, after all—and so are far easier to identify than insurgents hiding within the population. Similarly, there is no "hearts and minds" campaign in a zombie world wherein you work with local communities to turn against the insurgents by drilling wells in villages, building roads and clinics, and conducting key leader engagements with local political, tribal, civic, and security leaders. Additionally, while there is no discernible end in a zombie world, a war veteran can at least mark out what the path to victory could look like by simply killing more zombies. The world of the zombie is almost exclusively strategy free from a macro sense and is a series of tactical and operational moves that, for the vast majority of veterans who are not officers or even senior officers, is a satisfying worldview because it mimics the perspective of their own deployments. Additionally, survival is almost exclusively about small-unit action, which echoes the veteran's experience. Further, there are few moral hazards from killing zombies, and the complexities and moral ambiguities of counterinsurgency are largely absent. When it comes to humans, the veteran is also well disposed because, outside of his small group of survivors, almost all people are hostile to him and seek to take what he and his group have collected. In these situations, the veteran relies once more upon his war zone experiences as guides to his behavior. There is very little negotiation with these groups, there is very little collaboration, and questions of governing, strategy, and a solution to the zombie apocalypse never really come up. Outside of the TV series *The Walking Dead* and the film *World War Z*, most movies about zombies (e.g., *Shaun of the Dead*, *Dawn of the Dead*) don't last long enough for larger considerations to be evaluated, which satisfies the veteran's need to focus only on those things that resonate with him.

Movies

The entertainment industry is split when it comes to presenting irregular wars to the American public. There are stories of valor to be shared, but no conclusive ending to the war, and the moral ambiguities of these types of conflicts, and their inherently political nature, create opportunities for profit as well as political mischief. Great patriotic films about irregular wars, such as those of World War II, are much rarer in part because conclusive battles of a sufficient scale for films are extremely uncommon in irregular wars (and there is often no conclusive end) and movies generally require upbeat endings. What is unusual about the wars in Afghanistan and Iraq is that the commencing of the first, Operation Enduring Freedom, was due to our country being attacked (it's a great patriotic war, but it's also an irregular war), and the second, Operation Iraqi Freedom, was due to a concerted policy decision (inherently controversial). Additionally, the longevity of these conflicts and their inconclusive nature tax the patience of civilians, and war interest eventually wanes. Movies about irregular wars are most often about (1) conclusive acts of valor such as counterterrorism missions (e.g., *Zero Dark Thirty*), (2) patriotic movies focusing on clearing/ shaping operations (e.g., *Horse Soldiers* or *American Sniper*), (3) cultural/ education films (e.g., *The Kite Runner*), (4) antiwar films (e.g., *Green Zone*), (5) tragedy (e.g., *Lone Survivor*), or (6) returning home (e.g., *Thank You for Your Service*). They are often about discrete tactical events often tied to tragedies, or they showcase the exoticism of a country. Many films are antiwar, although most movies in this genre are almost exclusively about the war in Iraq.

It is profoundly difficult to accurately convey a war of counterinsurgency in a cinematic manner to a broad public. Conventional wars present simpler narratives of success (e.g., defeat the enemy's military, remove the enemy from X territory) as well as images that are easier to cinematically convey (e.g., sweeping movements of tanks, planes, ships, etc.). It is more challenging to demonstrate success in counterinsurgency when victory may be a whimper versus an epic battle and may take place years or even decades into the future. Further, while large clearing operations are necessary in counterinsurgency campaigns, victory is measured in the degree to which locals join their own security forces to secure their country and fight the armed insurgency and join in political efforts to lead their nation. Successful counterinsurgency campaigns are inherently about what locals do and how U.S. efforts bolster them, but movies and movie-watching publics are principally interested in seeing U.S. forces directly involved in combat. These types of movies almost exclusively focus on the actions of American soldiers and the enemy rather than the local population. Further, the time lines for these types of movies tend to be short and focused on a satisfying and conclusive ending. The objective is taken, the enemy is defeated, and the viewer can go home with some satisfaction. How does one convey the patient building up of indigenous forces over many years, the political reform efforts that diminish the sources of grievance the insurgency feeds off of, and the cultural nuances of convincing communities to turn against the insurgency? How does one do these things for a war that is almost always inherently controversial in domestic politics or becomes so over time? When the war is not seen as an existential threat to the home front?

Largely for these and other considerations, movies tend to focus on those aspects of counterinsurgency (COIN) campaigns that are as close as they can get to conventional combat narratives. The general construct of COIN campaigns in a military sense focuses on shaping, clearing, holding, building, and transitioning phases. The enemy's armed wing is "shaped" by direct actions: raids, precision strikes, and calibrated intelligence operations. It is "cleared" when Coalition and indigenous forces concertedly move across territory to remove or clear the enemy from a geographically defined area. Areas are "held" by security forces, Coalition and local, in a persistence presence posture to prevent the return of the insurgency and to protect the population. The phases of "building" and "transitioning" focus on bolstering local security and governing institutions through training and mentoring so that they can protect themselves. Movies that focus on acts of valor and are generally patriotic tend to focus on discrete counterterror missions or on a "day in the life" of a veteran. Movies such as *Zero Dark Thirty*, *Restrepo*, and *Act of Valor* are representative of valorous movies, and *American Sniper*, *12 Strong*, and *The Hurt Locker* are seen as generally patriotic. Some commercially successful movies also focus on local culture, such as *The Kite Runner* for Afghanistan, but they are quite rare. Antiwar films are much more common and focus almost exclusively on the War in Iraq and include *Green Zone*, *War Machine*, and *Lions for Lambs*, among others. The genre that seems most popular for movies about counterinsurgency are tragedies that either take place in country as part of combat operations or are about how the war affects combatants and their families and supporters on the home front. War zone tragedies include *Lone Survivor*, *The Outpost*, and *The Patrol*, among others. The bulk of these types of movies emphasize the costs of war on the home front, including *Taking Chance*, *The Messenger*, *Brothers*, *Thank You for Your Service*, and *In the Valley of Elah*, among several others. A notable trend is that successes in Iraq, such as the Anbar Awakening and the overall turning around of the war due to the surge and the use of COIN strategies, are not really conveyed by these films other than *The Surge: The Whole Story*, which is a documentary. The combination of indigenous action (e.g., Iraq's western tribes rising up against al-Qaeda in Iraq) and good news from the Iraq Campaign (considered politically contentious because there were many people who would not welcome positive news from the Iraq War and so weren't inclined to look for it or celebrate it) meant that these and other episodes of the wars weren't ever really conveyed to the public via cinema.

The appetite of veterans for movies while on deployment is insatiable, and it was customary for many to have sizable personal movie libraries whether as DVDs or on thumb drives, share drives, or on their computers/phones. As the war matured, the Post Exchange offices (stores to purchase sundries) on major bases in both wars carried extensive inventories of movies. As you can imagine, most veterans in the wars in Afghanistan and Iraq were young men seeking some sort of diversion from the war, but they were also looking for insights into fighting and Arab/Afghan culture, some way of staying connected to the home front, or relaxing and thinking about something other than war. In general, there are approximately seven major categories of movies Afghan/Iraq veterans tended to watch overseas: (1) movies about other wars; (2) coming-of-age movies; (3) comedies; (4) dramatic, violent, and apocalyptic movies; (5) cultural films; (6) films about their own wars (Afghanistan and Iraq); and (7) movies about returning home. As will be reviewed in chapter 6, "The Vietnam War," many veterans consumed movies about the Vietnam War, but other wars were also quite popular and reinforced the general theme of yet another generation of Americans serving their country in war. Further, since so many veterans are young men, and war service has a way of not only maturing a person but also accentuating how much one's life has changed from one's former civilian life, coming-of-age movies are particularly popular. Living in a world of violence naturally also makes veterans drawn to such movies as part study and professional development but also as part of attrition escapism. Cultural films are also valued, although they are more about war and violence than anything else, but they also provide valuable insights into how to navigate the complexities of dealing with local populations as part of counterinsurgency operations. Comedies are also a vital necessity as part of escaping war for something lighter to watch; they also frequently have coming-of-age themes and romance, and they remind veterans of their prewar life. Finally, since the wars in Afghanistan and Iraq have gone on for so long, movies eventually came out about their own conflicts, which became, for veterans who served later in the wars, crucial "lessons-learned" movies.

Movies about Other Wars (Real or Fictional)

The TV series *Band of Brothers* was particularly popular among veterans of the Afghanistan and Iraq wars, as were many other movies about World War II such as *Saving Private Ryan*, but movies about ancient warfare and colonial wars were also appealing. Many of these movies were viewed with an eye toward learning lessons about leadership, small-unit action, the world of war in general, and, in some cases, wars that successfully concluded. Some of the more exotic movies that are entirely fictional were also a means of escapism and touched on familiar war themes. One advantage of serving in war is that you develop a great interest in other wars and are drawn to the details of those conflicts. The movie *300* ricocheted throughout the U.S. military and deeply resonated with veterans with its themes of small-unit action, selfless service, unconstrained masculinity, and single-minded purpose. The movie *Black Hawk Down* also resonated due to its account of a contemporary war (Somalia) and the fact many leaders of Special Operations in the wars in Afghanistan and Iraq served in that effort. The movie *Master and Commander*, which is about the British navy in the nineteenth century, was principally seen as an instructional movie about military leadership. Many of these movies have culminating battles or conflicts, which also resonated with veterans of wars with no discernable conclusion. Superhero movies were also quite popular partly as a means of escape but also because they frequently successfully ended with a positive conclusion in a manner that was fairly uncomplicated.

- Movies about other wars (real or fictional): *300, Master and Commander, Live. Die. Repeat: Edge of Tomorrow, Black Hawk Down, The Last of the Mohicans, Saving Private Ryan, Jarhead, The Last Samurai, Enemy at the Gates, Thin Red Line, Troy, Zulu, Avatar,* Avengers series, Starship Troopers series, Alien series, Matrix series, Terminator series, Underworld series, and Lord of the Rings/ Hobbit series.

Coming-of-Age Movies

Movies that emphasized coming-of-age themes resonated with many veterans as wars mature boys and young men into war veterans. There is sometimes a lament in this transition, a longing for one's former self before the brutal knowledge of war was conveyed. Additionally, many war veterans enjoy the great camaraderie of war and come to see their fellow veterans as brothers, with all the joking, hilarity, and teasing that comes with those sorts of relationships. Many of the most frequently watched movies echo these themes of male camaraderie and humor, such as *Old School* and the Hangover series. Other movies echo themes of modern ennui, such as *Office Space*, and are seen as more curious windows into the difficulties of civilian life, which both intrigue and shock war veterans; they know this is their future when they leave the service.

- Coming-of-age movies: *Good Will Hunting*, *Hangover*, *Office Space*, *Old School*, *Dead Poets Society*, and *School Ties*.

Comedies

Comedies are a necessary escape for most war veterans, especially on deployment, and echo the joking and teasing that takes place among men at war. The gallows humor of war is absent from these movies, which also mix in themes of coming of age, love, and the preposterousness of life in them. The catchphrases learned from these movies, such as, to paraphrase from *Anchorman*, "60 percent of the time it works 100 percent of the time," bond men with each other and help break the tension on deployment.

- Comedies: *Van Wilder*, *Animal House*, *Anchorman*, and *Get Hard*.

Dramatic, Violent, and Apocalyptic Movies

The war veteran is steeped in violence, and he is taught it formally through instruction and from hard experience. Combat and war tap into primal elements of mankind that, for most war veterans, are unleashed for the first time. This knowledge of violence is enhanced through the struggle for survival in war, which is why apocalyptic scenarios are so enticing to veterans, as their preoccupation with zombie movies makes clear. Movies such as *The Road*, *The Crazies*, and *The Purge* tap into these elemental urges, and their emphasis on small-unit action, day-to-day survival, camaraderie within a small group, and constant violence resonate with war veterans intensely. The movie *Captive State* is apocalyptic as well as insurgency focused as humans work against a totalitarian alien invasion. The movie *Children of Men*, with a similar theme of an insurgent movement working against a dominant government in an apocalyptic environment, resonates particularly strongly among counterinsurgency veterans. Other movies focus on individual actors committing violence, such as John Wick and the protagonist in *Ghost in the Shell*, as well as the classic 007 movies. War veterans are attracted to these movies because of the movies' emphasis on individual-level violence and the definitive nature of the missions, which is particularly satisfying in an era of prolonged conflict.

- Dramatic, violent, and apocalyptic movies: Batman series, *A Quiet Place*, Terminator series, Rambo series, Taken series, *Cloverfield*, and *10 Cloverfield Lane*.

Cultural Movies (War Related)

As veterans of the wars in Afghanistan and Iraq, today's war vets have also become greatly acquainted with the nuances, history, and culture of Central Asia and the Middle East. As they have implemented counterinsurgency operations, conducted key leader engagements, built infrastructure, mediated tribal disputes, and partnered with local leaders, they naturally became curious about how best to do this type of work. The movie *Lawrence of Arabia* was particularly influential among war veterans because the cultural knowledge of Arabia was being conveyed in a war setting (World War I). Additionally, the fact that Lawrence was working alongside tribal leaders resonated among veterans working with their own tribal leaders in Afghanistan and Iraq. The Godfather series also connected with many war veterans due to simply seeing how much of business in Afghanistan and Iraq was conducted using such similar methods. I frequently heard veterans say, "If you want to understand Afghanistan/Iraq, watch *The Godfather*."

- Cultural movies: *Lawrence of Arabia*, *Argo*, *The Kite Runner*, and the Godfather series.

Afghan/Iraq War Movies

Since the wars in Afghanistan and Iraq have gone on for more than two decades, movies focused on the conflicts eventually came out even as both wars were still being fought. While many of these types of movies are political or documentaries, a large portion of them focus on fighting in both countries by veterans themselves. Many of these movies are focused on discrete operations, such as the Osama bin Laden raid in 2011 as portrayed in *Zero Dark Thirty*, or on tragedy such as *Lone Survivor*, or simply on operations in theater such as *Restrepo* and *Act of Valor*. The movie *Team America*, which uses puppets to convey the odd contradictions of the war on terror and its more humorous elements in a somewhat profane way, connected with many war veterans. The TV series *Generation Kill* is probably the most realistic portrayal to come out that conveys more of the complexity of counterinsurgency operations early in the Iraq war, although most of its emphasis is on fighting conventional Iraqi military forces instead of a robust insurgency.

- Afghan War/Iraq War/war on terror movies and TV series: *Team America*, *American Sniper*, *Lone Survivor*, *Zero Dark Thirty*, *Act of Valor*, *Restrepo*, *The Hurt Locker*, and *Generation Kill* (TV series).

Movies capture many elements of the counterinsurgency war veteran's experience but cannot do so completely due to the limitations of the medium and the interest of the market. These types of movies tend to emphasize stories about missions that can be conveyed in a succinct and definitive manner, such as counterterrorism missions and combat narratives. Overly political films are quite common as well as those that cover tragic outcomes of war in country or on the home front. However many movies have come out about the wars in Afghanistan and Iraq, the difficulties of accurately conveying the complexities of fighting insurgencies contributes, however unintentionally, to a less than complete picture of how to successfully win in these types of conflicts. These blind spots perpetuate incomplete thinking about the war and misrepresent the terms of the conflict in a cycle that repeats itself as new rotations of soldiers, sailors, airmen, and Marines deploy to fight again on unending tours of duty. However much these veterans learn about war in a direct and visceral manner, it will be hard for them to see their stories told completely and accurately on the home front through the medium of movies.

Returning Home

The experience of returning home from war was frequently captured by filmmakers but often as part of a larger narrative focused on combat. The challenges Chris Kyle faced in *American Sniper*, played by Bradley Cooper, included the costs of constant rotations, the toll of dealing with morally ambiguous situations in which you must make decisions to kill, as well as how to balance these challenges with having a family. Other accounts such as *The Hurt Locker* brought home the profound disconnect between the violence of Iraq and the stable and predictable world of the home front. The film *Thank You for Your Service* also brought home the great costs of posttraumatic injury and navigating the world between war and peace. The 1946 movie *The Best Years of Our Lives* stood out for how it dealt with the process of coming home in a humane and sophisticated manner. No contemporary movie about the wars in Iraq and Afghanistan captures the brilliance of its portrayal of the three main characters and how they navigated their homecomings. The movie was the highest-grossing film not only in 1946 but for all of the 1940s, and one of its actors received two Oscars for his performance. Adjusted for inflation, *The Best Years of Our Lives* is one of the one hundred highest-grossing films in U.S. history.[4]

- Returning home movies: *American Sniper, The Hurt Locker, Taking Chance, Thank You for Your Service, The Best Years of Our Lives, The Deer Hunter,* and *Born on the Fourth of July.*

Video Games

There are two broad types of video games that war veterans generally prefer: first-person shooter and war strategy. The first is by far the most popular, and these games are largely about conducting combat and counter-terror operations in the first-person from the perspective of a soldier, Marine, or a member of Special Operations Forces. The most popular tend to be the Call of Duty series, but other titles include *Resident Evil* and *Halo*, which are, respectively, zombie themed or based in the future with aliens. The veteran is attracted to these types of games in large part because they are almost exclusively about combat with little of the ambiguity of counterinsurgency operations. They also allow war veterans to experience combat in a virtual environment if their own personal war experiences didn't provide them the kinds of combat experiences they wanted. The missions in these types of games are also fairly clear cut and can be achieved in a generally straightforward manner. This is particularly satisfying for veterans of protracted conflicts that are inconclusive. These kinds of games also allow veterans to fight alongside their friends in collaborative team play, which serves as a way of bonding and letting off steam. In some respects, they are a way for war veterans to ease their transition home. Another aspect of these games that appeals to veterans includes the lack of an overarching strategy other than attrition; this is another example, much like zombie movies, of attrition escapism for counterinsurgency veterans. Additionally, there are few, if any, interactions with civilians in these games, which make them even more appealing to veterans of wars focused on the moral complexities of counterinsurgency and their primary effort of protecting civilian populations from the insurgency; most war veterans prefer to focus on combat actions against the enemy.

War strategy games are also quite popular with veterans in part because they live the reality of these exact sorts of choices every day as they implement strategies against the enemy chosen by generals and admirals. War veterans naturally wonder why they did something in the course of a campaign or wonder how a particular course of action was decided upon and become professionally curious about these sorts of broader questions. Further, it is customary for more senior officers to study military theoreticians such as Sun Tzu and Carl von Clausewitz as part of their professional training. The challenge in these types of games is that however well they convey the complexities of conventional war, they struggle or avoid altogether the realities of fighting insurgencies. It is particularly hard for these sorts of games to convey the nuances and multifaceted nature of political aspects of these sorts of wars. How one models the sentiments of the civilian population in a video game is a challenge that does not appear to have been met. One of the more popular of these types of games is *Command & Conquer: Generals*, which has a series of games in the genre. One of its most popular is called *Zero Hour*, and among the forces it allows you to play (which also include the People's Republic of China and the United States) is the Global Liberation Army (GLA), which is a simulated terrorist group. The GLA has terrorists, hijackers, angry mobs, bomb trucks, saboteurs, demolition traps, black markets, and fake (covert) structures among more conventional capabilities such as cannons, tanks, SCUD launchers, rocket buggies, and such. Many of these capabilities are used in insurgencies, but absent the sentiments of the population, which is the goal of counterinsurgency, and the ability to convey political strategy, which the armed insurgency is fighting on behalf of, the modeling of these games can be quite limited. Overall, many strategy games reinforce a conventional warfare narrative, which complicates comprehensive thinking about how to conduct counterinsurgency campaigns effectively. In and of themselves these games allow veterans to take a macro worldview of some of the aspects of the wars they are participating in, while allowing them to dabble in attrition escapism, but, at their heart, they contribute to a misunderstanding of war and counterinsurgency in particular.

Conclusion

War has always been a subject of great fascination for movie producers as well as video game designers, and conventional wars in particular have always had a special place in both creative fields. This type of war readily lends itself to these genres due to their clear narratives of success defined as defeating the enemy's military. They present compelling battle scenes, put U.S. forces in the action, provide clear conclusions, and present an enemy that is easy to capture visually. These types of wars also resonate with U.S. culture on many levels and, due to their size and their sometimes existential nature, compel the great interest of many Americans. Not only are irregular wars more complex, but their nature of having an enemy that hides within the population, of rarely presenting large-scale battles, of inconclusive endings and long time lines, and of not involving the great energies and interest of the American people, are also difficult to capture visually and in game format. Largely for these and other reasons, insurgency veterans rarely find their experiences accurately captured by both mediums even as they attract veterans in general. While combat themes and small-unit action are a natural draw, the inherently political nature of counterinsurgency work—with its emphasis on building indigenous forces, working with government officials, and implementing intelligence-driven operations to search for an elusive enemy—rarely appears. However challenging it may be to accurately capture the experiences of counterinsurgency veterans, video games and movies provide a necessary outlet for veterans on deployment to simply escape the realities of war, reflect on life, and long for a simpler civilian life. The world of zombies and similar apocalyptic movies resonates with counterinsurgency veterans largely as attrition escapism and its attractions while they participate in inconclusive insurgency conflicts. They resonate because they reflect the critiques war veterans often have of civilian society and, due to the veteran's special knowledge of war, allow veterans a place of prominence in a brutal survivalist world they inherently know. How cultures remember war, whether it is through movies, video games, or books, helps craft the myths and legends of the conflict and shape how future wars are thought of and how they are fought, sometimes to their detriment.

War Memoirs **5**

> "A nation chooses its war story when it chooses the men who
> will fight its war."

—SAMUEL HYNES, *THE SOLDIERS' TALE:*
BEARING WITNESS TO MODERN WAR, 182

> "I was writing the book for [the dead], for those who were
> there, and for those who wanted to know what it was like—
> in that order."

—ALEX BOWLBY, *THE RECOLLECTIONS OF RIFLEMAN BOWLBY*, 222

THERE ARE FEW OPPORTUNITIES FOR CIVILIANS to truly understand the experience of war beyond direct participation. What they
often hear is mediated through the news, movies, the internet,
and books, and it is frequently incomplete and sometimes wrong. In some
cases, a civilian may get an opportunity to speak to a war veteran directly,
which can certainly improve understanding, but they must usually rely
upon secondhand or even thirdhand accounts. Whatever medium through
which the war is portrayed privileges certain aspects of the conflict over
others, with the news, for example, emphasizing headline-grabbing events
on a short-term time horizon. As a genre, movies tend to focus on visually arresting images and simple narratives and, with respect to irregular
wars, often present shaping and clearing operations (e.g., combat) but not
holding, building, and transitioning, which are vital stages of any successful
counterinsurgency strategy. They also tend to focus on the actions of U.S.
personnel versus a balanced portrayal of indigenous efforts as well. When

it comes to books, though, a genre that spans centuries of conflict, a more thoughtful civilian has a chance to hear about the war experience unfiltered from a direct participant and less influenced by market conditions, which accentuate certain narratives. Book publishers are certainly profit-making enterprises and, even in this form, certain narratives are still emphasized over others; however, the unvarnished voice of the veteran and the ability to delve more deeply into the subject is likely the best way for the civilian to learn about war. As a genre, war memoirs occupy a special place in literature as well as in the military, for they are the first drafts of history by the men in the arena. Veterans cherish them as windows into the world of violence and death and read them carefully for lessons learned and those special insights into humanity that a close association with mortality brings. War memoirs also play a vital role in helping war veterans transition to civilian life where they can process their experiences and contribute their narrative to the annals of history.

When the war veteran returns home from overseas and leaves the service, he is bombarded with a number of significant life adjustments. He must navigate the different mores of a stable and peaceful civilian society; find a home, job, and perhaps a companion; and shed a number of psychological, moral, intellectual, and personal adaptations to combat. As he goes through this process, he inevitably reflects upon his combat experiences of losing friends, killing the enemy, and being injured, as well as missions accomplished or lost. He also thinks about his time in uniform, the camaraderie of friends, injustices he has experienced, and the hardships and privations he has endured. He has just left a world that was completely different from his civilian life and witnessed horrendous devastation. He has seen beautiful vistas completely unlike his home country, he has witnessed the best and worst of human nature, and he has struggled mightily on behalf of a mission to which he gave his all. His war might be over or it might continue on after he left the service, but his participation in it is done. He won't be going back, and so he begins to reflect on his experiences. This reflection period may happen right away, may be delayed as other responsibilities of life take hold, or may even take decades. Some veterans prefer to keep their thoughts on their experiences to themselves while others feel the strong need to write about them as a way to process their time overseas: "[V]arious veterans discovered that writing of their experiences offered a meaningful opportunity to ventilate traumatic memories and still-painful emotions. . . . Other veterans also turned to penning a memoir in the hope that it would provide a means of expunging lingering mental suffering."[1] Many veterans keep journals of their experiences in uniform or often write letters home. Some write articles about their experiences while others privately write down their thoughts but never publish them. One of the more influential methods the veteran uses to reflect upon his experiences in war is by writing a memoir.

The war memoir is a type of literature wherein the author recounts his firsthand experiences with the subject he writes about focusing principally on a specific chapter in his life. It is unlike an autobiography wherein the author recounts his whole life. The motivation to write is multifaceted and quite personal to each veteran, and, while processing painful episodes in war is often a reason, the veteran frequently has other goals. Chief among these are to remember his deceased comrades and create a living memorial of sorts by recounting their lives in print: "They wrote instead to fix an image of the fallen for eternity, a literary means of ensuring that their names live for evermore. . . . [T]he creation and publication of a war memoir also allowed the veteran to sanctify his own memories of his comrades, placing their memory and sacrifice upon a public pedestal of remembrance."[2] Memoirs are often dedicated to the deceased comrades of the veteran and frequently recount their shared time in service as well as their final moments in combat. It is also a means for the veteran to process his grief and his loss in a manner that is public and communal that invites similar acknowledgments of grief by his compatriots in the unit. It is also a celebration of his deceased comrade's life and accomplishments, as well as an homage to the role his comrade played in the history of his nation: "The memoirs of former frontline combatants have been referred to as 'survivors' songs,' a description which perfectly encapsulates the nature and function of these narratives as dual proclamations of mourning and celebration."[3]

Many veterans also write memoirs for the comrades of their unit, command, and generation as part of a collective experience of recounting their shared war service. Their book is but one of many about the conflict but, however much it is the veteran's personal story, it is also the story of a generation that went to war: "War memoirs thus operated as an act of communion, reaching out to other veterans across the services. . . . War memoirs were intended to offer tribute to the community of veterans by publicly acknowledging the extent of the sacrifice they had made for the nation."[4] It was also a method for the veteran to share his views with that club of combat veterans who know only too well the experiences they have shared and that "these books are communications among the members of that secret army, the men who have been there and will understand, as other generations will not and cannot."[5] The war veteran's memoir communicates not only to the public and his fellow generation of veterans but also to future veterans. It seeks to share the hard-won combat knowledge the veteran has collected and to reassure the veterans of the future that they can rise to the challenge of war service.

> In the spirit of hoping to be of some use to subsequent generations, several veterans constructed their memoirs as a text of tactical reference for future combatants. . . . Other veterans also reached out to communicate with new generations of combatants on an emotional level, seeking to provide quiet reassurance that it had all been done before and could be done again.[6]

The act of writing a war memoir is also a form of nostalgia for the veteran for when he played his small role in the great events of history, when he had fewer responsibilities, and when he was younger, fitter, and more alive than his present civilian life of comfortable living. It is also a means for the veteran to share his experiences with his family who grow up with the war even though they hadn't served there because it is such a central part of their father's and husband's life. Spouses and children often play a role in facilitating the writing process, and for many veterans, as they get older and their life settles down, they finally have time to reflect upon their time in uniform. Confederate general Edward Porter Alexander, for example, recounted such a motivation when he began to write his memoirs as an artillery officer in General James Longstreet's division: "All my life my children have been begging me & I've been promising to write out my recollections . . . of the war . . . [and I was] writing only for my children & intimate friends."[7]

> Constructing a war memoir thus offered an opportunity to reconnect in some measure with memories of the veteran's wartime "band of brothers." . . . Writing a memoir thus performed an important function for the veteran during the post-war decades. In allowing the reincarnation of treasured bonds of wartime comradeship, [a] military memoir could provide a vital solace to the veteran in the present day.[8]

Typically, anniversaries of key events the veteran participated in and the slow passing away of his friends prompts the veteran to also write. It is an opportunity for him to reach out to old colleagues and units, to organize his notes and recollections, and to set the record straight, as he sees it, for posterity.

The War Memoir

*"Allen's [*Toward the Flame*] narrative has the virtue that all good battle memoirs have: it makes real the part of a war that one man, fighting, sees."*

—SAMUEL HYNES, *THE SOLDIERS' TALE:*
BEARING WITNESS TO MODERN WAR, 97

There is a familiar pattern to the writing style, themes, references, and narrative format of many war memoirs as a genre. The first aspect of most memoirs is that they are generally written not by formally trained men who aspire to be writers but regular citizens who may never have contemplated writing at all. As the World War II and Korean War veteran and then Princeton professor of literature Samuel Hynes put it, "War writing, it seems, is a genre without a tradition to the men who write it."[9] Generally lacking formal training, they often recount their experiences in a chronological manner and largely eschew larger questions of politics and strategy. As the Vietnam War veteran and memoirist Philip Caputo puts it, "It has nothing to do with politics, power, strategy, influence, national interests, or foreign policy. . . . It is simply a story about war, about things men do in war and the things war does to them."[10] These tendencies have much to do with the second aspect of many war memoirs; they are largely written by junior officers and enlisted personnel who, as members of small units, are deeply involved in combat. As Hynes puts it, "Infantrymen's narratives are narrower in the range of their vision, smaller in scale, more identified with groups than with individuals, more determined by the contingencies of battle, more concerned with survival than with action."[11] The British World War I veteran and memoirist Edmund Blunden also regarded many stories by war veterans as "very local, limited, [and] incoherent."[12] Veterans from other types of units beyond the infantry also exhibit similar tendencies.

Since most war memoirists are young men in combat with little to no formal training in writing, the incidents and themes they mention reflect the conditions of war that are most unlike those they would encounter in their civilian lives. As the philosopher and World War II veteran J. Glenn Gray puts it, "What are the secret attractions of war, the ones that have persisted in the West despite revolutionary changes in the methods of warfare? I believe that they are: the delight in seeing, the delight in comradeship, the delight in destruction. . . . These three had reality for me, and I have found them also throughout the literature of war."[13] These "delights" are incredibly experiential and often quite jarring and frequently provide visceral visual memories for most war veterans. Partly for this reason, they are often the subject of discussion in memoirs due to their novelty: "The eye is lustful because it requires the novel, the unusual, the spectacular. It cannot satiate itself on the familiar, the routine, the everyday."[14]

> You don't expect war to be composed of such odd incidents; but it is out of remembered astonishments like these that war narratives are made. *Strangeness* is the great constant in remembered wars. The young man who goes to war enters a strange world governed by strange rules, where everything that is not required is forbidden, a world without women or children or old people, a violent and dangerous world where, out there in the darkness or just over the hill, strangers wait whose job it is to kill you. Strangest of all is the presence of death, and the ways it is present . . . death is a recurrent subject in the soldiers' tale.[15]

There are frank discussions of dead bodies, violence, and decay, as well as amazing vistas and other natural beauties; injustices experienced from other men, units, commanders, and the like; and loss and devastation. Many of these accounts are delivered in a cool and detached manner, sometimes tinged with anger, in a matter-of-fact style. This partly reflects the combat adaptation of the veteran of detaching himself from the emotional impact of things. Further, if what he sees is the result of violence from the enemy, the veteran is processing the effect with an eye to what lessons he can learn and discerning what the other fellow did not learn and consequently fell prey to in combat. This attention to detail is taught to the veteran and then is constantly validated by his war experiences where men who do not focus on the details are injured or killed.

> Everyone who remembers a war first-hand knows that its images remain in the memory with special vividness. . . . One remembers with special vividness too because military training is very largely training in alertness and a special kind of noticing. . . . When a man imagines that every moment is his next to last, he observes and treasures up sensory details purely for their own sake.[16]

The fascination with death, how it happens, how people survive it, and how the enemy tries to kill you is a constant subject of discussion. Inevitably, because death is so common, the veteran's eye naturally gravitates to the novel and unusual even within that macabre subject. The descriptions of these types of scenes is almost set piece, presented in a detached manner but in a way as to elicit strong responses. As Hynes sees it, "The style in which these sights [dead soldiers] are described remains flat and uninflected; but *realism* somehow doesn't seem quite the right term for such grotesque occasions. For this kind of reality of war, perhaps we need a new term. Suppose we call such visions 'Battlefield Gothic.'"[17] The gruesome details recited in a matter-of-fact manner also pertain to the deaths of friends, as if the extra detail is part of the commemoration of their passing: "Soldiers remember and retell the deaths of their comrades with a terrible exactness—where a man was hit, how he fell, the bloody details of spilled brains and dismembered limbs."[18]

The experience of serving in the military, fighting for one's nation, and being part of history can also be a powerful motivator to contribute a memoir to posterity. For many veterans, this may be the only time in their lives when they are part of great events, of shifts in history which shape the courses of nations and people.

> It's easy to see why men remember their wars. For most men who fight, war is their one contact with the world of great doings. Other men govern, sign treaties, invent machines, cure diseases, alter lives. But for ordinary men—the men who fight our wars—there will probably be only that one time when their lives intersect with history, one opportunity to act in great events.[19]

Partly for this reason, there is also a tendency to exaggerate their role (see chapter 8, "Stolen Valor and Fake Veterans") and the significance of their part in the broader effort. Having served in Afghanistan a few times, I often heard people refer to the province they served in, mostly in the south, as the place where al-Qaeda leader Osama bin Laden had plotted the attacks of 9/11; he had apparently done this planning in virtually every province in the region. Similarly, there is a propensity to dismiss the actions of units not affiliated with the veteran, which is easy to do, in part, because veterans often only know their small role in the greater movements of the conflict. However, this tendency reinforces the centrality of their role and their story to history unfolding. The proximity to death and mortality also prompts veterans to recall experiences with special clarity. These observations are reinforced by strong emotional feelings since they are so often tied to extremely challenging circumstances such as combat, death, and the exhilaration of success.

Young men at war feel life and death with an intensity that is beyond peacetime emotions. They know comradeship, a closeness to other men that ordinary life frequently does not provide. They see their friends die, and they feel grief that is different from what they have known before, back home, where folks die naturally, and mostly old. They feel fear, and the exhilaration of fear overcome. And they are changed.[20]

The confluence of the multitude of intense feelings veterans experience in war leave their imprint on their memoir prose. Death, the strange, the historic, and those things that occur to him that are without precedent in his civilian life merit mention. They also write memoirs because the experience of war is the greatest adventure of their lives, and they want others to know it: "Men like danger, hardship, and fear: we must accept that; it's an *adventure*."[21]

The act of writing a war memoir by a veteran is a process of recounting his tour(s) in such a manner that it allows him to relate his experiences to at least four principal audiences: fellow veterans, future veterans, the broader public, and posterity. The veteran collects his photos, journal entries, emails and letters home, unit reports, after-action reviews, and newspaper articles and begins to reach out to fellow veterans who served with him. Most memoirs follow a familiar pattern of pre-deployment life (usually entailing discussions of why they joined and military training), the beginning of the deployment (introduction of geography, the enemy situation, key personalities), and first brushes with death and combat (loss of innocence, first kill, working through tactical problems). There are frequently references to friendships in the service, exotic scenes or unusual sights, and expressions of some injustice, as well as statements about poor strategy or tactics. There are sometimes discussions of local culture, the mention of the death of a friend or colleague, perhaps a brief discussion of personal difficulties, and, finally, a discussion of coming home. Specific missions provide the fodder for specific chapters, which always have a beginning and an end: "[P]enning a war memoir allowed the veteran to shape and order his recollections of the past, imposing pattern and coherency upon experience."[22]

Some experiences in war are so unlike those in civilian life that veterans use rhetorical mechanisms to bridge the gap in understanding. It was not uncommon, for example, for World War I veterans to use literary references as a way of bridging this understanding.[23] In the wars in Afghanistan and Iraq, it was quite common to use movie references to serve the same purpose. Movies such as *The Godfather* were often cited to explain how Afghan and Iraqi society operated, with its emphasis on loyalty, clannish behavior, less than legal means of operating, tribal identity, and willingness to use violence. The Star Wars movies were frequently used to describe desert scenes as well as the infamous bar scene when explaining the odd assortment of characters who show up in war zones. The movie *Black Hawk Down* and the TV series *Band of Brothers* were often enlisted to describe combat scenes or the personalities of fellow comrades or leaders in the veteran's chain of command.

> [F]inding the war "indescribable" in any but the available language of traditional literary terms . . . and [i]nhibited by scruples of decency and believing in the historical continuity of styles, writers about the war had to appeal to the sympathy of readers by invoking the familiar and suggesting its resemblance to what many of them suspected was an unprecedented and (in their terms) an all-but-incommunicable reality. Very often, the new reality had no resemblance whatever to the familiar, and the absence of a plausible style placed some writers in what they thought was an impossible position.[24]

Part of the effort to improve understanding also includes references to what Hynes mentions as the "imagined war-in-his-head," which is the veteran's understanding of what war is—based upon movies, books, and popular history: "[E]very young man who goes to war finds the experience strange and disorienting beyond his expectations, and so must redefine his war terms and turn the imagined war-in-his-head into another, stranger story."[25] For many veterans in Afghanistan and Iraq, these "wars-in-the-head" included the movie and book *Black Hawk Down*, the movies *Full Metal Jacket* (and the book *The Short-Timers* it was based on) and *Platoon*, and the TV series *Band of Brothers*, among other reference points. These helped shape the contours of these memoirs by establishing expectations of how wars are recounted and how they are incorporated into the broader national culture. The Vietnam War in particular resonated with many veterans as they wrote their memoirs since it was the last conflict U.S. forces waged against an insurgent force. For the veterans who fought in Afghanistan and Iraq, the Vietnam War and World War II were often their "imagined war-in-[their]-head": "Everyone fighting a modern war tends to think of it in terms of the last one he knows anything about."[26] The iconic scenes of long-range patrols in the jungles of Vietnam were reference points for Afghan veterans, for example, who conducted similar patrols in Afghanistan's mountains and verdant valleys. The insertion of military personnel into the jungle via helicopters was also echoed in Afghanistan and Iraq as military personnel were inserted into villages, towns, and deserts. Similarly, World War II resonated due to the proliferation of movies and books about the conflict, but, in this regard, the "war-in-[the]-head" of that conflict had more to do with thinking about combat, small-unit action, and killing the enemy. The unconstrained patriotism of that era also resonated with veterans due to the attacks of 9/11.

Afghan and Iraq War Veterans

> *"It seems unlikely that memorable war stories will come out of the wars that the Western world is fighting in our new century; the invasions of Iraq and Afghanistan go on and on, but they're Little Wars, in which one side has most of the technological weapons and the other side has most of the casualties. They're victim wars, for both sides; there will be no new myths, no epics here. If that is so, writers and artists and filmmakers, the myth-tellers of our culture, will surely continue to return to the two World Wars, and we will return with them to learn again that war is terrible, and yet that in war men may act beyond the limits of their ordinary natures."*
>
> —SAMUEL HYNES, *ON WAR AND WRITING*, 67

Since the invasions of Afghanistan in 2001 and Iraq in 2003, veterans of both of these conflicts and the broader global war on terror have increasingly turned to memoirs to recount their experiences. Even though these books are shaped by the usual forces that impact the drafting of war memoirs (e.g., untrained writers; a focus principally on tactics, themes of death, camaraderie, and injury; etc.), characteristics unique to the generation of veterans who served in these conflicts have impacted the broader genre. The longevity of the wars in Afghanistan and Iraq have led to multi-memoir veterans, accounts of both wars in single memoirs, and multiple tours discussed in single volumes. The inclusion of women in more and more roles in the U.S. military has also led to a significant increase in female-authored memoirs. The breadth of counterinsurgency operations has prompted the inclusion of greater insights into indigenous cultural practices; this has also led to expansive discussions of tribal politics, raising and training local security forces, reconstruction activities, development efforts, and good governance work. Even those who write these memoirs are different since they all volunteered to join the military—many of whom did so after the attacks of 9/11—instead of being compelled to serve through a draft. Finally, the war in Afghanistan was launched following attacks on the homeland, and the United States faced a nonstate actor (Taliban) rather than a nation-state; this introduced other themes of patriotism that were undertaken in an irregular warfare context whereas past narratives of attack have usually been about nation-states.

In my research, I have found approximately 168 memoirs written by U.S. military veterans of the wars in Afghanistan and Iraq published in book form, representing the work of 155 separate authors. While many veterans of these conflicts have written multiple books, only those that were memoirs of their time in service in a war zone were included in the database I created.[27] Approximately eighty-eight memoirs (52 percent) were written about the war in Iraq, forty-nine (29 percent) were exclusively about Afghanistan, and thirty-one (19 percent) were about both conflicts. Consistent with campaigns of prolonged ground warfare, roughly eighty-six memoirs (51 percent) were written by U.S. Army personnel and thirty-nine (23 percent) by Marines. Due to the multiservice nature of U.S. operations in both countries, members of the U.S. Navy have written thirty-two memoirs (19 percent), and U.S. Air Force personnel have written eleven (7 percent). Predictably, fifty-four (32 percent) of the memoirs were written by members of the infantry, twenty-five (14 percent) by U.S. Navy SEALs, twelve (7 percent) by members of the U.S. Army's Special Forces and twelve (7 percent) by members of military intelligence, and ten (6 percent) by U.S. Army Rangers and ten (6 percent) by members of the Armor community. Remaining memoirs are in the single digits, but many have been written by pilots (seven) (e.g., fighter jets, helicopters); medics (four); and members of the cavalry (three), artillery (three), military police (two), and logistics (two), as well as several single memoirs covering such diverse areas as administration, communications, mortuary affairs, and members who have served as a mechanic, a drone pilot, and a Judge Advocate General.

Virtually every single U.S. military rank is represented among the authors of these war memoirs. Understandably, service members who just joined the military have not written memoirs (E-1, E-2, and O-1), nor have some senior officers (O-8). Commissioned officers wrote most of the memoirs at eighty-seven (52 percent), and enlisted personnel wrote eighty-one (48 percent). Among officers, O-3s (captains, lieutenants) wrote the most war memoirs at twenty-nine (17 percent), followed by O-5s (lieutenant colonels, commanders) at twenty-two (13 percent), O-6s (colonels, captains) and O-2s (first lieutenants, lieutenant junior grade) at nine (5 percent) each, O-4s (majors, lieutenant commanders) at seven (4 percent), and O-10s (generals, admirals) at five memoirs (3 percent). Among enlisted personnel, E-5s wrote the most memoirs at twenty-one (13 percent), followed by E-4s and E-6s at seventeen (10 percent), E-7s at eleven (7 percent), and E-8s at five (3 percent). The five ranks that wrote the most memoirs of the wars in Afghanistan and Iraq (O-3s/O-5s/E-5s/E-6s/E-4s) are those best placed to conduct combat operations either in leading or in support of shaping and clearing operations. Among O-5s, this is the last rank where an officer can direct military forces and have an impact on the ground in such a way that lends itself to the memoir format, such as an infantry battalion commander or a SEAL team commander. Additionally, many people leave the service at lower ranks, deciding not to have a military career or retire as an O-5, giving them time to write. Many other ranks do not write as many war memoirs due to a lack of time or career considerations so as not to endanger their advancement opportunities. Another factor is that the publishing industry generally wants to print combat narratives versus other themes that are central to successful counterinsurgency operations but perhaps not as compelling to U.S. readers. Subjects such as building indigenous security forces, efforts at reconstruction and development, and longer-term studies on areas with a greater focus on local views are not generally published if written by military personnel.

There are several distinct categories of memoirs within the predominantly combat-focused genre of war memoirs. Chief among these are eleven memoirs written by general or flag officers, six written by Congressional Medal of Honor recipients, and thirteen written by female veterans. Only seven of the memoirs are predominantly focused on conducting stability operations (or training indigenous security forces) versus combat, and three are written by veterans who feel they have been mistreated in their careers. Themes such as overcoming serious injury are also common among some memoirs, such as in *Tough as They Come* by Travis Mills, who served with the U.S. Army in Afghanistan as a staff sergeant and who is a quadruple amputee. Hynes refers to these types of books as a "Sufferer's Tale" or a "literature of wounds."[28] Overcoming such an injury and then returning to war, which happened on a number of occasions, is awe inspiring: "[T]he will to survive great injury and pain is a long act of courage, as great as courage in battle, and the story of his wounds is the heart of the story."[29] Eleven of the veteran authors wrote two memoirs, including one female veteran, and two veterans wrote three memoirs each.

The practical impact of this is that later memoirs by these authors reflect greater wisdom about war, counterinsurgency, deployments, culture, and strategy, which moves beyond the familiar themes of innocence lost, first brushes with death and mortality, and an emphasis on combat in most war memoirs. Traditionally, war memoirs are mostly written after a war ends, but due to the longevity of the wars in Afghanistan and Iraq, some memoirs cross over into providing advice to policy makers on how to prosecute the war more effectively versus having a retrospective quality to their prose. Additionally, due to the heavy use of reservists in both conflicts, many authors bring extra perspectives to their writing from civilian jobs such as with the U.S. government that may have some impact on the war such as the U.S. Department of State, the Intelligence Community, and the U.S. Department of Defense, among other agencies. Publication of war memoirs from these wars significantly increased in the later years of the conflicts as veterans found time to write following retirement or after leaving the service. Most memoirs were published in 2019 (twenty-one, or 13 percent), with 2020 at seventeen (11 percent), 2014 and 2016 at thirteen each (8 percent), and 2018 at eleven (7 percent).[30]

The memoirs of Afghanistan and Iraq veterans capture the changing conditions of both wars and, depending upon when the war veteran served there, have certain themes that reflect the stages of the campaigns. The memoirs reflect the shift from direct combat by the U.S. military to indirect through indigenous security forces. As the military gained greater knowledge of indigenous culture and counterinsurgency, these themes are reflected by increased references to local partners (e.g., tribal leaders, security officials, etc.) and vignettes of meetings, friendships, and partnerships with them. As the war matured, there are greater expressions of frustration with growing rules and regulations and more references to life on giant forward operating bases. Development activities are increasingly referenced, as well as a general war weariness not only in terms of multiple tours by the veteran but also regarding overall strategy in both conflicts. There are many references to prior tours in the same country as well as tours in the other war of Iraq or Afghanistan, and writers naturally make comparisons between both campaigns. There are also increased accounts by veterans who are wounded in combat but return to duty later in both wars. Finally, as the wars continue on, increasing numbers of them refer to the need to change policies not just with respect to adopting counterinsurgency strategies but also broadly in terms of dealing with outside forces that fuel the insurgencies (e.g., Iran in Iraq and Iran/Pakistan in Afghanistan) to shift the war in the favor of the United States.

Early memoirs are principally focused on combat by U.S. forces alone in an environment with limited rules of engagement. Their accounts are infused with an entrepreneurial spirit as units adapt to wartime conditions and begin to wrestle with the problem-sets of insurgencies and adapting to local culture. Their morale is high, patriotism is palpable, and there is a feeling of success as the initial goals of the war are accomplished. As the wars progress, the insurgency in Iraq breaks out, and a few years later (circa 2006) it begins in Afghanistan. Many of these memoirs also have combat themes; however, they are less about the conventional forces of the Iraqi state and the Taliban at the beginning of the conflicts and more about clearing villages and cities and on targeted raids in search of an elusive foe. As units begin to undertake reconstruction, development, and good governance tasks, local leaders start to show up in these narratives. However, the rise of suicide attacks (e.g., vest, car, truck) and improvised explosive devices (IEDs) also begin to take their toll. More and more accounts mention these types of attacks, and readers begin to see the frustrations of veterans executing a strategy, mostly in Iraq, that is not having the results they desire. As the surge and the application of counterinsurgency strategies begin in Iraq in 2007, there is a clear sense in the memoirs that a successful strategy is finally working. Violence is still high, but it is in the service of an approach that is achieving results; it is violence done to the insurgency versus violence from the insurgency. Local officials, security leaders, and tribal members are prominent in these accounts as a spirit of partnership infuses the strategy.

Similarly, in Afghanistan, beginning in 2010, as those surge forces arrive and new strategies are implemented on the ground (e.g., population protection, persistent presence, village stability operations) there is a similar sense of success. As U.S. forces prepare to pull out of Iraq by 2011, there is a view among some memoirs of a job well done while also some frustration that these later veterans did not have a chance to serve in direct combat. As a similar drawdown begins to develop in Afghanistan in 2013, the rise of the Islamic State of Iraq and Syria (ISIS) in Iraq gives pause to the withdrawal. Subsequent memoirs still focus on combat, although partnered with indigenous forces, but there is a sense of strategic muddle in Afghanistan, which some of these memoirs pick up on even though they try to return to familiar themes of combat. Increasingly, memoirs shift to the tolls of the war on veterans or recount scenes from earlier stages of the conflict as war memoirs are difficult to write when local forces assume most of the burden of fighting. Interestingly, there are not many memoirs, approximately three, that address the campaign against ISIS forces in both Iraq and Syria. This may have to do with the small footprint of U.S. forces in both countries as well as the fact that the war was largely executed through partnered indigenous forces where U.S. personnel operated more as advisors. Later memoirs begin to address the lives of veterans more holistically, focusing on their activities outside the military as well as post-military careers, and accounts of their wartime service are increasingly only a component of a broader story.

The varied accounts of the wars in Afghanistan and Iraq discussed by the memoirs of the veterans who served there cover a wide scope of U.S. and Coalition military activities in both countries. There are many that provide in-depth looks at the areas within which they are operating, but, on the whole, they suffer from some limitations at conveying the totality of the complexities of the wars. Most veterans who served in war typically serve one tour, and if they serve additional tours, they are often in other parts of the country, although not always. Partly for this reason, their accounts are often limited to the time horizons of their time in country, so they don't have a long-term perspective on where they are serving. Further, because publishers principally want to publish combat narratives, the emphasis of the war memoirs is on exactly that, and mentions of the local population and partnerships with local tribal and security forces are quite limited. Where locals are mentioned, they are typically key political and tribal leaders, security officials, interpreters, hard-luck cases, or insurgents. Robust backstories of locals are largely absent as well as time horizons beyond those of the veteran's tour. Further, a comprehensive look at the insurgency and the history of the village, city, district, and province are usually lacking, so the context within which the veteran is serving is quite limited. Additionally, most of these accounts do not convey a sense of the integrated strategy the unit is pursuing, although some accounts written by senior officers provide this sort of needed perspective.

Another tendency among the memoirs is seen through their choice of titles. There is a great deal of emphasis on combat narratives and the subject of death (as well as killing and hunting) in the titles. Among the titles, five books begin with the word *warrior* or with *American*. Other common usages are *ghosts* (at three mentions) and *battle*, *combat*, *hunter* or *hunting*, *kill*, *never*, *when*, *into*, and *Iraq* (two mentions each). These word choices reflect an analysis of what the American reading public desires and privileges the shaping and clearing narratives of the "clear, shape, hold, build, and transition" stages of successful counterinsurgency operations. Other titles, such as *Carnivore*, *The Reaper*, *Way of the Reaper*, *Kaboom*, *Knife Fights*, *One Bullet Away*, and *Rage Company*, convey this tendency as well. If an educated reader wanted to truly "understand" the nature of the wars in Afghanistan and Iraq, he would be hard pressed to appreciate its complexities from these accounts. More thoughtful treatments tend to be written by nonmilitary personnel, but even these often lack an understanding of military operations, strategy, local history, and the like.

Marines: The Most Literary Service

Of the nearly two hundred memoirs and novels written about the wars in Afghanistan and Iraq by U.S. military veterans, the United States Marine Corps stands out due to the literary accolades it has received.[31] It hasn't published the most—this honor is reserved for the U.S. Army—but the totality and diversity of the recognition its members have received speaks to a literary quality not often associated with the Marine Corps in popular opinion. Many of the books have been on the *New York Times* Best Sellers list, and some have even been made into movies attracting high-quality acting talent. They have been written by officers and enlisted alike and include memoirs, fictions, and graphic novels. The memoir *One Bullet Away* by Nathaniel Fick who served as a Marine captain in Afghanistan and Iraq received one of the early honors. He was selected in 2006 to receive the William E. Colby Military Writers' Award, which is given to "a first work of fiction or non-fiction that has made a major contribution to the understanding of intelligence operations, military history, or international affairs."[32] It was the first book from either war to receive the selection. The second Marine to earn such recognition was Seth W. B. Folsom, who also served as a Marine captain in Iraq, which led to his writing *The Highway War*; the book received the 2007 Military Writers Society of America's Gold Medal Award for Best Memoir. The final memoir, titled *Hillbilly Elegy*, was written by J. D. Vance, who served as a corporal in Iraq and published an account of his life in 2016 that included his tour in Iraq. In addition to being a number one *New York Times* best seller, it was made into a movie that was nominated for two Academy Awards.

Members of the Marine Corps also distinguished themselves in fiction and literature and have produced a number of quality contributions to the genre. The novel *Redeployment* by Phil Klay, who served in Iraq as a Marine captain, received the National Book Award in 2014, and Elliot Ackerman, who served in Iraq as a Marine first lieutenant, was a finalist for the same award in 2017 for his novel *Dark at the Crossing*, which addressed the growth of ISIS in Iraq and Syria. The graphic novel *The White Donkey: Terminal Lance* by Maximilian Uriarte, who served in Iraq, was also on the *New York Times* Best Sellers list and received the James Webb Award in 2016 from the Marine Corps Heritage Foundation. Uriarte also has a popular comic strip and website, and in 2020 he published another graphic novel titled *Battle Born: Lapis Lazuli*, which focuses on Afghanistan.

The U.S. Army and the U.S. Navy have also had former members earn literary distinctions but not to the same extent as members of the

Marine Corps. This includes Navy SEAL petty officer Marcus Luttrell, who received the William E. Colby Military Writers' Award in 2009 for his memoir *Lone Survivor*, which focuses on his tale of survival in Afghanistan. His memoir was also a number one *New York Times* best seller and was made into a popular and successful movie. The Colby Award was also given to R. Alan King in 2008 for his memoir titled *Twice Armed* about his service in Iraq as a U.S. Army civil affairs lieutenant colonel working with local tribes. The novel *Yellow Birds* by Kevin Powers, who served in Iraq with the U.S. Army, was a finalist for the National Book Award in 2012 and was also made into a successful movie. The final novel is titled *Fobbit* and was written by U.S. Army and Iraq veteran David Abrams, which was named a *New York Times* Notable Book of 2012 and a Best Book of 2012.

The Marine Corps has a romantic appeal to many men due to its high standards, esprit de corps, masculine ideal, aggressive reputation, and the exotic locales it serves in and dangerous missions it undertakes. It attracts members from all walks of life, from rural country roads, urban neighborhoods, and the halls of Ivy League universities. It also resonates with the broader American culture and draws from a wide swath of America. Further, a career in the Marine Corps can lead to work at the White House, at embassies around the world, and even with certain Intelligence Community agencies. Partly for this reason, it attracts recruits of a somewhat higher caliber who see opportunities after military service. Its insurgent reputation and focus on mission draws a personality type that simultaneously embraces adversity and hardship as well as a sentimental and romantic idealism for the United States. Further, the service, despite its public reputation in the eyes of some, thinks deeply about the problems it is given to solve and has a highly developed culture of intellectualism. It must, of necessity, think clearly about the problems it addresses because it also does not have the extensive resources of its sister services, and so it must be judicious and thoughtful in how it uses its capabilities. One only needs to think of former Marine general and secretary of defense James Mattis's views on the need to cultivate critical thinking and a sense of history as much as tactical knowledge. Additionally, as the smallest service (which has faced elimination in the past due to budget cuts), it cultivates robust capabilities in shaping its public image. This includes flying the *Marine One* helicopter for the president, collecting Toys for Tots during Christmas, protecting embassies around the world, and maintaining high physical standards for its members; the romanticism and elan the Marine Corps conveys draws budding writers or creates them.

Conclusion

> *"The author of* Wine, Women, and War *sets down his observations as a censor in the A.E.F.: 'Job of censoring enlisted men's letters. Full of humor, pathos and inspiration. Three classes: (1) To best girl. Magnifying hardship. Full of vainglory and heroics. (2) To boyfriend. Nonchalant, sophisticated, bold comments on wine and women. Spent a lot of time with both, apparently. Contemptuous of war and danger. Hard guy. (3) To mother. Usually brief. Laborious explanations and apologies for not writing oftener. Mostly truthful. No pretense of hiding homesickness. And a certain brusque tenderness that's hard on censor's eyes.'"*
>
> —WILLIAM MATTHEWS AND DIXON WECTER,
> *OUR SOLDIERS SPEAK, 1775–1918*

The vast majority of veterans who serve in war never contribute a public narrative of their time in uniform. Many will privately share their experiences with friends and family, and some will write short pieces in newspapers or other publications; however, very few take the time to write a memoir recounting their wartime service. Largely for this reason, the memoirs that are written assume much greater importance than simply one person's contribution to the first drafts of history. Over time, these memoirs begin to shape the public history of the event, the narratives that are created about it, and, eventually, how the wars are remembered. The emphasis of certain themes in these memoirs, privileged by those who write as well as those who publish them, begin to shape the histories of these wars in certain directions. These accounts are truthful and frank, but they are incomplete; however, in their totality, they begin to craft myths and legends of the conflict that may be either partially true or entirely untrue. As the veterans who served in these conflicts pass away, these vestiges of their service in war captured in book form will become the source material for future generations. As the veterans of the wars in Afghanistan and Iraq were shaped by personal accounts of veterans who served in Vietnam and other conflicts, future generations will experience a similar shaping and will find that their "war-in-[the]-head" is incomplete and requires a new contribution from their generation.

U.S. Army Sergeant First Class Thomas Arnold Green with his wife and son after returning home from service in World War II (Courtesy of the author)

U.S. Army Sergeant First Class Thomas Arnold Green during World War II (Courtesy of the author)

Honorable Discharge Emblem, or "ruptured duck" symbol (Courtesy of the author)

Cover of "Going Back to Civilian Life" (Courtesy of the author)

U.S. Navy SEALs prepare to undertake a mission in Afghanistan in 2012 (Courtesy of U.S. Navy)

25th Infantry Division on a mission in Uruzgan Province, Afghanistan, in 2005 (Courtesy of the author)

Shura with Afghan village elders in 2012 (Courtesy of U.S. Navy)

Delivering tractors to a district in Uruzgan Province, Afghanistan, in 2005 (Courtesy of Doug Dillon)

Cutting of ribbon for road-opening ceremony in Uruzgan Province, Afghanistan, in 2012 (Courtesy of the author)

IED explosion in Uruzgan Province, Afghanistan, in 2012 (Courtesy of the author)

Author with Uruzgan Province governor Jan Mohammed Khan in 2005 (Courtesy of the author)

American flag at Village Stability Platform site in 2012 (Courtesy of the author)

View from a Chinook helicopter en route to Dai Kundi Province in 2005 (Courtesy of the author)

U.S. Navy SEAL looking at horizon in southern Afghanistan in 2012 (Courtesy of U.S. Navy)

Combat Observation Post in Zabul Province, Afghanistan, in 2012 (Courtesy of the author)

Air drop of supplies for Village Stability Platform site in Zabul Province, Afghanistan, in 2012 (Courtesy of U.S. Navy)

Combat Observation Post Fenton along Route 10 in Fallujah, Iraq, in 2007 (Courtesy of the author)

Author with the mayor of Fallujah in 2007 (Courtesy of the author)

Minaret in the city of Fallujah, Iraq, in 2007 (Courtesy of the author)

Author with Jumayli Tribe Paramount Sheik Meshan in Fallujah, Iraq, in 2007 (Courtesy of the author)

Military surplus at the store Full Metal Jacket in northern Virginia (Courtesy of the author)

The Vietnam War 6

"Everyone fighting a modern war tends to think of it in terms of the last one he knows anything about."

—PAUL FUSSELL, *THE GREAT WAR AND MODERN MEMORY*, 314

WHEN I WAS GROWING UP in a small town in Florida during the 1980s, the Vietnam War was not even a distant memory for me since I had been born in 1976, a year after the South Vietnamese government had fallen to military forces from the Communist North. However, as a child during that decade when Ronald Reagan was president, the battles over what the war meant and what should have been done to win seemed to rage on. I cannot say I had a sophisticated view of the war at that time, other than to bomb the heck out of the north, but I learned a lot about it by how it was portrayed in movies (the easiest method for a young boy to learn anything about such a complicated subject). The films *Platoon* and *Full Metal Jacket,* for example, captured my imagination as did the ubiquitous Vietnam veteran who appeared in so many other movies, frequently portrayed as, unjustifiably, slightly unhinged. I also grew up watching the *M*A*S*H* TV series as well as the movie, which, although ostensibly based upon the Korean War, spoke directly to the issues of the Vietnam War. The movie *Rambo* stood out, principally for its violence, but more now because it is essentially about coming home, how the Vietnam veteran was shunned and even persecuted, and how an ungrateful community (sheriff) hunted him without trying to understand him. The meaning of the war and how it was remembered also ricocheted throughout American culture. Countless books about the war were written, and certain myths and legends of the conflict were generated and gained traction with the public. The U.S. military sought to move on and crafted a narrative of the war's conclusion that allowed it not to address its own shortcomings, and the generals who led the war fought over their own histories of involvement in the war and about what should have been done. All these elements of how war is remembered are beginning to take hold for the wars in Afghanistan and Iraq even as they are still fought. However, as a young boy in the 1980s and into the 1990s, I was generally unaware of these controversies. My understanding of the complexities of the Vietnam War was not particularly deep, and it was only when I went to Afghanistan and Iraq that I became a serious student of the conflict, building a strong sympathy for the soldiers, sailors, airmen, and Marines who served there trying to make the war a success.

The initial entry point to the Vietnam War for most veterans of the Afghanistan and Iraq wars, the generation largely born after the war or too young to remember it, were the movies about the conflict. Even today, the classics *Full Metal Jacket*, *Platoon*, *We Were Soldiers*, *Apocalypse Now*, *Good Morning, Vietnam*, *The Deer Hunter*, *The Green Berets*, and *Rambo* are regarded as seminal films about the war. Taken as a whole, the movies cover boot camp (*Full Metal Jacket*), combat (*Full Metal Jacket*, *Platoon*, *The Green Berets*), the odd realities of war (*Full Metal Jacket*, *Platoon*, *The Deer Hunter*, *Good Morning, Vietnam*, *The Green Berets*), and the process of coming home (*The Deer Hunter* and *Rambo*), among many other topics. For most veterans on their first tour, the movies *Platoon* and *Full Metal Jacket* particularly resonated because they are about small-unit action in an insurgency war. The world of captains, lieutenants, sergeants, and privates is largely the world of the front-line soldier. The canonical scene of patrols in the jungle as part of shaping, clearing, or reconnaissance missions is the iconic image of that war for most veterans. In some ways, it became a metaphor for the war: soldiers always looking for an enemy in the jungle who also hid within the population, the search for victory always elusive, morally complex situations, and debates among unit members about strategy as emblematic of larger debates about the direction of the war on the home front. In typical veteran fashion, catchphrases from these movies became reference points and helped veterans contextualize their own firsthand experiences with war. Joker's iconic statement from *Full Metal Jacket* ("I wanted to be the first kid on my block to get a confirmed kill!") is often referenced, and Animal Mother's "You talk the talk. Do you walk the walk?" captured the sentiments of most veterans about who had *really* experienced the war. The brutality of Gunnery Sergeant Hartman in the opening boot camp scenes in *Full Metal Jacket* captured the transition to a war zone mentality for many veterans; countless veterans would actually welcome going through such a test today.

What these movies don't capture, or only reference in passing, is a fully accurate presentation of counterinsurgency strategies that were used later in the Vietnam War and efforts to implement them. Movies such as *Full Metal Jacket* almost inevitably focus on shaping and clearing operations; this is where the most combat takes place and is most visually appealing. Their focus is invariably on the year 1968 (the Tet Offensive) or earlier and don't capture later innovations in the war that fought insurgent strategy more comprehensively (e.g., the Civil Operations and Revolutionary Development Support [CORDS] program). There is a scene in *Full Metal Jacket*, for example, in which local civic and political leaders are buried after being assassinated by the Viet Cong, which suggests the political warfare aspects of the insurgency, but these vignettes are rare. The movie *Apocalypse Now*'s Colonel Kurtz is shown to "understand" some of the requirements of how to successfully fight the Viet Cong insurgency, targeting their shadow government leadership, but he is portrayed as "crazy" because he goes against the military system of thinking; his innovations make him a loose cannon, however right he was in his actions. The pro–Vietnam War movie *The Green Berets*, produced by and starring the actor John Wayne, was the only movie of the time—it was released in 1968—that portrayed the political warfare dimension of the conflict as much as the combat. By focusing on the U.S. Army's Special Forces, it highlighted their unique role in raising indigenous forces, and by showing how the family of a local leader the Green Berets had befriended was killed by the Viet Cong, it was a useful illustration of insurgent terror tactics.

Inevitably, most movies about the Vietnam War have an undercurrent of antiwar sentiment, and they typically focus on the elusive hunt for the hidden insurgent, which is a hallmark of General William Westmoreland's "search and destroy" strategy; however, there is no discussion of population protection, which occurred later in the war largely under the leadership of General Creighton Abrams. There also don't appear to be any major movies about the war in the later years after 1968 even when U.S. participation in the war continued for seven more years. Most of the movies about the Vietnam War known to the American public are excellent, but they principally focus on fighting in Vietnam as part of search-and-destroy missions, not about winning in that war—which is focused on population protection, raising indigenous defense forces, and crafting a dynamic political strategy to foster support for the government. Fighting the insurgency is still essential, albeit largely through indigenous forces; however, the population is the key, and fighting the armed wing of the insurgency is only in support of that goal. No movies really address the insurgent safe havens of North Vietnam either, which, as a subject, is hard to know when it is denied to members of the Western media and even harder to make resonate with the American viewing public.

When I watched the movie *Rambo* before my deployments to Afghanistan and Iraq, I greatly appreciated its action, drama, and violence. The tactics the main character used against the local police force, his creativity, and his fierce determination were sights to behold to my younger eyes. Similarly, when I watched *The Deer Hunter*, I was drawn more to the violence of combat and the infamous Russian roulette scene and the prisoner-of-war experience than the opening backstories of the characters and their return home. Once I deployed a few times and had gone through my own process of coming home, I viewed these movies with fresh eyes and greater maturity. I was immediately drawn to the early scenes of the movie as Rambo, somewhat rootless since his return from Vietnam, looks for an old combat buddy only to find that he has died of cancer from Agent Orange, the defoliant used in Vietnam to strip trees of their leaves to reveal hidden insurgents. The look of confusion and sadness on his face left a deep impression. His aimless but peaceful journey through a nearby town resonated as one searches for what is next in life after the war. Seeing him harassed as a vagrant—after he had served valorously for his country and received a Congressional Medal of Honor, no less—was similarly frustrating to witness. Seeing Rambo reveal and apply the special knowledge of violence he had learned from war and visit justice on those who would violate their oaths was extremely heartening. The opening scenes of *The Deer Hunter* wherein the backstories of the main characters are developed and their innocence established before they go to Vietnam was very impactful. It is hard to lose this innocence of life from experiences in war, and there is forever a yearning for a return to it. Additionally, the last scenes of the movie, in which the men wrestle with their journeys home from war and grapple with the brutal realities of what they experienced, resonated on many levels. The camaraderie and loyalty of the men, how Robert De Niro's character was the calm, unifying presence of the group, served to underscore again how war disparately impacts men who serve in it. I liken these reactions of mine to the way love songs sound once you've had and lost love. They sound trite, sappy, and somewhat unrelatable, but after losing one's love, they take on a whole new meaning and have an emotional impact that is visceral. The same is true for war veterans when they watch any movies connected to war after experiencing it firsthand. The Vietnam War of the generation who fought after 9/11 was a series of movies that are themselves only representations of aspects of reality. For many veterans, the memoirs, histories, and other accounts of the war helped fill in the gaps.

Literature

"I like reading books about the last war in this one."

—PAUL FUSSELL, *THE GREAT WAR AND MODERN MEMORY*
(QUOTING COLIN PERRY TALKING ABOUT READING
WORLD WAR I BOOKS DURING WORLD WAR II)

While the visual appeal of movies about the Vietnam War explains why veterans found them so enticing, firsthand accounts of combat by veterans of that conflict written in memoirs were also readily consumed by Afghanistan and Iraq veterans. The vast majority of war memoirs are written by junior officers and enlisted personnel who are recounting their combat experiences, typically from their first tour, which are instantly relatable for veterans of similar rank preparing for their own deployments. Additionally, even after a war deployment, many veterans find these types of books eminently relatable and readable as they process their own war experiences. Many of the most prominent war memoirs of the Vietnam War that veterans gravitated toward include *A Rumor of War* (1977) by Philip Caputo, a Marine infantry officer; *If I Die in a Combat Zone* (1973) by Tim O'Brien, a U.S. Army infantryman; *Once a Warrior King: Memories of an Officer in Vietnam* (1985) by David Donovan, a U.S. Army officer and military advisor; *The Killing Zone: My Life in the Vietnam War* by Frederick Downs (1978), a U.S. Army officer; *Combat Recon: My Year with the ARVN* (1991) by Robert D. Parrish, a U.S. Army officer and military advisor; and the less well-known but impactful *The Advisor* (1973) by Captain John L. Cook, a U.S. Army officer and military advisor. The complexities of finding and fighting an elusive enemy hiding amid the local population as well as in the jungle are quickly made apparent as they participate in combat operations, principally patrols in the jungle. The memoirs of Caputo, O'Brien, and Downs are particularly relevant here. These narratives of combat in support of shaping and clearing operations resonate with war veterans who have undertaken similar activities, and they are as close as one can get to conventional war narratives of straight combat in an insurgency war. Additionally, these books focus on the world of junior officers and enlisted personnel working through the complexities of their missions, managing the application of violence, and wrestling with the usual first-tour challenges of homesickness, facing death, and the politics of small units.

The wars of Donovan, Cook, and Parrish differ markedly from these straightforward narratives of combat and focus on "the other war," the war of fighting the hidden insurgency of the Viet Cong by raising, training, and combat advising local security forces; combating the insurgency's shadow government; working alongside political leaders; and conducting intelligence-driven operations. Their memoirs are more subtle and deliberate; combat is small scale and doesn't dominate the narrative. Locals are mentioned much more frequently; they are given personality and life (even names!), and they are vital partners to these veterans as they raise local popular forces in rural Vietnam (Donovan), partner with Vietnamese security officials (Cook, Parrish), and uncover the hidden insurgency (Donovan, Cook). The villages, history, and culture of Vietnam become real and vital, and the partnerships of these veterans with the communities they are working in become real places to the reader. They are also looking for an elusive enemy that hides within the population, but their operations are crafted by, with, and through local security, intelligence, political, and village leaders; they are on the hunt for hidden Viet Cong leaders and their shadow governments. Traditional Vietnam combat narratives, especially of the early war years, focus principally on unilateral combat operations by U.S. military forces. As Vietnamese military forces are built up later in the war, in many respects much too late, there are very few narratives of these partnered operations wherein U.S. forces fight alongside indigenous forces, although Parrish's is a welcome exception since he embedded with the South Vietnamese army. Another feature of Donovan's and Cook's books is that their tours are largely taking place away from the U.S. Army's bureaucracy, with all its attendant inflexibility. Each book references certain tendencies in the U.S. Army as an institution that make counterinsurgency more difficult, such as how some of its members disrespect the local population (Donovan) and how careerism (Cook) inhibits an effective war strategy. These themes of local entrepreneurship despite the U.S. Army's bureaucracy resonate with many contemporary veterans.

The longevity of the U.S. presence in Vietnam also allowed some veterans to not only serve there but also write thoughtful books about the conflict with the goal of shaping U.S. policy in Indochina even as U.S. forces were still fighting. These deeper studies, which were published later in the war, emphasize less the personal narrative of the author, such as in a memoir, and more the intellectual foundations of the insurgency and counterinsurgency strategy. They discuss the micro-histories of the areas they analyze, study the enemy's strategy holistically (political as well as military), and showcase the "other war" narrative of the Vietnam War focused on fighting the Viet Cong's insurgency versus exclusively North Vietnamese conventional forces. There are narrative aspects of the books that are tactical, but they principally use them to illustrate larger strategic insights about the conflict such as fighting the insurgency holistically. *War Comes to Long An: Revolutionary Conflict in a Vietnamese Province* (1972) by Jeffrey Race is the most highly developed book of this type. Race served in Long An Province, which is south/southwest of then Saigon (modern-day Ho Chi Minh City), as well as in Phuoc Tuy Province east of the capital with the U.S. Army. He would eventually spend two years in country and became fluent in the Vietnamese language as well. He then left the service and returned to Long An to study both sides of the conflict as part of his dissertation research for a PhD.

He conducted interviews with American and Vietnamese government officials, spoke with captured and reconciled members of the Viet Cong, reviewed interrogation and intelligence reports, read government studies, and drew upon his firsthand knowledge of the area. His research uncovered how the dueling narratives and histories of the conflict were mostly talking past each other and how the Viet Cong crafted a nuanced local political strategy that garnered the support of the population (although it also regularly oppressed the population). This strategy was politically agnostic with respect to Communist ideology and made appeals to the self-interest of villagers, such as by resisting government efforts to aggregate land that had previously been distributed to landless farmers back to large landowners. They tended to respect local traditional political leadership structures, although they also sought to impose their own on the population, in contrast to political leaders imposed on villages by the central government. The South Vietnamese government likewise eliminated the election of local leaders in the late 1950s, and so officials lacked local democratic legitimacy and were more concerned about political sentiments in Saigon than local conditions in areas they led and represented (this echoes similar political arrangements in Afghanistan and Iraq). Further, simply by being in the province, the Viet Cong developed a sympathetic understanding of the local population's concerns when many centrally appointed officials were too scared or simply decided not to perform their duty of local service. The end goal of the Viet Cong was always to impose a Communist dictatorship on the population, but these short-term strategic adjustments appealing to self-interest rather than ideological purity were more successful as a strategy (there are echoes of this approach in how the Taliban behaved toward the population in Afghanistan) later in the war.

A similar book in this vein is Robert Andrews's *The Village War: Vietnamese Communist Revolutionary Activities in Dinh Tuong Province, 1960–1964* (1973), which is a study of the Dinh Tuong Province in the Mekong Delta. Andrews served as a Special Forces officer, but it was as a member of the U.S. Information Agency that he traveled throughout the Upper Mekong Delta with six South Vietnamese determining the political, economic, and social factors the Viet Cong exploited to gain power. His comprehensive analysis of how the Communist Viet Cong were organized, gained power, influenced local populations, and conducted political warfare at the local level is seminal and is almost exclusively focused on studying how the enemy operated. It is a unique contribution to the study of the war. The book *The Village* (1972) by Bing West, a Marine officer, brings to life the small wars of counterinsurgency at the village level as Marines combat the armed wing of the local insurgency as part of the Combined Action Platoon program. The effort provided population protection through persistent presence, raised local security forces as part of that initiative, and fought the armed insurgency. It is a study in small–unit action and the interpersonal dynamics of men in combat as well as about partnership with local political, civic, and security officials. These books as well as Race's thoroughly enriched the collective understanding of the U.S. military about the nature of the Viet Cong's insurgency strategy at the local level. The United States eventually adopted elements of a comprehensive approach (e.g., population protection, development, raising local security forces, embedded partnering, etc.), which fought the "other war" through its adoption of the Civil Operations and Revolutionary Development Support program. This effort was also assisted by the decimation of the Viet Cong in the Tet Offensive when their hidden cadres rose up against the South Vietnamese government and were largely killed.

There are four books about the Vietnam War that particularly resonated with veterans of the wars in Afghanistan and Iraq and served as bridges between their contemporary wars and the war in Indochina. The first is *A Better War: The Unexamined Victories and the Final Tragedy of America's Last Years in Vietnam* (1999) by Lewis Sorley. Sorley graduated from West Point, served in Vietnam with the U.S. Army as an officer, and eventually earned a PhD in national security policy. He focuses his study on the later years of the war in Vietnam during and after the Tet Offense under the tenure of General Creighton Abrams. He recounts in telling detail how the U.S. military improved its understanding of the nature of the insurgency conflict it was involved in and adapted its institutions and thinking to that end. His research showed that, due to later innovations in the war that fought the insurgency holistically through the adoption of a population–centric strategy and the raising, training, and combat advising of indigenous secu-rity forces, the Northern Vietnamese government was forced to rely upon conventional forces and conventional invasions. These efforts were further buttressed by the destruction of the Viet Cong during the Tet Offensive, further forcing the North Vietnamese to rely upon their own forces rather than local cadres. He also details how, through improved intelligence, the United States was better able to monitor and thwart conventional invasions of the south by the north. In addition to better tracking efforts on the Ho Chi Minh trail, the insight of identifying and destroying food caches in the south, assembled to feed invading northern troops, significantly hamstrung the north's efforts. Sorley's book directly led to the creation of the Village Stability Operations/Afghan Local Police program in Afghanistan begin-ning in 2010, which fought the local insurgency comprehensively through population protection, persistent presence, the raising of local security forces, and the empowerment of local officials.[1] The intellectual linkages between the Village Stability Operations initiative in Afghanistan and the Combined Action Platoon program (U.S. forces partnered with Vietnam-ese Popular Action Forces at the local level) is clear.

The second and third books, *Matterhorn* (2010) and *What It Is Like to Go to War* (2011), are written by the same author, Karl Marlantes, who served as a Marine infantry officer in Vietnam. Marlantes received the Navy Cross for his service as well as a Bronze Star, two Purple Hearts, two Navy and Marine Corps Commendation Medals with "Vs" for valor, and ten Air Medals. He also graduated from Yale University and had been a Rhodes Scholar. *Matterhorn* is a novel about the Vietnam War as told by a young Marine officer on his first tour, echoing Marlantes's own experiences. It is almost exclusively about small–unit action in the jungles of Vietnam and is focused on the personal dynamics of the characters as they conduct shap-ing and clearing operations in the jungles. While many novels had been written about the Vietnam War, such as *Close Quarters* (1977) and *Paco's Story* (1987) by Larry Heinemann, *Fields of Fire* (1978) by James Webb, and *The Short-Timers* (1979) by Gustav Hasford (on which the movie *Full Metal Jacket* is based), this contemporary publication reintroduced the Vietnam War to a new generation of war veterans. Many of the most prominent novels of Vietnam also focused on shaping and clearing operations and often had scenes of patrols in the jungle, and Marlantes's book continues this trend. His book also demonstrated to contemporary veterans as well as the literary world that war veterans could write popular as well as critically acclaimed fiction. His work inspired other veterans to write their own fiction based upon their war experiences. Further, the persistence of Marlantes in publishing his novel, originally written shortly after he returned from Vietnam, was also an inspiration. He kept at it after decades of rejection even in the face of a lack of interest in the war (1970s), the fact that other novels and movies had addressed the conflict (1980s), and desires to repurpose it to the Gulf War (1990s) or to the post-9/11 wars (2000s). His determination to tell his story and the story of Vietnam veterans generally resonated with many veterans who also struggle to tell their story even as society moves on from their conflict(s).

Marlantes's *What It Is Like to Go to War* (2011) is nonfiction and is a firsthand account of the struggles he went through over several decades after coming home from war. It is also a biography and recounts his life growing up in Oregon, his attending Yale University and receiving a Rhodes scholarship, and his decision to go to Vietnam to serve as an infantry officer. His open and sometimes startlingly frank stories of his struggles coming home, often shared in a confessional style of writing, expressed in words what so many contemporary veterans experience. He gave voice to those private moments of crisis—moral, physical, and spiritual—that veterans sometimes experience. The harrowing story of his struggles coming home, supplemented by interviews about his books, legitimized the same struggles of Afghan and Iraq veterans. Here was a bona fide war hero, a man among men, and a Rhodes Scholar recounting his own struggles in a way that was accessible to veterans and not obscured in the language of psychology. His discussion of joining "the club"—those who had been to war—resonated with war veterans as they felt this same transition in their own lives. His frank admittances of ill discipline with women and drugs and his general disregard for Marine protocol resonated with many returning war veterans who felt this rootless animosity to the patterns of stable life. His veneration of combat and of war, and of how it transformed him and how he misses it, and his struggles with anger, numbness, and seeing dead Viet Cong bodies captures in written form the weird world where combat adaptations persist into civilian life.

The fourth book was written by John A. Nagl, a U.S. Army veteran of the war in Iraq, although his book was published before his deployment and, while not about Iraq, clearly provided important insights into the conflict by studying the U.S. experience in Vietnam. *Learning to Eat Soup with a Knife: Counterinsurgency Lessons from Malaya and Vietnam* (2002) was an outgrowth of Nagl's dissertation at Oxford University, where he had been a Rhodes Scholar. He compared the U.S. Army's experience fighting the Viet Cong in Vietnam with the experiences of British forces fighting an insurgency in Malaya. He demonstrated that efforts to actively study the insurgencies and their strategy and incorporate these insights into strategic and institutional design considerations led to greater success in the campaigns. He showed how the U.S. Army, in the field as well as an institution, had become an "un-learning" institution and how eventually, due to leadership changes and poor battlefield outcomes, the army became a better "learning institution." The parallels between U.S. experiences in Vietnam in this regard and those in Iraq and Afghanistan are, unfortunately, very clear, and the necessity of helping the U.S. Army once again become a learning institution was evident. Nagl's popularization of these ideas eventually helped create counterinsurgency schools in Iraq and Afghanistan to train U.S. personnel and helped with the broader efforts of the United States learning more about the cultures, histories, and politics of the countries they were operating in as well as the nature of fighting and defeating the insurgencies Coalition forces were confronting.

How wars are remembered by society influences how future conflicts are fought. How they are chronicled in movies, books, TV shows, and the like craft the myths and legends of the war and contribute to what the World War II/Korean War veteran and author Samuel Hynes refers to as the "war-in-his-head" of the veteran. Outside of firsthand experience, what the veteran thinks about war is influenced by these past accounts of conflict and war, sometimes to his detriment. While most capture some aspects of the wars they cover, certain narratives resonate more with American culture than others. This tendency is particularly acute in wars of counterinsurgency, which don't engage the full energies of the American people, are not considered existential threats, rarely have conclusive battles, and are often controversial and politically contentious. Success in conventional wars is fairly easy to describe (i.e., destroy the enemy's military forces); success in counterinsurgency requires fighting as well but is really about getting the local government to fight the war successfully. Success is complex, takes time, requires local partners, and is slow to achieve. Largely for these and other reasons, these types of wars are particularly susceptible to mis-remembering as accounts of combat are written about and chronicled in movies at far higher rates than pacification campaigns and population protection. As new generations came of age in the United States following the end of the Vietnam War and firsthand experience with the conflict receded in the military due to retirements, how the war was remembered influenced how new veterans thought about their own wars. These "myths and legends" became the reference points for many Afghanistan and Iraq veterans of what fighting an insurgency by U.S. forces really entailed and will impact how these wars are remembered and chronicled for future generations.

The Vietnam War's Generals

The legacy and memory of the Vietnam War, as is true for all wars, was also shaped by those generals who played prominent roles in its execution. The memoirs, articles, and interviews they conduct, both during and after the war, also shape what is remembered about wars and contributes to the myths and legends of the conflict and helps create the "war in the head" of the next generation. Generals William Westmoreland and Creighton Abrams (both commanders of the United States Military Assistance Command in Vietnam, from 1964 to 1968 and 1968 to 1972, respectively) and their legacies significantly shaped the thinking of the strategies and execution of the wars in Afghanistan and Iraq. Further, as new generations of veterans turned to studying the Vietnam War in search of insights into how to fight the insurgencies in Central Asia and the Middle East, the legacies of these two generals were revisited. However, even then, certain lessons were learned more readily than others, and the execution of war strategies in Afghanistan and Iraq were also hampered by many similar constraints. Institutional considerations and civil-military structures impacted all three wars but were not seriously addressed in the campaigns in Afghanistan and Iraq outside of modest in-country reforms. However much discretion generals and flag officers have as commanders, they are still limited in their choices by the institutional considerations of their services and the civil-military structures they operate within.

The dual legacies of Westmoreland and Abrams and how they are remembered today capture the institutional tendencies of the U.S. Army to remember conventional warfare lessons rather than counterinsurgency lessons. Westmoreland's tenure in Vietnam from 1964 to 1968, when he largely adopted a conventional warfare strategy against an opponent that largely chose a strategy of insurgency, squandered precious time, energy, and resources. Efforts should have been spent on building indigenous forces, undertaking a proper counterinsurgency strategy focused on population protection, and, working with the State Department, resetting the Vietnamese government to be more legitimate, effective, and capable. While conventional North Vietnamese forces were a factor with which he had to contend, his overemphasis on defeating these forces using conventional warfare strategies incorrectly conceptualized the revolutionary/

insurgency nature of the conflict. While the Tet Offensive in 1968 is regarded by popular history as a calamity (and its leading to President Johnson's decision not to run for reelection reinforces this impression), the military success of U.S. and Vietnamese forces at crushing what had been the formerly concealed Viet Cong insurgency in open warfare is not generally known. U.S. pacification programs, which had begun just before Westmoreland's departure in 1968, were better able to operate due to the Viet Cong's decimation. However, the limitations on U.S. forces and their inability to address the safe havens of North Vietnam, Laos, and Cambodia conventionally sowed the seeds of instability, which no amount of in-country stabilization could really address.

The tenure of General Abrams, who served as Westmoreland's deputy in 1967 before becoming commander of U.S. forces in 1968 until he departed in 1972 to become the U.S. Army's chief of staff, is regarded much more favorably by historians. By embracing a more holistic counterinsurgency strategy, while also benefiting from the weakening of the Viet Cong insurgency following its losses during the Tet Offensive, he pulled U.S. war strategy from defeat to a position closer to victory. While search-and-destroy missions continued, they were better informed and focused on Northern Vietnamese conventional units, which were not local and larger compared to the hidden insurgency. His tenure and his successes, though, became subsumed within the narrative of U.S. withdrawal and Vietnamization wherein the South Vietnamese government assumed greater responsibility of the war effort. As was seen in the wars in Afghanistan and Iraq, the initial years of squandered strategy undermined political support for the conflicts in the United States, so when later innovations took place wherein institutions adapted to the unique requirements of fighting the insurgency, there was little popular support to undertake an improved strategy. However, the legacies of both men were not remembered the same way by history.

The publication of General Westmoreland's memoir *A Soldier Reports* (1976) privileged his narrative of the war, and he had a supreme self-interest in defending his tenure in light of the war's unfortunate conclusion. For the rest of his life, General William Westmoreland justified, explained, and defended his initial strategies of seek and destroy and an attrition-based strategy. He defended it in his memoir, justified it in a lawsuit against CBS News, and never wavered from his views. His spirited defense was based upon his military assessment of Vietnam as seen through a conventional warfare lens. American commanders in Vietnam faced not just an insurgency but also invading North Vietnamese conventional forces. For Westmoreland, these larger forces required more of his attention, clearly echoing the Korean War's dynamic, rather than counterinsurgency work. His views echoed the assessment that an invasion of North Vietnam should have taken place to eliminate it (as well as Laos and Cambodia) as a safe haven for the Viet Cong and included a criticism that civilian meddling (e.g., selecting of targets to bomb, Congress not supporting the South Vietnamese government by cutting off aid in 1974–1975, etc.) hamstrung U.S. military efforts. His views found fertile ground in conservative political assessments of the Vietnam War.

Abrams did not write a memoir of his time in Vietnam, and he passed away in 1974. He was not able to provide an amplifying version of the Vietnam War, and, as is often the case, successful pacification is not remembered by popular culture, whether it's in movies, TV series, memoirs, newscasts, and such. The later innovations of the conflict were not remembered in popular culture or the institutions of the U.S. military. A strategic mis-remembering of the war's later institutional adaptations and improved strategies took place, which were only really rescued by Lewis Sorley and his books *A Better War: The Unexamined Victories and Final Tragedy of America's Last Years in Vietnam* (1999), *Thunderbolt: General Creighton Abrams and the Army of His Time* (1992), *Vietnam Chronicles: The Abrams Tapes, 1968–1972* (2004), and *Westmoreland: The General Who Lost Vietnam* (2017). Sorley literally gave a voice to Abrams by editing and publishing the tapes he made of military strategy sessions he held while he led the U.S. effort in Vietnam as well as his end-of-day journal. Sorley also focused on the later years of the war, 1968–1972, when most popular histories such as Stanley Karnow's *Vietnam: A History* (1983) and David Halberstam's *Best and the Brightest* (1972) didn't cover them but still had outsized influence on popular opinion about the war. The book *A Bright Shining Lie* by Neil Sheehan is an exception to this tendency. Sorley's documentation of Abrams's tenure provided a necessary balance to Westmoreland's account and detailed how U.S. culture and politics explained the conclusion of the war. There are merits to Westmoreland's views with respect to foreign safe havens the insurgency used and civilian efforts to influence U.S. targeting efforts, but his tenure is more remembered for lost opportunities.

The Institution of the U.S. Military

A central narrative of the Vietnam War, as is true in the wars in Afghanistan and Iraq, is the misconception of the initial conflict being exclusively a conventional war, or counterterrorism in Afghanistan's case, with its attendant emphasis on enemy-centric warfare rather than population-centric operations.[2] Violence was something done to the enemy compared to something that was done by, with, and through indigenous partners with the population against the enemy. Further, the inherently political nature of insurgency warfare was not well understood, and acts of political warfare were seen as simply acts of violence versus attempts to intimidate the population and undermine confidence in the government. Compelling political strategies seeking to make the indigenous government a legitimate, effective, and capable force in the lives of the population were never really achieved in a dynamic fashion; regime types of overly centralized systems were not reformed to decentralize and democratize structures. Additionally, because these initial misjudgments were made, U.S. forces and their leaders, using positive indicators of conventional war that measured enemy killed, among other factors, as measures of success, downplayed the need to raise, train, equip, mentor, and combat-lead indigenous security forces at all levels. Further, due to the sense that these conflicts would be short in duration, enemy safe havens such as North Vietnam, Laos, and Cambodia for the Vietnam War and Pakistan for the Afghan War and Syria and Iran for the Iraq War were never comprehensively addressed. This often had to do with the political sensitivities of expanding operations to these countries but was also due to a misunderstanding of the terms of the initial conflict. Measures of performance, which are often easier to quantify (e.g., enemy killed, money spent, patrols completed, improvised explosive devices found, etc.), were used more frequently than measures of effectiveness (e.g., villagers joining local protective forces, government leaders taking the initiative, insurgents joining the government, etc.), which, in insurgencies, is what the population decides to do as part of its risk/reward calculations and thus is the key measure of success. These tendencies are made all the more acute by constant rotations of personnel due to careerism and the institutional needs of the services.[3] As each new unit, leader, and command showed up in Afghanistan and Iraq, as well as in Vietnam, corporate memory degraded, and, lacking expertise in either country, inevitably military personnel measured their performance and effectiveness in conventional warfare terms, which furthered their own careers.

Another factor that complicated the Vietnam War and was a central element of the difficulties of the Afghanistan and Iraq wars were the civil-military structures that promulgated the initial war plans for both countries. The removal of the Joint Chiefs of Staff as a corporate body from the chain of command in 1958 as part of the Defense Reorganization Act, seen as a means of strengthening civilian control, removed a necessary mediating bureaucratic layer between the forces fighting the war and the leaders who make strategic plans. The struggles over roles and missions of the Joint Chiefs of Staff, which enriches strategic thinking and forces necessary conversations about war plans, were removed at the strategic level. Further, by making the chain of command go from the president to the secretary of defense to the combatant commander, civilian leaders became more culpable for general war strategy when the Joint Chiefs were professionally better placed to undertake such tasks. The Joint Chiefs as a corporate body also functioned as a shield to mitigate the political interference of civilian leaders in military operations while also shielding civilian leaders from the state of the war by allowing them to defer to the Joint Chiefs of Staff if war strategy needed to change. It also allowed the service heads, the Chiefs of Staff and the chief of Naval Operations, to oversee personnel changes in a more active manner as war revealed those leaders who fell short of expectations. They were still able to remove (fire) personnel, but since they were not directly involved in the execution of war strategy, it was made all the more difficult. Further, making the commander in the field fighting the war report to the U.S. Army's chief of staff reinforced accountability and empowered the chief of staff to be an advocate, supporter, confidante, and strategic leader on behalf of the commander in the field. He was also able to keep the commanding general fighting the war apprised of the political and strategic dynamics of Washington, DC, as well as serve as a better advisor to the president and commander in chief due to his greater knowledge of the war's dynamics.

The Vietnam, Afghanistan, and Iraq wars were also fought in the context of a large, professional standing military system with its own institutional interests and competing missions. Historically, the U.S. military would grow its forces for conflicts using the draft, volunteer units, and reservists. The large standing military that was created after World War II, and the careerism it created, privileged the need to provide careers for its members and focus on nation-state and strategic priorities. This tendency is well documented in the book *The Army and Vietnam* (1986), written by the then U.S. Army lieutenant colonel Andrew Krepenvich Jr., wherein he detailed how the competing priority of deterring and being prepared to fight the Soviet Union in Europe prompted the U.S. Army in particular to not resource the Vietnam War correctly. Its primary mission was being prepared to fight the Soviet Union and so the less important mission of the Vietnam War constantly suffered from the rotations of U.S. Army personnel as part of careerism. It was also done as part of an effort to make sure they had well-rounded careers in order to be prepared to face the larger, strategic threat of Soviet Communism. It's no small thing that the pejorative word *lifer* was hurled by draftees (since reservists were not heavily utilized in the Vietnam War) at active duty careerists for their tendency to focus on their next assignment versus the war they were fighting. The young army officer plucked out of his unit mid-tour (as referenced in Tim O'Brien's Vietnam War memoir *If I Die in A Combat Zone*, for example) was emblematic of this tendency. The shift to an all-volunteer force in 1973 furthered these tendencies as the institution of the military, and the U.S. Army in particular, was not systematically confronted with alternative perspectives as draftees forced it to reconcile its institutional priorities with that of war fighting. The military increasingly selected its members from smaller and smaller talent pools that echoed its priorities, and more members were part of extended family networks serving in uniform. These developments further complicated the ability of the U.S. military to adapt to the unique challenges of the insurgency wars they were involved in versus the conventional wars they were designed to fight for the nation.

Conclusion

The impact of the legacy of the Vietnam War on U.S. strategic thinking and how the war was remembered by American culture greatly influenced a new generation of policy makers and veterans. The myths and legends of that conflict, fostered by movies, books, and TV shows about the war, created narratives and strategic reference points that directly influenced the direction of both wars. Some insights were adopted by strategic thinkers, in part because they were well chronicled, or often ignored due to the mis-remembering of the Vietnam War and the fact that lessons were never truly institutionalized or captured in a manner that endured. Additionally, some of the lessons that had been "learned" from the Vietnam War, such as greater deference to the U.S. military for war strategy execution, turned out to be mistakes in both conflicts. It is hard to say how the wars in Afghanistan and Iraq will end, if they end at all, and so how the U.S. experience will be recorded has not yet been finally established. Some conclusions or narratives of the wars have begun to solidify and focus on having too few troops in the initial phases of the conflict, strategies that did not initiate counterinsurgency efforts early (population protection, building indigenous security forces, a political warfare strategy, etc.), and the need to address enemy safe havens in surrounding countries. More has yet to be written about these and other issues, but the final histories of both conflicts and the U.S. experience remain to be written.

Militaria

*"The walls were all paneled and lined with a double row
of bunks, on which lay blankets, ruffled from recent use. A
greatcoat or two hung on the walls, and (joy!) there were five
'pickelhaubes' [German helmets] lying about. . . . While
Bickersteth showed him the good points of the trench, and made
a case for staying there, I ran back to the dugout determined at
least to find a souvenir. In the shaft I met Wells, and together
we seized on the last remaining 'pickelhaube.'"*

—CHARLES EDMONDS, *A SUBALTERN'S WAR*, 76–78

*"This Jap had been hit. One of my buddies was field-stripping
him for souvenirs. I must admit it really bothered me, the
guys dragging him around like a carcass. I was just horrified.
This guy had been a human being. It didn't take me long to
overcome that feeling. A lot of my buddies hit, the fatigue, the
stress. After a while, the veneer of civilization wore pretty thin."*

—STUDS TERKEL, *"THE GOOD WAR": AN ORAL HISTORY OF
WORLD WAR II*, 61 (QUOTING E. B. SLEDGE)

WHEN I WAS GROWING UP in a small town in Florida in the
1980s, World War II, although distant to me in time, was
omnipresent as were the stories of my grandfather who had
served as a communications sergeant in the U.S. Army during the conflict
in Europe. I did not get to know my grandfather because he passed away

when I was less than two years old, but the pictures of him during the war and the stories he shared and impressions he left with his children, including my father, greatly impacted my view of military service. One item that stood out in the stories I heard was my grandfather's regret that he was not able to take a Walther P38 pistol he had acquired, which was a German officer's sidearm, back from the war. It was a much-sought-after item due to its quality, but the idea that an enlisted man, my grandfather, could come into its possession after (I assumed in my young mind) killing an officer or coming across his corpse was enthralling to me as a child. It was the first weapon I had ever heard about, and I quickly recognized its unusual design whenever it came up in a TV show, movie, documentary, or book on World War II. I was sad my grandfather hadn't brought one home from the war. The fact that he apparently frequently lamented his inability to do so spoke volumes, and I secretly pledged that one day I would get one for him even if it was posthumously. Similarly, the small reminders of my father's service in the U.S. Army, such as an old ammunition box repurposed for medical supplies, an old name tag sewn into my kindergarten blanket, and an old shooting trophy, reinforced these connections to the military. The urge to "bring something home from the war" is a powerful feeling for war veterans and is a timeless constant for combatants across the centuries. It is physical link for the veteran to his experiences and a reminder of a visit to an exotic land, of a brush with death, of the feeling of camaraderie, of friends lost, and of a vanquished foe. On the home front, his war zone souvenirs are points of curiosity that transport the veteran to a faraway land and add to his mystique among civilians.

On October 5, 1946, the latest issue of the *Saturday Evening Post* was published, and on its cover was the newest painting by the noted artist Norman Rockwell depicting a scene familiar to many World War II veterans. The image was of a young man named Willie Gillis, a fictional character Rockwell created to depict the evolution of a civilian to military service to war service and then back to civilian life. In this respect, Gillis was taking advantage of the postwar GI Bill to receive a college education. He was sitting on the windowsill of his college dorm room deeply immersed in reading a textbook, and, as with many Rockwell paintings, the rich details of the image contained the clues to his identity and past experiences. On the wall to the left were his discharge papers from the U.S. Army and the cloth rank of a sergeant first class (E-7), as well as the red, white, and blue Army Service Forces Patch. To the right was a set of golf clubs symbolizing a reprieve from war service and an opportunity to relax. However, there were three items dangling from a hook above his head, war souvenirs of the military campaign in Europe, which offered the most interesting insights into his background. They were a German army helmet, a German ceremonial dagger on a chain, and a small Nazi flag. Gillis presumably acquired these souvenirs, or militaria, from his service overseas, grabbing them in battle or perhaps parlaying for them with fellow soldiers.

Many veterans feel an acute need to seize and possess something of the enemy from their combat tour. The enemy is a mystery to the veteran upon first arriving in country. He has heard the stories of battle from other veterans, studied the enemy's ways, and is generally acquainted with the mission he has been given. Upon first contact with his opponent, when the rush of combat ensues, the enemy begins to assume shape; he is now real, and as bullets zip by the veteran, the abstraction recedes. Upon discovering the body of the dead enemy, the veteran is confronted by the visceral reality of his mission. There, in a crumpled mass, is the man who tried to kill him. He is covered in visible wounds, his kit and weapon by his side; the bodies of his comrades are destroyed by gunfire, and the violence of the encounter surrounds him. What was abstract has now become quite real and personal, and the veteran has now transitioned to a combat veteran; he has experienced battle, death, and killing, which forever distinguishes him from his civilian self and his civilian colleagues. At this moment, the veteran grabs some memento of his encounter, some tangible evidence of his success—proof that he has passed "the test" and, depending upon his courage and the ability of his unit, has passed with flying colors: "Your enemy's possessions are yours: that's a soldier's creed."[1] He quickly grabs what he can—perhaps a helmet, a knife, or some personal effect of his opponent—and jams it into his pocket or backpack, moving on to the next ridgeline, village, and mission. The veteran and his unit were able to impose their will on the opponent, depriving him of his objective, his life, and his cause, and the tangible proof of the veteran's success is what he has taken from the enemy.

This proof of successful contact with the enemy becomes a mark of distinction for war veterans among other veterans. For those who have not been in combat, the veteran's souvenir carries huge weight and becomes a symbol of respect, awe, and sometimes envy. It is also a window into the world of the enemy: how he fights, thinks, and organizes, and what he believes. It is an object of great fascination. Past conflicts are replete with these items whether they are helmets, daggers, weapons, uniforms, battle flags, maps, or enemy photos. It was not uncommon, for example, for captured enemy equipment to be paraded before adorning crowds by the victors in war. Many souvenirs are much more than simply battlefield pickups and are part of intelligence-gathering efforts by the U.S. military. Diaries, letters, books, photographs, manuals, and orders are among hundreds of items military intelligence collects to fill in the picture and to uncover the mystery that is the enemy and his plans, abilities, and motivations.

> The doughboy's duffel also bulged with articles that were not G.I. There were [German] spiked helmets by the score, shrapnel splinters, cooties embalmed in a drop of candle-wax. Among the Army of Occupation the demand for Iron Crosses was so brisk that Germans had been constrained to manufacture them for the overseas trade; late in the winter of '19 the exchange value was quoted as having fallen to one cake of American soap. A joke of the trenches said that the French might be fighting for freedom, but the Yanks were fighting for souvenirs.[2]

War veterans also bring back mementoes of close calls with death such as bullets and shell fragments or deeply meaningful items from their time in country such as a stone, some dirt, or an item connected to the death of a comrade. It is also common for war veterans to bring back U.S. military equipment, whether it is a rifle or grenade or something more mundane such as an overcoat, fleece, or other items that can be used on the home front. In some cases, war veterans even send or bring home body parts of the enemy or from the local population, a decidedly more visceral (and also illegal) reminder of his victory over the enemy.

> Parts of destroyed suicide planes were scattered all over the ship. During a little lull in the action the men would look around for Jap souvenirs and what souvenirs they were. I got part of the plane. The deck near my mount was covered with blood, guts, brains, tongues, scalps, hearts, arms, etc., from the Jap pilots. One of the Marines cut the ring off the finger of one of the dead pilots. They had to put the hose on to wash the blood off the deck. The deck ran red with blood. The Japs were spattered all over the place. One of the fellows had a Jap scalp, it looked just like you skinned an animal. The hair was black, cut very short, and the color of the skin was yellow, real Japanese. I do not think he was very old. I picked up a tin pie plate with a tongue on it. The pilot's tooth mark was into it very deep. It was very big and long, it looked like parts of his tonsils and throat were attached to it. It also looked like the tongue you buy in the meat store. This was the first time I ever say a person's brains, what a mess. One of the men on our mount got a Jap rib and cleaned it up, he said his sister wants part of a Jap body. One fellow from Texas had a knee bone and he was going to preserve it in alcohol from the sick bay. The Jap bodies were blown into all sorts of pieces.[3]

Similarly, "[i]n 1944, *Life* magazine, that arbiter of popular opinion, could print a photograph of a pretty American girl with a 'Jap skull' on her desk, souvenir from a boy-friend in the Pacific."[4] Another prominent example is when a soldier in World War II sent President Franklin Delano Roosevelt a Japanese soldier's leg bone fashioned into a flute. However, what is collected in conventional wars differs from what is collected in wars of counterinsurgency.

Nation-states and conventional wars make and leave far more items for collecting than insurgencies, and depending upon the nature of the war and its political circumstances, some items gain more currency than others. Nazi paraphernalia, for example, has always carried extra weight with some collectors compared to items from Imperial Japan. Insurgencies, by their nature, are far less formal; they lack many of the weapons of nation-states (e.g., tanks, airplanes, etc.), and because their strategy is one of indirect fighting, operating within the civilian population and husbanding resources to fight another day, they tend to be light guerrilla forces, which means their gear is simple and sometimes civilian in nature. Because so much of guerrilla warfare is about small-unit action, one would expect more battlefield finds for the U.S. soldier. However, because insurgents don't typically wear formal military uniforms with patches, unit insignia, helmets, and the like, what usually remains after a firefight is a weapon (e.g., AK-47s, sniper rifles, and Russian RPD and PKM machine guns), civilian clothing, and perhaps a document and a picture or two. More mature insurgencies may have some artillery, rockets, recoilless rifles, vehicles, and such. Insurgents also tend to conduct operations in such a manner as to maximize surprise, to fight at a moment of their choosing, and to keep their casualty numbers low. Additionally, insurgents tend to blend in with the civilian population, making it harder to identify them and any military gear unique to their forces.

Most successful counterinsurgency (COIN) strategies require a deep understanding of local culture and the interests of the population and focus on bolstering local security forces. These methods require, along with a compelling political strategy to gain the support of the population for the government, a focus on the needs and interests of the people. Because of this, members of the military, as a matter of course, must understand and develop some sympathy for indigenous populations and their culture, mores, history, and politics. Largely for this reason, souvenirs from COIN campaigns tend also to be heavily drawn from indigenous populations, and this can include such things as local clothing, farm implements, and cultural items. Additionally, because a central feature of insurgent strategy is to avoid direct combat and engage in indirect action (e.g., improvised explosive devices [IEDs], ambushes, etc.), war souvenirs tend to be components of IEDs, booby-traps, and examples of propaganda, among many other items. Another aspect of collecting is that as much as war veterans enjoy the admiration of other veterans for what they've collected, some items resonate with the home front and civilian population there more than others. In this regard, a war veteran encounters how the war was chronicled at home, which tends to emphasize items of visual appeal that appear in newsreels, objects tied to combat and the enemy, pieces that convey or buttress notions of masculinity (the items become talismans of testosterone), and artifacts associated with death. There is an inherent and sometimes grisly fascination with these types of items on the home front.

When soldiers, sailors, airmen, and Marines came home from World War II, they not only brought their war trophies and souvenirs with them but also carried most of the gear they had been issued, including uniforms, clothing, boots, backpacks, socks, and sea bags, among many other items. Many of these military articles as well as souvenirs were repurposed for use on the home front. Weapons were used for hunting or home protection; clothing was used for home, farm, or industrial work; helmets were used for motorcycle riding (German helmets are still used in this regard); and daggers and knives were used for a variety of work. Finding no need to keep the bulk of their issued gear, veterans off-loaded their items to "War Surplus Stores," which sprang up in the thousands in the wake of the war's conclusion.[5] Additionally, as time went on, some of their more unique "war bring backs" started to show up in these surplus stores. The War and Navy Departments also unloaded excess articles they had manufactured, which created, overnight, a robust market after demobilization. These stores built on an already established tradition dating before the Civil War of army and navy stores selling new military uniforms and accessories, which, eventually, expanded to include "war surplus" items after World War I. In 1872, however, the business model of largely local stores changed when Francis Bannerman, the son of a local scrapper in Brooklyn, bought new and used surplus military items in bulk following the Civil War.[6] He then opened the first military surplus store and proceeded to aggressively buy all sorts of military items, from rifles, cannons, and bullets to uniforms, boots, plates, and field gear. When the Spanish-American War broke out in 1898, a war my great-grandfather served in as part of the 1st Kentucky Volunteer Infantry, Bannerman outfitted several volunteer regiments with surplus Civil War uniforms.[7] He also created the first surplus catalog to sell his wares across the nation.[8] As veterans from World War I and World War

II returned home, returning with not only surplus government-issued gear but also war souvenirs, these types of stores expanded even further.

As time goes on and the veteran transitions from a young man to middle age, the visceral memories of war service, combat, and his time in the military recede. However, as the responsibilities of life such as family and career become more important, the veteran's mind begins to range back to a seemingly simpler time when he was in the service: "And the most honest and self-aware of them, when they reflect on their lives as soldiers, confess to feeling nostalgia for that strange, exciting world."[9] These feelings of nostalgia and the interests of a new generation in a war they have only heard about—often draped in the language of myth, legend, and infamy—prompts the veteran to wander back to the items in his collection. A new generation has discovered the allure of war: "Millions of men in our day—like millions before us—have learned to live in war's strange element and have discovered in it a powerful fascination. The emotional environment of warfare has always been compelling; it has drawn most men under its spell."[10] He also increasingly contemplates his own mortality as the milestones of life go by and he reflects on his dead comrades. Additionally, his actions in the war and the achievements of his unit sometimes gain greater historical relevancy or even notoriety; his time in the service is now enshrined in the history and fabric of his country. In this moment, he might set out to re-create his old uniform, with its medals, patches, and special nuances; perhaps build a shadow box (a method of displaying one's military achievements) to share with family members; or commemorate the service of his unit by collecting memorabilia from his service, branch, or warfare community. Furthermore, the process of collecting these sorts of items leads him to reconnect to old comrades, reestablish contact with his old unit, and enjoy the esteem and camaraderie of men for his service and achievements. He may also be invited to speak before his old unit, now filled with a new generation of soldiers, sailors, airmen, and Marines, and bask in their respect, curiosity, and interest in mentorship and the passing of lessons learned to a new generation. Further, as history places his war contributions into a larger context, his own interest in the conflict in all its detail becomes something of a passion for him. He only knew one part of the war and, even then, likely only a narrow portion, so his interest in the history of his war compels him to understand it on a deeper level. Additionally, depending upon how the war was accepted by his nation, he may feel a need to defend the actions of his generation. All of these factors lead many veterans to collect memorabilia from their time in the service.

While many veterans are able to place their war experiences in context and process their time in uniform in their own way, often setting the experience aside as life continues, some do everything they can to erase the memory of their time in war. For many of these veterans, their war experiences are so painful and so wrenching that they do all they can to get rid of anything connected to their time in uniform. These men not only sell all their issued gear but also frequently delete all photos of the experience, throw away letters and mementos, and sometimes avoid their former colleagues. A friend of mine whom I served with in Afghanistan in 2005 went through a similar experience. He had successfully finished a year of service in Afghanistan, but when a fellow army veteran and friend of his, who had also served in Afghanistan, died in a motorcycle accident off base within three months of coming home, he decided then and there to delete his experiences. He expressed his shock and dismay that his friend had survived the whole deployment only to be struck down in such an unimportant and banal manner. While he was still on active duty, and thus couldn't escape his experience completely, he deleted all the photos of his time in Afghanistan. Interestingly, many of these types of veterans often return to a military surplus store, sometimes years later, to re-create some aspect of their time in the military (such as assembling a complete uniform from their time in the service) or to search for other connections to their own personal history.

Conversely, there are many men who marinade in the experience of war, collecting as many items from their time in the service and in war that their wallet and family allow. For many of these men, their war service is often the pinnacle of their lives where they were tested, experienced the highs and lows of combat and the surreal experience of war, were men of consequence, were respected by their peers, served a vital function for their unit and their country, and played a small part in the great drama of history. These types of men are fascinated by war, theirs and others, and seek total mastery of whatever aspect of it they focus on. Similarly, amateur historians who appreciate their country's history—but who may not have served—also collect items of this sort, and the competitive nature and shared experience of collecting forms a new sort of brotherhood for many of them. For many of these men and women, collecting also has aspects of it that touch on veneration for the service of their fathers and grandfathers. While they did not serve themselves, they grew up in the legacy of the conflict and the memories and consequences of the service of their ancestors. For many of these people, collecting is as much a journey of learning as the veneration of ancestors. This also often prompts them to adopt the role of "setting the record straight" about a particular unit, veteran, or campaign that, in their opinion, was not dealt with correctly by the history books.

Iraq/Afghanistan Veterans

In early 2004, I entered the office of one of my colleagues at the U.S. Department of State who worked in the Verification and Compliance Bureau. I had long been contemplating the best way to get to Afghanistan, and I would eventually volunteer to go there starting in January 2005, but on that day I was visiting him for another work-related issue. As I entered his office, I noticed he had a most unusual rug on the floor. It was yellow, orange, brown, and red, roughly hewn, and covered in all sorts of pictures of AK-47s, rocket-propelled grenades (RPGs), and other Soviet weapons, and a long line of armored personnel carriers leaving what was an image of the country of Afghanistan. I quickly asked him what it was, and he said it was an "Afghan war rug" that he had picked up on a trip to the country. The carpets were traditional to Afghanistan and had been made for centuries, but this one wove in contemporary details of Afghanistan's experience with the Soviet invasion. It was enthralling. The traditional motif of the carpet was in contrast to the cool modern style of my colleague's State Department office and was my first introduction to a piece of militaria from the war in Afghanistan. This item is a must-have for Afghanistan War veterans because it can easily be displayed in one's office or home among many other such carpets. It's a useful reminder to nonveterans that he served "over there" and they didn't.

The war in Afghanistan following al-Qaeda's attack on the United States in 2001 has created a new generation of war veterans drawn to collecting militaria and introduced a number of new items that are unique to that conflict. In a broad sense, many of the items are tied to the Soviet experience in Afghanistan in the late 1970s through to the late 1980s. The country is awash in Soviet military gear from typical weapons such as AK-47s to complete tanks. Similarly, there is a unique mix of international weapons which had been given to the mujahedeen, which adds an exotic appeal to what could be found. There is also great interest in the British historical experience in Afghanistan as well as anything connected to Alexander the Great and his conquest of the region. These collecting tendencies are not that surprising since the Soviet and British experiences in the area were due to nation-state interventions; they simply had more to leave behind. It was very common for veterans to bring back old British rifles from their tours (this was allowed via military regulations), as well as anything tied to the Soviet experience including uniforms, the optics of weapons, bayonets, helmets, gun sights, maps, and the like. When it came to the Taliban, they left fewer items behind from their time dominating the country, but their militant arm constantly left detritus as battles, skirmishes, and ambushes took place in the intervening years. Parts of IEDs, mortars, RPGs, grenades, and bullets were very common to bring back, as were Taliban night letters (messages used to intimidate the population) and ink stamps used by Taliban commanders on official communications. Afghan cultural items were also quite common to bring back, including burkas, traditional Afghan clothing such as the *shalwar kameez* and turbans, prayer beads, jewelry, carpets of various kinds, election ballots, and money. It was also common to collect items from indigenous security partners, so military clothing, ranks, medals, and such were frequently collected from Afghan army and police forces and were often exchanged as gifts. Other items such as lapis lazuli (a semiprecious blue stone), rocks of various kinds, dirt and soil, and wooden crafts were also collected.

The invasion of Iraq in 2003 began as a nation-state war and devolved into a war of counterinsurgency with the state under intense pressure from multiple insurgencies. Many of the initial items collected by veterans included these outward expressions of Iraqi national sovereignty, which included anything with Iraqi president Saddam Hussein's picture on it, items connected to the Republican Guard, and anything connected to their military (e.g., uniforms, ranks, etc.) and the state (eagle symbols were common). Due to the extensive amount of Soviet equipment in Iraq, there were also plenty of items of Cold War interest (also true in Afghanistan), which also resonated with veterans who grew up during that time. Insurgent-related items such as parts of IEDs, mortars, RPGs, bullets, grenades, and such were also common to bring back. The constant interest in bringing back AK-47s, RPD machine guns, PKM machine guns, and the like was there, and many of these made it back to the United States in the early years of the conflict. Gold- or silver-plated AK-47s particularly resonated with collectors. Cultural items such as tribal clothing, the garb of sheiks, and prayer beads, as well as carpets, were also of great interest. Much like Afghanistan, uniforms from the Iraqi army, police, and other security forces also resonated with collectors less, over time, as symbols of a vanquished foe than the uniform of an indigenous security partner going through a shared experience of war. More macabre items from both wars also made it home. A U.S. Air Force customs inspector I came to know mentioned investigating cases of fresh camel heads being sent home and, in one case, a set of boots with the feet of either a suicide bomber or a victim of an explosive attack still in them. Both packages made it back to the United States only to be discovered due to their horrendous smell and the oozing of an opaque liquid from the FedEx box.

The Show of Shows
The pinnacle of militaria collecting in the United State is a once-a-year event called the Show of Shows, which recently took place in early 2020 at the Kentucky Exposition Center in Louisville, Kentucky. The three-day event attracts militaria collectors from around the world due to the quality (and sheer quantity) of its items. It has more than 1,965 tables with nearly two thousand individual dealers selling objects from the Revolutionary War to the war on terror. The event is sponsored by the Ohio Valley Military Society, and its members get privileged access to the tables before the public can participate. The Show of Shows is the preeminent show in the nation, but other shows gain regular interest from collectors, including the Max Show: Military Antiques Extravaganza held in York, Pennsylvania; the Militaria Relics Show in Nashville, Tennessee, which has 310 tables; the Original Baltimore Antique Arms Show, which has one thousand tables; the Ohio Valley Military Society show in Wilmington, Ohio, which has four hundred tables; and smaller venues such as the Hallowed Ground: Militaria and Historic Arms Show in Gettysburg, Pennsylvania. These events are social gatherings as much as opportunities for business and attract veterans, collectors, and the interested public.

In addition to the extensive militaria at the Show of Shows, there is almost a carnival atmosphere as collectors and dealers from around the world reconnect. There is the usual fare of conventions (funnel cake, hot dogs, and sodas), badges, and plastic bracelets to make sure you paid, but there are other indicators that this meeting is unique. Before you enter the main room, there is a prominent sign showing two U.S. soldiers from the World War II era holding various militaria items. Below them is a clarification, which reads as follows:

> This is a show for those interested in historic arms and military antiques, including war souvenirs taken from defeated enemies. These objects hold the interest of collectors today for the same reasons that our servicemen took them during and after the war: they are historic artifacts. Please do not confuse collector interest in these war trophies for any sympathy with the regimes that created them.

A nearby poster reinforces this emphasis on history with another two World War II–era soldiers holding captured German militaria, and it states, "Their Victory, Their Souvenirs. Collectors Preserve THEIR Story." There are also prominent veterans at the event such as a Medal of Honor recipient, a prisoner of war, and veterans of World War II, Vietnam, and the Gulf War who are manning a table at the back of the convention. The program for the event includes their biographies as well as a special place to affix their autograph. There are also a number of military enthusiasts dressed in the complete uniforms of soldiers, sailors, airmen, and Marines. They do all they can to make sure the clothing items, insignia, and weapons are contemporary to the service member they are portraying. The program also noted the passing of prominent members of the militaria world such as one who specialized in Japanese World War II headgear and another who created a publishing business focused on militaria who almost single-handedly created the field of Third Reich militaria. This world of collecting is almost exclusively male, and among the thousands of attendees at the event very few were women; more often than not, they were wives of collectors or sellers themselves or the rare interested girlfriend.

It becomes very clear upon perusing the tables that conventional wars are heavily represented among the items and that among those types of conflicts, the German military of World War II dominates the field. Items from the Soviet Union are evident, and there are a few tables of Japanese militaria, and many tables have U.S. military gear, insignia, and the like. However, German militaria dominates for many reasons. As a modern nation-state and as a regime that took over the German state, the Nazi Party did everything it could to intertwine itself into German national symbols and sovereignty. It propagandized its people and sought to harness the legitimacy of the German nation to bolster its political position. Partly for this reason, the regime created an abundance of items of steel, stone, and porcelain to reward loyalists, to intertwine with national symbols of achievement such as military decorations, and to shape the culture of the nation. The German military also had, in the words of World War I veteran and British writer Siegfried Sassoon, "decoration complexes." Metal military badges and awards were common and have endured as time went on.

Statues of German military leaders and those venerating German military service, as well as portraits, books, and posters, were also quite common. The proliferation of these types of items has led to dedicated dealers who only focus on German militaria, and books such as *German Combat Badges of the Third Reich* and *Prussian Blue: A History of the Order Pour le Mérite* (the highest award for valor during Imperial Germany) orient collectors to what is most highly sought after. Another reason for the prominence of German military items rather than Nazi items is that generations of U.S. soldiers undertook occupation duties in Germany after World War II, which gave them access to these pieces further buttressed by their steady income as professional soldiers. This stands in contrast to U.S. Japanese occupation duty, which was largely away from mainland Japan and its population. Most Japanese items at the show were military-themed sake cups, odd optics that were brought back, and assortments of pouches. The German economy also created far more objects out of metal than the Japanese government, thus contributing to the longevity of items from that regime. Further, the clear defeat of the Nazi regime and its horrific crimes serves as a draw for some collectors who are, for a variety of reasons, attracted to the unrestrained evil of the regime. What is all the more remarkable is that the Japanese government attacked the United States, suggesting that items from that regime would most likely be collected, but the shared cultural and other similarities of Germans with many Americans may explain an enduring interest in the German military.

A second notable trend is that unconventional wars and wars of counterinsurgency are largely absent. There are some items from the Vietnam War, principally items from U.S. combatants, and only a few objects from the war in Iraq. On one table, I spotted a complete Fallujah Police shirt, arm bands, and ranks while another sported an item from the Iraqi Republican Guard. Items from the war in Afghanistan were largely absent. This has to do with a lack of items from those conflicts, and their relative newness, in addition to the fact that they did not have a definitive ending brought about by the United States. Further, as unconventional wars, they never enlisted the full energy of the U.S. population, who did not see them (setting aside the attacks of 9/11) as an existential threat to the security and interests of the United States. Additionally, these three wars eventually became politically unpopular, so other than direct participants, interest in collecting items from them remains low. The Gulf War was also largely absent from the collectors' tables due to its brevity. Similarly, the Korean War lacked representation, most likely due to its unpopularity (in its day, it was not seen as an existential threat the whole nation rallied around) and its inconclusive nature. Further, there are virtually no items from the domestic populations of these countries, such as clothing, farm implements, uniforms, weapons, and cultural items, or from the partnered security forces the U.S. military fought alongside. These are simply uninteresting to domestic and international collectors. The lack of militaria from these types of conflicts contributes to an incomplete picture and an incomplete remembering of these wars, which reinforces narratives of combat and not counterinsurgency, direct war versus partnered fighting, and the actions of the military versus a holistic approach to the conflict.

While militaria can encompass a wide swath of objects taken from war zones and issued by the military, events such as the Show of Shows also attract vendors who specialize in military-related items that are also quickly snatched up by collectors. These items aren't military in any way, but they provide a useful insight into the mind-set of many attendees. One of the more notable objects is a tailored patch not issued by the military but related to veteran topics and issues. The slogans on these patches, sometimes referred to as "morale" patches, are a mix of irreverence, political incorrectness, life wisdom, and, frankly, insults. They come in a series of distinct categories: (1) they are tough on terrorists, (2) they focus on freedom and liberty, (3) they extol combat, (4) they celebrate military life, and (5) they support the Second Amendment. The following is a select list of many of the patches for sale at a variety of militaria shows:

"Waterboarding Is How We Baptize the Terrorists"
"Pork Eating Crusader"
"F★★★ the Taliban"
"Keep Calm and F★★★ Al-Qaeda"
"Not My Circus, Not My Monkeys"
"Pork-Eating Infidel"
"Special Forces: Mess with the Best, Die Like the Rest"
"Liberty or Death"
"I Find Your Lack of Ammo Disturbing"
"Don't Tread on Me"
"Cover Me, You Limp D★★★ Motherf★★★★★!"
"F★★★ Calm Die in Battle and Go to Valhalla"
"Harden the F★★★ Up"
"Come On, You Sons of Bitches, Do You Want to Live Forever?"
"Whisky Tango Foxtrot"
"I Am a Veteran: My Oath of Enlistment Has No Expiration Date"
"Infidel Strong"
"Warning: This Veteran Is Medicated for Your Protection"
"Spraying and Praying"
"Keep Calm and Shoot 'Em in the Head"
"Die Historic, Live Again. Valhalla. Admit One"
"United States Waterboarding Association"
"I Love M-60"

"Come and Take It"
"Infidel"
"Punisher"
"Keep Calm and Reload"
"We Do Bad Things to Bad People"

As quickly becomes evident, many of these types of patches reinforce a counterterrorism versus a counterinsurgency narrative and glorify combat. Many of them echo the adjustments veterans go through to inure themselves to hardship and pain and morally strengthen themselves to deliver death to the enemy. They also extol the culture of weapons and the idea of being self-sufficient from the government. They are decidedly politically incorrect and reflect the attitude and opinions of some Americans of how best to get tough on terrorists. In general, there were few overtly political signs at the convention; those that existed tended to criticize politicians as a group and the Democratic Party in particular.

A final feature of militaria shows is that many dealers specialize in certain, highly collectable items. There was a dealer who only focused on World War I and II Liberty Loan posters, another on ship models from World War II that were used to train ship spotters and navy crew, and another on military-related comic books such as *SGT Rock*, *G.I. Combat*, *All Out War*, *The Unknown Soldier*, *Fightin' Marines*, and *Star Spangled War Stories*. It was quite common for dealers to have a certain item on their table to draw the attention of customers, such as a demilitarized machine gun (although it wasn't for sale) or, sometimes, even a female at their booth. Collectors tended to want items connected to officers versus enlisted, combat arms versus support, and anything related to a battle that is well known to the public such as the Battle of the Bulge. There is still an enduring interest in the Cold War, although strictly only Soviet Union hardware, including spy equipment, such as cameras, and anything with the Communist hammer and sickle on it. Trench art, which is art made by World War I veterans from readily available material on their deployment such as artillery casings, also drew great interest, and there was at least one dealer there who specialized in such items. There also appear to be a mix of dealers who sell militaria on the side and many others who are full time and professional. There are also clear "celebrities," such as Thomas T. Wittman, who owns Wittman Antique Militaria, which specializes in German militaria, as well as Alex Cranmar, who, with his father, owns International Military Antiques, the nation's largest militaria company.

Alex is also a successful actor and is a regular on the *Pawn Stars* TV show, appraising military items that are brought onto the show.

Conclusion

Events such as the Show of Shows form part of a troika of masculine subculture in the United States—the other two are gun shows and war reenactments (e.g., the Civil War)—and attract many veterans. All three contain elements of nostalgia, interest in history, masculinity, and commerce. Gun shows are the most politicized, while militaria shows and reenactors are clearly conservative but not overtly political. In many ways, these events serve a useful function for men to use their hobbies and interests to maintain friendship and camaraderie networks. Aspects of these events present an alternative (and, they would think, genuine) perspective on key historical events—mostly underserved perspectives not captured by professional historians. The scholarship and dedication to finding out the truth about wars, battles, key leaders, weapons systems, and the like is exemplary and presents the men who specialize in key subjects with positions of authority in a community that celebrates their expertise. Community militaria and war surplus stores, such as Full Metal Jacket in northern Virginia, also serve as a useful and necessary hub for veterans to socialize. They are familiar places where the language of the military is understood and respected, and they function as safe havens for many veterans who are no longer in the service and are unable to connect to civilians in the same manner. For many veterans, militaria items serve as crucial connections to their war experiences; they are symbols of having cheated death, of having lived another day, and of having played a small part in the great drama of human history. While their meaning will change over time, for the war veteran, his militaria collection has a deeper, personal meeting that only he knows.

Stolen Valor and Fake Veterans 8

> *"Should any who are not entitled to these honors have the insolence to assume the badges of them, they shall be severely punished."*

—GENERAL GEORGE WASHINGTON, 1782[1]

WHEN A WAR VETERAN ENCOUNTERS someone who makes bogus claims of combat valor or military service, it is especially hard for him to conceal the odd mixture of hatred, glee, and curiosity that he feels so viscerally. The first instinct of a war veteran upon meeting a fellow veteran in the civilian world is one of camaraderie based upon a shared experience, but as the veteran learns more about the person and his claims of false service, warm feelings give way to cold inspection and a thinly veiled contempt for the creature. Why does stolen valor and the fake veteran antagonize the war veteran so much when polite civilian society generally ignores (if not tolerates) him or, on the rare occasion, defends the pretender? Why does the war veteran seem so determined to unmask the faker, even taking delight in doing so? The reasons are multifaceted and often quite personal, but they run the gamut from an affront to the integrity of war service, medals earned, and qualifications achieved to a view that the fake veteran profits off the sacrifices of others, many of whom shall never be known. In an era of ready access to information on veterans through the internet and social media and the prestige of combat experience (which is enhanced due to so few Americans serving in the military let alone in war zones), a heady mix of opportunity exists for the fake veteran.

Since the founding of the American Republic, stolen valor has coexisted with real valor, and while common themes exist throughout our nation's history, false claims expanded as our country's hardscrabble colonial militia of the revolutionary era gave way to a globally deployed professional military. As our military forces institutionalized and served in ever larger numbers of conflicts, opportunities for stolen valor and fake veterans in general grew with them. Over time, additional wars meant more medals, more opportunities for valor and heroic acts, and greater numbers of veterans returning home. This inevitably raised the prestige of war service and thus the incentive for fake veterans to assert themselves. As the U.S. government created and then extended benefits to returning war veterans, additional fakers sought to take advantage of these opportunities, making false claims to fraudulently get a government paycheck or subsidy. Further, as large standing U.S. military forces became the norm after World War II when, heretofore, they had been temporarily raised in reaction to conflict, the number of medals further proliferated as part of a general recruiting, retention, and rewarding effort; careerism required some method of recognizing non-war achievement. Additionally, as recruitment for our military shifted to an all-volunteer force in 1973, moving away from the draft, medals became even more central to a workforce retention and promotion strategy for the U.S. Department of Defense. The shift to an all-volunteer military and fewer large-scale conflicts following the Vietnam War also led to a slow reduction in Americans' general knowledge of the military. As understanding of the military declined, greater opportunities were created for fraudsters to claim military service. Further, as the number of Americans participating in wars decreased overall after World War II, as well as after the Vietnam War, valorous service not only became rarer (the number of American servicemen who had served in war was simply lower) but also became more valued and valuable, especially to those who trafficked in confidence games.

It's hard to determine the extent to which stolen valor and false claims of military service have existed throughout our Republic's history. Evidence is often fragmentary and mostly anecdotal, and claims have shifted as the country's military institutionalized over time. However, there are instances where one can discern a general pattern. Other than the Badge of Military Merit, which was created by General Washington during the Revolutionary War on August 7, 1782, medals were largely absent from U.S. inventories until World War I.[2] Even then, the decoration was only awarded three times, discontinued, and then later reestablished as the Purple Heart on February 22, 1932 (on the two hundredth anniversary of General Washington's birth).[3] Some large table medals were individually authorized by Congress for heroes of the Revolutionary War and the War of 1812, such as Captain John Paul Jones and his capture of HMS *Serapis* and Commodore Edward Preble's attack on Tripoli.[4] These types of medals were also awarded to a ship's captain, officers, and crew and were gold, silver, and bronze, respectively.[5] However, broadly speaking, individual medals that could be worn on a uniform were absent. Part of this thinking was an outgrowth of the American Revolution itself: "For nearly a century after the United States military services were born, the U.S. military establishment eschewed the European custom of adorning the uniforms of its soldiers, sailors, and Marines with 'bits of colored ribbon.' For the most part, these medals were viewed as an aristocratic braggadocio and beneath the dignity of our brave new form of republican government."[6] In an effort to recognize superior performance in combat and extraordinary fidelity, the U.S. military instead relied upon brevet ranks or Certificates of Merit.[7]

A brevet promotion meant that a member of the military, usually an officer, was assigned a higher rank in recognition of merit but would not typically receive commensurate pay or, in most instances, the right to command troops.[8] The respect that came with the higher rank bolstered the morale of troops and was a tangible sign of the value of the member's contributions. During the Civil War, for example, the use of brevet promotions was extensive since there were no widely available military medals to recognize meritorious or valorous performance. One example of this is Union general Joshua Lawrence Chamberlain, a postwar Medal of Honor recipient who secured the left flank of Union forces in the Battle of Gettysburg in 1863. He was breveted as a major general toward the end of the war, but, upon the war's conclusion, his Regular Army rank was brigadier general. During the Mexican War (1846–1848), the U.S. Congress authorized the president to "present a certificate to enlisted men who specially distinguished themselves."[9] The Certificate of Merit was similarly issued to recognize superior accomplishment but provided no tangible record on the uniform of military personnel.[10] It wasn't until the Civil War that a formal medal was authorized, struck, and awarded to military veterans. On December 9, 1861, a bill was introduced in Congress that created a Medal of Honor to "further promote the efficiency of the Navy."[11] The next year, President Lincoln authorized the creation of a similar decoration for the U.S. Army.[12] Interestingly, the Confederate States of America (CSA) created a similar decoration to recognize valorous acts on October 13, 1862.[13] The Confederate Congress passed "an act to authorize the grant of medals and badges of distinction as a reward for courage and good conduct on the field of battle."[14] Due to other priorities, competing demands for the material, the lack of a final design, and the end of the CSA, no formal medals were awarded.[15] However, a Roll of Honor had been created to recognize valorous achievements (votes were cast by members of prospective honorees' units).[16] While not all units participated in the process, this was later resolved in 1977 at the Eighty-Second General Convention of the Sons of Confederate Veterans in Dallas, Texas, which agreed to present "Certificates of Honor" to the descendants of those on the Roll of Honor.[17] The meeting also resolved to award the Confederate Medal of Honor by formal application submitted to the Confederate Medal of Honor Committee of the Sons of Confederate Veterans.[18]

By the 1920s, the practice of breveting was discontinued, and superior performance was instead recognized, increasingly, through the awarding of medals.[19] In 1905, the U.S. Army authorized the awarding of a medal for those soldiers who had received Certificates of Merit, thus creating the third medal in the U.S. inventory.[20] That same year, the War Department issued an executive order "establishing the principle of recognizing service in wars and campaigns by issuing distinctive medals," thus creating the first authorization of campaign ribbons.[21] The U.S. Navy and Marine Corps followed suit and, in 1908, also authorized the issuance of campaign medals.[22] In later years, the recipients of the Medal of Honor created a membership organization called the Medal of Honor Legion, later renamed the Legion of Valor, which was the first organization whose membership was solely based upon receiving a military decoration.[23] While there are examples in which the medal was awarded for circumstances less than valorous, the prestige of the decoration and the relatively small number awarded limited false assertions.

Prior to World Wars I and II, most false claims of military service and valor in the United States were quite limited to either, on the rare occasion, the Medal of Honor or simply assertions of having participated in war and sometimes key battles. On December 19, 1959, for example, a man named Walter Williams passed away, having claimed to be a Civil War veteran: "[T]he city of Houston gave a historically large and lavish funeral procession to the man hailed as the last living Civil War veteran. A week of mourning was proclaimed throughout the city. A subsequent investigation, however, found that Williams had never served in the Civil War. He was only five years old when the war began and ten years old when the war ended—too young even to be a drummer boy."[24] Mr. Williams had the dubious honor of likely being the last living fake Civil War veteran and of having conned a whole city into believing his tale of war participation. Because the U.S. military, and the U.S. Army in particular, historically surged its numbers during wartime, relying largely upon conscripts and the raising of volunteer units, one incentive that was used to attract volunteers and to reward wartime service to the nation was to offer a pension: "The conscript militaries of the Civil War, World War I, and World War II, which demanded male citizens perform military service, pioneered many social welfare programs in the United States. These were crafted for veterans as rewards for faithful service or compensation for loss."[25] As the years went on, this situation inevitably led to fraudulent claims of service in order to receive financial and other government benefits. In 1879, for example, the U.S. government determined that of 4,397 affidavits submitted over a three-year period by "veterans" applying for a wartime pension, approximately 3,084 were determined to be false, and only 1,313 (30 percent) were legitimate claims.[26]

In 1917, the U.S. Congress undertook a wholesale reform of the military awards system.[27] In addition to conducting a review of previously awarded Medals of Honor, it created a series of military decorations below the Medal of Honor to recognize different levels of heroism.[28] The review of the Medals of Honor led to the rescinding of 911 due to their having been awarded frivolously, and it also formally defined the criteria to receive the medal to "heroism, above and beyond the call of duty in combat."[29] The president and Congress also created five new military decorations to recognize valorous action in war. President Wilson signed an executive order in January 1918, which created the U.S. Army's Distinguished Service Cross and Distinguished Service Medal.[30] The U.S. Congress confirmed this action and enacted it into law in July 1919 and, in February of that year, created similar decorations for the U.S. Navy (the Navy Cross and the Distinguished Service Medal).[31] The crosses were for valor, and the service medals were for meritorious service in a position of great responsibility. Congress also created the U.S. Army's Citation Star, which was a small silver star that could be issued by any general officer to a soldier who had "exceptionally distinguished himself by his conduct, or who performed with gallantry."[32] A decade later, this citation was upgraded to the Silver Star Medal and restricted to combat valor, and it became the fourth-highest award and the third-highest award for valor.[33] Another aspect of this wholesale revision of the military awards system was that foreign governments sought to recognize the superior achievement and courage of U.S. military personnel serving in the Great War. Since this was expressively prohibited, Congress also consented to the awarding of foreign military decorations to U.S. military personnel, as well as the awarding of U.S. decorations to foreign military members.[34] As the awarding of military decorations increased—and the prestige that went with them—during and after World War I, fraudulent claims of service followed suit.

> In April, facsimiles of the Victory Button, given every man who had served in uniform [in World War I], were being hawked at twenty-five cents apiece: "Pay a Quarter and Be a Veteran." Fake heroes, with medals and bandages, were hauled by military detectives off speakers' platforms in the Fifth Liberty Loan. One man was sporting Marine chevrons, Infantry collar insignia, and Navy service stripes. Another dazzled the public with an array of nineteen decorations, including "a pretty medal with the Lord's Prayer on the back." Peddling and begging were the common resource of these fakers.[35]

General George Washington's Order of Military Merit was revived and upgraded in 1932 by then U.S. Army chief of staff General Douglas MacArthur to the Purple Heart Medal and awarded to military personnel killed or wounded in combat action.[36] During World War II, the Silver Star Medal was further authorized for the U.S. Navy, Marine Corps, and the Coast Guard.[37] These new medals formed the basis of what is referred to as the Pyramid of Honor, the order of precedence for valorous military decorations.[38] The U.S. Congress created the Distinguished Flying Cross for the U.S. Army Air Corps in 1926 and, eventually, the Air Force Cross in 1960, once the U.S. Air Force was created following passage of the National Security Act of 1947.[39]

The number of valorous and meritorious medals created during World War I increased even further as World War II began. In order to recognize meritorious service below that of the Distinguished Service Medal as well as valorous conduct not meriting the Silver Star, Congress authorized the creation of the Legion of Merit in 1942. The Army Air Corps created the Air Medal in 1942 to recognize heroic or meritorious achievement or service involving aerial flight; this prompted U.S. Army leaders to also recognize similar achievement for land forces, and they created the Bronze Star in 1944. Subsequently, the Legion of Merit was then typically awarded to more senior officers and enlisted personnel while the Bronze Star was limited to more junior personnel. In a memo to President Franklin Roosevelt, U.S. Army chief of staff General George C. Marshall outlined his reasoning for the creation of the Bronze Star:

Memorandum for the President
(Through the Secretaries of War and Navy)
February 3, 1944 [Washington, DC]
Subject: Medals and Decorations.

The Secretary of War has informed me of your desire that he discuss our present decorations with high ranking officers in order to arrive at a more definite policy. The subject was brought to your attention by the joint Army and Navy recommendation for the establishment of a new Bronze Star decoration.

The latter proposal was initiated by me personally after I had obtained the comments of overseas commanders and had observed first hand the effect of the awards of the Air Medal upon combat personnel of the Air Forces. The prompt award of this Medal has been of tremendous value in sustaining morale and fighting spirit in the face of continuous operations and severe losses.

The awards of the Air Medal, however, have had an adverse reaction on the ground troops, particularly the Infantry riflemen who are now suffering the heaviest losses, air or ground, in the Army, and enduring the greatest hardships. The most satisfactory solution I can find is some such decoration as the proposed Bronze Star. Otherwise to meet the situation we would inevitably be forced to lower the standards for the award of our present decorations for exceptional heroism.

Decorations and service ribbons are of real value to the war effort only if promptly bestowed. In the first World War we were quite niggardly about it during the fighting and then after the Armistice, particularly during the early 1920's, a flock of awards was made, too frequently the result of pressure, political and personal. The Victory Medal with its bronze and silver stars was authorized too late to have any effect on the efficiency of the Army. I received a ribbon for service in Germany twenty-three years after I returned to the United States.

From my point of view there are three important factors to be considered:

   a. Make the awards immediately, at the time, so as to sustain or stimulate morale. There will be a minimum of misapplication if done in the field at the time. There are too many eye witnesses present.

   b. Permit these young men who are suffering the hardships and casualties to enjoy their ribbons, which mean so much to them, while in uniform. They cannot wear them once they return to civilian attire.

c. Keep a balance among the services involved in battle, the best to the man who is actually in the fighting. Something else, less impressive, to the men who labor behind the lines.

There is definite and urgent need for the Bronze Star to provide the ground people with something corresponding to the Air Medal. I want to use it now, while it will do some good, not after the war is over.

There will inevitably be unfavorable reactions or misapprehensions resulting from the wearing of numerous ribbons by men who have been transferred from theater to theater, or especially those on duty in Washington who serve for short periods overseas—participating in actual landing or bombing operations in many cases. But these are a very few people, and I am concerned about the thousands who never see Pennsylvania Avenue and are doing their best in some difficult or dangerous or isolated post overseas. The fact that the ground troops, infantry in particular, lead miserable lives of extreme discomfort and are the ones who must close in personal combat with the enemy, makes the maintenance of their morale of great importance. The frequency of air thrusts against the enemy and the steady and heavy losses made it advisable to take special measures for the Air people.[40]

Other decorations were created to recognize meritorious but non-combat service during the war with the establishment of the Navy Commendation ribbon in 1944 and the Army Commendation ribbon in 1945 (both became full medals in 1960). Even as the number of decorations increased and standards were created to verify claims of valorous service, false or embellished claims continued: "Everybody embellishes the truth a little bit. I don't lie, but I don't always tell it a hundred percent. So I says I was in on the invasion of Okinawa. That's true. The outfit I was in made a diversionary trip to the southern end of Okinawa."[41] The famous World War II Marine veteran and author E. B. Sledge also encountered the need by some to "enhance" their war service: "Conversation could be risky, I soon found, when some 'wannabe' combatant told his tall tales, and I asked him how he felt the first time he saw a buddy killed by a shell. Blank looks from the wannabe and gasps from the girls told me that civilian conversation carried its own perils."[42] The totality of these medals and ribbons built on the standards established in World War I and were created to recognize ever-expanding levels of valorous achievement during the war as well as

meritorious accomplishment. Even with these greater decorations the human need to embellish even respectable war service continued.

Unlike past conflicts, however, while U.S. forces did demobilize following victory in Europe and Asia in World War II, their numbers did
not completely fall to prewar levels. Instead, as part of the creation of the
U.S. Department of Defense in 1947, which merged the War and Navy
Departments, and the need for larger troop levels as the Cold War began,
new recruiting, retention, and recognition needs added additional requirements for recognizing performance. In 1939, for example, the U.S. Army
and U.S. Navy had 189,839 soldiers and 125,202 sailors, respectively.[43] Just
eight years later, U.S. Army numbers were at 990,000 soldiers, and the U.S.
Navy had 484,000 sailors.[44] This not only increased the number of medals
awarded but also expanded their use beyond the narrow field of valor in
war to recognize merit and performance during times of peace—and on a
far larger scale. Further, as efforts were undertaken to improve "jointness"
and "unification" of the services—terms coined to indicate experience
working with other services (e.g., U.S. Army, U.S. Navy, U.S. Marine
Corps, and U.S. Air Force)—in order to break down service parochialism,
a new tranche of medals were created. These medals included the Air Force
Commendation Medal in 1958, the Joint Service Commendation Medal in
1963, the Meritorious Service Medal in 1969, the Defense Superior Service
Medal in 1976, and the Defense Meritorious Service Medal in 1977. Other
devices were soon added to some medals, such as a bronze "V" for valor
during combat or as a combat-distinguishing device, bronze or silver stars
denoting multiple tours in war zones, the Combat Action Ribbon, and
the Combat Infantryman's Badge, among many others. These and other
enhancements to uniforms recognized other valorous achievements during
war and became a further means by members of the military to distinguish
themselves. As competition for promotion within the military services and
careerism more broadly increased now that large standing military forces
were the norm, the importance of awarding medals increased substantially.
This tendency became even more pronounced as more and more positions
became "joint" in that members of multiple services could apply for them,
and such assignments became essential to future promotion.

Contemporary Stolen Valor and Fake Veterans

*"But many of those who claim covert or heroic actions
in Vietnam present authentic medals and official-looking*

documents, including DD-214s, to support their claims. Some have license plates on their cars that indicate they are former POWs or recipients of the Purple Heart or Medal of Honor. Others have medals framed and mounted in their offices to impress those who don't realize such things can be purchased at almost any sizable flea market and through collectors catalogs, as can other military paraphernalia and 'in-country' mementos."

—B. G. BURKETT AND GLENNA WHITLEY,
*STOLEN VALOR: HOW THE VIETNAM GENERATION
WAS ROBBED OF ITS HEROES AND ITS HISTORY*, 351

As gender roles in the United States began to change in the 1960s and as ostensibly "male" professions became open to women and the responsibilities and rights of men were transformed, stolen valor adjusted with it. In general, the phenomena of "stolen valor" and "fake veterans" is an overwhelmingly male affair and is inextricably linked to perceptions and the changing nature of masculinity. While the process of gender equality continues to this day, many professions, such as the military, are more closely associated with men and quintessentially "male" attributes than others. Additionally, as the U.S. economy shifted from industrial to postindustrial—which is to say, from emphasizing physical strength to mental strength—valorous service, and military service in general, became more attractive in the competition among men for position, prestige, and power. With the definition of masculinity in flux in broader society, military and war credentials in particular provided an anchor for some as part of their self-evaluation of their masculinity. This comment from a Vietnam War veteran captures some of these changing circumstances:

For other men, not joining the Army left them with the distinct feeling that they had missed a critical "rite of passage" in coming to terms with their manhood. Understanding the long-term consequences of missing that ritual passage is beyond my capacity. But the fact that this feeling came at a time when the very idea of manhood was rightfully being challenged by the feminist movement has to be factored into any new conceptualization by our culture of what it means to be a man. This is a take that seems to me to be as profound as any we will face in the next ten years.[45]

War service confers a special status upon people, and men in particular, that no amount of money, material possessions, and position can overcome. As men compete for advantage in life, war service provides an almost unassailable leg up in the subtle art of male dominance among men.

This tendency is particularly acute for men of lower socioeconomic status who lack typical achievements that convey prestige, such as advanced education, position, money, and power. However egregious stolen valor claims are, they continue to persist even as the ability to check false assertions has improved immeasurably due to the internet, social media, and crowd sourcing.

The generation of veterans who served in the wars in Afghanistan, Iraq, and the war on terror more broadly were all volunteers serving in a military that was broadly institutionalized, where careerism was the norm, and where a robust selection of military medals and decorations existed to recognize those who passed the test. While society is still working to achieve gender equality, most participants in these conflicts grew up after the feminist movement started and in a culture more favorable to gender equality. The war in Afghanistan was due to our nation having been attacked by the terrorist group al-Qaeda, and the war in Iraq was undertaken out of concern that its regime had weapons of mass destruction and would reconstitute them. As these veterans returned home, often after repeated tours, they, like their predecessors, moved on to the next stages of their lives and careers. They enrolled in universities, started businesses, volunteered in their communities, ran for public office, deployed again, and started families. Once again, the prestige of war service was introduced widely into the American consciousness, and the value of war service was enhanced once more in the competition for life. Extensive government and private support (e.g., education, disability support, etc.) existed for returning veterans, and as they began these new chapters in life, veterans started to encounter fake veterans and people who proclaimed stolen valor. These encounters had many of the familiar themes of the past but were updated for this generation with its pervasive social media and the internet, changed gender roles and expectations, the repeated nature of deployments, and other attributes of contemporary and deployed life.

In March 2019, for example, at Cape Canaveral National Cemetery in Florida, in a familiar scene that has played out across the nation thousands of times, veterans gathered to commemorate Vietnam veterans.[46] An impressive speaker had been chosen to deliver the convocation, a retired Green Beret master sergeant and medic named Craig "Doc" Glynn, who had, in addition to serving in Vietnam, served in Somalia, Iraq, and Afghanistan.[47] His "service" was not limited to multiple tours in war zones; he had also received the Distinguished Service Cross (the nation's second highest valorous decoration behind the Congressional Medal of Honor), two Silver Stars, ten Bronze Stars, and nine Purple Hearts, among other military decorations.[48] However, even though "Doc" Glynn had served in Vietnam as a U.S. Army medic, his military service ended in 1972, and, as further research uncovered, he had repeatedly mentioned his false claims of heroic military service over a number of years. In this instance, the stolen valor claims of Craig Glynn not only were embellishments on an already respectable military record but also included wholesale fabrications of exceptional valor and additional war duty. He benefited from the fabrication by gaining local fame and notoriety and, most likely, other advantages as well.

One of the first fake war veterans I ever met was a taxi driver in Washington, DC, who made a bold claim that he had been a "combat medic in Korea" as he drove me to my destination. I was wearing civilian clothes at the time, and as I settled into the back seat, I noticed a series of U.S. Army patches glued to his dashboard. Curious, but not willing to tip my hand at having a military background, I asked him whether he had served in the military. With great pride and a practiced cadence, he dutifully informed me of his claims as we wound our way through DC's streets. He appeared to be in his mid- to late sixties, with his grey hair pulled into a ponytail, but he did not seem old enough to have served in the Korean War. I asked him when he served in Korea, and he told me "1970–1971." Continuing my mien of gentle curiosity, I said, "I hadn't realized there had been that much combat in Korea at the time." Upon this recognition on my part of the history of Korea and the conflict in general, he opened up and said he had been drafted in 1969 and, much to his relief, had been sent not to the war in Vietnam but to South Korea instead. He said he had been a truck driver near, or perhaps in, the de-militarized zone (the border region between South and North Korea), and because the Korean War was not officially over, he considered it still a war zone.

I continued to express my interest in his story, and I asked when he had become a "combat medic," which he then addressed by stating he had received some "first-aid training" in Seoul, the capital of South Korea—thus, in his mind, creating the story of being a "combat medic in Korea." It was clear from our conversation that he had been extremely happy not to go to Vietnam when he had been drafted, but he knew that, decades later as we sat in his vehicle, no one would find a brief stint in relatively peaceful South Korea particularly compelling or interesting. However, upon the passage of time, a reprieve from combat service had now become one of his most interesting life experiences, so he glued U.S. Army patches to his dashboard in an effort to prompt passengers to ask about them. He also took the risk of gambling that no current veterans, or at least anyone knowing anything about the Korean War, would ever be a passenger. In the end, his experiences in the U.S. Army were authentic, but he had "juiced up" his story to make it sound more interesting and to create an aura of importance around him.

In 2014, I was walking down the street in the Farragut North area of Washington, DC, when I saw a man in his early thirties sitting on the curb with a cardboard sign stating he was an army veteran with PTSD (post-traumatic stress disorder). Along the edge of the placard, he had listed a series of bases where he had presumably served, and he was asking for spare change. He caught my attention not only due to what his sign said but also because our ages were somewhat similar and it seemed to me that he must have served in the Iraq or Afghanistan wars. Once we exchanged greetings, I asked him whether he had served in Iraq (versus Iraq War since we were obviously veterans of the war), to which he promptly said, "Yeah, in southern Iraq." I already suspected he hadn't served in the U.S. military, but his answer further suggested he hadn't served in Iraq. I asked him whether he had served in Mosul, Iraq, or Ninewa or Diyala Provinces (all of which are in northern Iraq). He said he had served in Mosul; I replied that Mosul was in northern Iraq. Without giving him a chance to respond further, I asked him where he had served in Afghanistan. He responded that he had "served on the border with Iran," which sounded very dramatic. I mentioned I had also served in Afghanistan and knew the country well. I asked him whether he had served in Khowst, Paktika, Paktia, or Nuristan Provinces (all of which are not on the border with Iran in western Afghanistan but on the border with Pakistan in the east). He said he had served in Paktika Province, which I promptly informed him was not on the border with Iran; he was clearly growing frustrated with my inquiries. I finally asked him about a base he had listed on his placard, a location he called "Ft. Louis." He somewhat dismissively said, with great assurance, it was in Washington State and was a U.S. Army base. I promptly responded, "Not spelled like that." Once we had reached an understanding, I went on my way, dismayed at seeing, once again, another case of stolen valor in America.

The final fake veteran I've met was in my local shopping mall in my hometown of Vero Beach, Florida. One of the vacant stores there had been converted into a community space where a collection of local veterans' charities had gathered to raise money by selling various items such as T-shirts, bumper stickers, and challenge coins; it was also a meeting place for veterans to share camaraderie. Along a wall that separated the store into two spaces was an area with pictures displayed of local residents who had joined the U.S. military. Having grown up in Vero Beach, I was curious to see whether I recognized any of the pictures and quickly set about look-ing at the roughly one hundred photos. As I did so, a man approached who worked at the store, inquiring about whether I needed anything. I remarked that I was struck by how many local residents had joined the military and how impressed I was with that fact and how positive it was to have a space at the mall for veterans to connect and to help local charities. At this point in the conversation, I had not mentioned my own military service, and I was dressed as a civilian. The man, who appeared to be in his sixties, dutifully informed me that he had served in "Special Forces." Frankly, I already knew he hadn't but was willing to help him tell his story, if only to reinforce my own initial impression. I asked him whether he had been a Green Beret. He responded by saying that he was "Special Forces," which, of course, means U.S. Army Special Forces or Green Be-rets. After I expressed how impressed I was with this accomplishment, he went on to tell me he got his orders direct from the Pentagon. To this I responded, "Doesn't everyone in the military?" He then informed me that his were conveyed orally and so no written record existed of his orders and, conveniently, of his missions. After this final statement, I knew my initial impression had been correct. I indicated that I was done with the conversation and proceeded to look around the store and then departed.

While rules and regulations govern the proper wearing of military decorations within the U.S. military, and the Uniform Code of Military Justice enforces it, there have typically been few (if any) laws that govern the civilian use of military decorations or fraudulent military claims. In an effort to combat the fake veteran/stolen valor challenge, President George W. Bush in 2005 signed into law the Stolen Valor Act, making lying about one's military experience a crime.[49] Seven years later, the Supreme Court invalidated the law as an infringement on freedom of speech. President Barack H. Obama then signed into law an amended version of the Stolen Valor Act in 2013, which still made lying about one's military record or making false claims of military service illegal, but only if it gained some sort of "tangible benefit." According to the Valor Guardians website, the medals that were expressly prohibited from being lied about include the Medal of Honor (U.S. Army, U.S. Navy, U.S. Air Force), the Distin-guished Service Cross, the Navy Cross, the Air Force Cross, the Silver Star, the Purple Heart, the Combat Infantryman's Badge, the Combat Action Badge, the Combat Medical Badge, the Combat Action Ribbon, and the Combat Action Medal.[50] Because the law cannot sanction those who falsely claim military service or valorous achievement if they do not get tangible benefits, the only recourse is to expose their claims and use

community shaming. This is largely why so many veterans attempt to police their own community via in-person confrontations or via the internet
through websites such as Valor Guardians. Since the law is unable to protect the integrity of valorous and military service, the veterans community
has undertaken it themselves.

Stolen Valor: By the Numbers

> *"Books about war psychology ought to contain a chapter on
> 'medal-reflexes' and 'decoration complexes.' Much might be
> written, even here, about medals and their stimulating effects on
> those who really risked their lives for them. But the safest thing
> to be said is that nobody knew how much a decoration was
> worth except the man who received it."*
>
> —SIEGFRIED SASSOON, *MEMOIRS OF AN INFANTRY OFFICER*, 72

The phenomena of stolen valor and fake veterans is replete with anec-
dotes and stories but has not been systematically analyzed, although some
clear trends have been identified. Chief among these are that stolen valor
assertions are overwhelmingly made by white males who have a great
propensity to claim some affiliation with Special Operations Forces and,
predictably, some sort of valorous combat service. There also appears to be
a general trend for former members of the military to make false statements
as much as (if not more than) civilians with no prior service. However,
according to retired Navy SEAL senior chief Don Shipley, who is an ex-
pert in verifying stolen valor cases, claims have shifted over time: "When
'Rambo' came out, everyone was a Green Beret. After 'The Hunt for Red
October,' everyone was a submariner."[51] Shipley also noted that stolen
valor cases tend also to be junior enlisted men, that it is "primarily a white
problem," and that people in authority, such as pastors, sheriffs, and politicians, regularly show up in stolen valor cases.[52] Due to the prominence of
Special Operations Forces in military operations in Afghanistan and Iraq,
including the raid on al-Qaeda leader Osama bin Laden's compound in
Pakistan in 2011, it is not surprising that the special operations community
continues to attract fake veterans and stolen valor claims. Following the
Vietnam War, for example, it was also common for fake veterans to assert
prisoner-of-war status as a means of gaining favor.

This section of the chapter will focus its analysis on examining the cases of one hundred stolen valor and fake veteran examples from 2018 taken from the military veteran website Valor Guardians (www.valorguardians. com), which was started by Jonn Lilyea, a retired U.S. Army infantry platoon sergeant. The website is one of the most prominent of a number of websites devoted to investigating false military claims and posting the profiles of fake veterans as part of an effort to shame them. It serves as a central point for several other veteran-affiliated websites that focus on exposing stolen valor and fake veteran cases. They maintain a comprehensive list of these cases in a section called "Valor Vultures," and they post the fake claims of the individual and the documentation disproving their claims. They principally rely upon three sources of information to verify claims: (1) official documents forwarded to them, (2) Freedom of Information Act requests to federal and/or state sources, and (3) personal validation by third parties.[53] The posts often have the photo of the offender, evidence of their claims or assertions, and then the documentation demonstrating the person's actual military service, if they have any at all.

The first one hundred profiles listed in the "Valor Vultures" section of the Valor Guardians website from 2018 were systematically analyzed. Fully 97 percent of the stolen valor cases were men, and 84 percent of the overall number were white, with 8 percent black, 7 percent Hispanic, and 1 percent other. A large majority of the cases had actually served in the U.S. military at some point (79 percent), and of these 14 percent (eleven) had served in a war zone at some point in their military career. Only three (4 percent) of the seventy-nine who had served were former officers, with the highest rank being an O-3, and 96 percent of the seventy-nine were prior enlisted members of the military with the highest rank being an E-6. Approximately 41.8 percent (thirty-three) of prior service cases had served in the U.S. Army, 36.7 percent (twenty-nine) had served in the U.S. Navy, 15.2 percent (twelve) had served in the U.S. Marine Corps, 5 percent (four) had served in the U.S. Air Force, and 1.2 percent (one) had served in the Coast Guard. The most frequently cited claim was thirty-four examples of having been a U.S. Navy SEAL; thirteen stated they were members of the U.S. Army's Special Forces, nine said they were U.S. Marines (six specifically mentioned MARSOC, Raider, Reconnaissance), eight said they were U.S. Army Rangers, three stated they were "veterans," and two said they were members of U.S. Air Force Pararescue. All other mentions were in single digits. Fully 33 percent of all the cases asserted service in a war zone, with thirteen claiming time in the wars in Iraq and Afghanistan, twelve in Vietnam, four in Beirut, two in Grenada, one in Desert Storm, and one in Somalia. The most claimed military decorations were twenty Purple Hearts, nine Silver Stars, seven Bronze Stars, six Combat Action Ribbons, and three Combat Infantry Badges. Higher-level valorous decorations were not frequently cited, and only two Navy Crosses, two Distinguished Service Crosses, one Congressional Medal of Honor, and one Soldier's Medal were mentioned from the one hundred cases. Of the seventy-nine who had previous service, thirteen (16.5 percent) claimed a higher military rank than they had earned, five claimed an Airborne qualification, and one asserted a Pathfinder qualification.

In general, a contemporary stolen valor or fake veteran is someone who had previously served as an enlisted member of the U.S. military, principally the U.S. Army, who was a white male, claimed some affiliation with Special Operations Forces (usually Navy SEAL), and asserted they had received a Purple Heart, a Silver Star, or a Bronze Star. While only one-third falsely claimed service in a specific, named war, it's clear that many more had to have done so to claim the decorations or qualifications they asserted. Past research on stolen valor echoes many of these conclusions: "[A]n inordinate number of pretenders claim to be members of elite forces: Green Berets, SEALs, CIA, or other intelligence operatives assigned to supposed covert operations like the Phoenix Program."[54] Additionally, while there was only one false claim of having received a Congressional Medal of Honor, other trends echo past research: "[T]he FBI estimated that for every real Navy SEAL there are 300 imposters; for every one of the 120 Living Medal of Honor Recipients, there are twice as many phonies."[55] All of these sorts of assertions are easy to make in part due to "[t]he lack of proper record keeping by the services, the limited access to the truth by the public, and the inherent desire not to question a veteran's service make stolen valor easy to get away with."[56] What is notable about the one hundred cases that were analyzed is that the number of Congressional Medals of Honor and similarly high-ranking valorous decorations were not claimed at higher levels. This is likely due to the Legion of Valor, which operates to this day since its founding in 1890, which maintains a list of those who have received these types of awards and advocates on behalf of integrity in the medals system. Because of this robust ability to verify fraudulent claims for higher valorous awards, fakers usually concentrate on lower-tier awards such as the Purple Heart, Silver Star, and the Bronze Star since there is no central database for those who have received these decorations. Additionally, so many more members of the military have received these decorations compared to the Congressional Medal of Honor that the story of the fake veteran is more plausible to the casual listener.

However, even these awards are getting easier to verify due to the internet and social media.

Why Do They Lie?

> *"In the civilian sector those bits of colored ribbon are often little understood. Most civilians with no former military service couldn't readily distinguish a badge awarded for being a good marksman from a medal given for uncommon courage. Those bits of colored ribbon, however, serve as both a resume and as a form of currency in the military profession."*

—DOUG STERNER AND PAM STERNER, *RESTORING VALOR: ONE COUPLE'S MISSION TO EXPOSE FRAUDULENT WAR HEROES AND PROTECT AMERICA'S MILITARY AWARDS SYSTEM*, 2

While the database of stolen valor claims from Valor Guardians listed some reasons for false claims, it was not consistently documented. However, based upon the examples listed in this chapter and in other reports there appear to be six broad categories of things fake veterans seek when they lie: (1) money, (2) prestige, (3) love/romance, (4) power, (5) sense of belonging, and (6) respect. Or they're crazy. These echo similar findings from clinical psychologists such as this perspective from Dr. Loren Pankratz in Portland, Oregon: "They do it for all sorts of reasons. . . . It's a spectrum. There are losers, pathological types, guys trying to impress women. What they all have in common is this internal need to impress themselves and a feeling of power that they can pull it off."[57]

Many of the documented claims take place at public events recognizing the service of veterans. These claims are efforts to financially gain (such as in business, panhandling, or government assistance) or are tall tales among other veterans to earn respect, status, or belonging. One aspect of stolen valor is that in the postmilitary world of veteran communities (e.g., Veterans of Foreign Wars, American Legion, etc.), it is generally frowned upon to overly emphasize one's former military rank among veterans. All veterans are navigating postmilitary life, and now that they are civilians, rank, while a feature, is not the key element of their present reality. Rank is important, and some garner more attention than others; however, among veterans, valorous medals often trump rank since the circumstances of life have changed. Stolen valor claims also confer greater status when one's former military rank may not. Additionally, not all veterans have the opportunity to serve in war, and even those who did sometimes don't have war experiences that are interesting to their fellow veterans, or the position they served in during the war may not garner that much interest.

The need to embellish one's service record is very powerful among some veterans, which is evident since 79 percent of the stolen valor cases in the dataset are former military, and it is especially strong in a civilian environment that is particularly veteran heavy. In a sense, a new but informal hierarchy is created upon leaving the service. It is never fully fixed, but those who have served in war feel they have an advantage, and those with valorous decorations feel it more acutely, and those in combat arms feel they have an edge versus those who were support. The competition and friction between those who are "combat/war" veterans and those who are not is real within veteran circles. This sentiment is captured well by the World War I veteran and writer Siegfried Sassoon: "Any man who had been on active service had an unfair advantage over those who hadn't. And the man who had really endured the War at its worst was everlastingly differentiated from everyone except his fellow soldiers."[58] The need to belong to the "warriors club," as stated by Vietnam veteran and author Karl Marlantes, is powerful, but so is the need for public esteem of having served: "I shan't get maimed: either I shall get killed or I shall get a few pleasant putty medals and enjoy being stared at in a night club."[59]

What is notable about false claims is that those who assert them want the listener to know they risked their life, showed courage, and performed their duty when called upon in one of the most stressing circumstances of life. It is as much a commentary on the person's courage, character, and valor as it is about their masculinity. Largely for this reason, fake veterans do not usually assert time in support services such as logistics, medicine, transportation, and the like. Additionally, they don't assert participation in war via indirect means, such as artillery, or in highly technical fields such as fighter jets because, however deadly against the enemy, the *personal* valor of the person in terms of risk to bodily harm is lower, especially so in today's contemporary wars with air superiority. Further, assertions about stolen valor that are technical, such as being a fighter pilot, are easier to disprove, and most combat pilots are officers, which means a fake veteran also has to assert time in college. For fake veterans, it is all about asserting an idealized identity that is not their own: "Whether it is a pick-up line in a bar or a boast on Memorial Day, people often learn that a little fib of military service can go a long way in achieving certain advantages. It is a way of instantly giving yourself a better image—perhaps becoming the person you wish you were."[60] Another reason fake veterans are drawn to special operations is that they represent, as part of changing views of gender and gender roles, in idealized form, an extreme view of masculinity. When what is understood as masculinity is in flux, the culture appears to embrace an extreme version of it. Very rarely do fake veterans assert a regular infantry identity, and if they do, it is often enhanced by Ranger or Airborne .qualifications. Further, the elite status of Special Operations Forces and the fact so many of their operations are murky to the broader public or secret makes it easier for fake veterans to not disclose details of their time in service.

The Language of Stolen Valor

There are certain telltale signs that someone is a fake veteran or is talking about stolen valor in the language they use to describe their time in the military. On the surface, what they say appears to be coming from a veteran who has been to war or served at some point, but, upon closer inspection, there are several key elements that are often common among these types of stories. Frequently, these kinds of claims are buttressed by militaria, whether it is uniforms, patches, medals, paperwork, and such, which enhance the truthfulness of the story. The key point to remember, though, is that while the fake veteran might have *some* knowledge of the military, and we expect as much since so many previously served, the basis of their assertions, typically special operations related and war zone heroics, is completely absent. Thus, the first sign is a general lack of details, or, if details are offered, they are oddly familiar since they are frequently drawn from popular culture such as movies, books, and TV shows. It is very common for fakers to reference widely known battles (e.g., the battles for the city of Fallujah, Iraq, in 2004) or tragedies (e.g., bombing of the Marine barracks in Beirut in the 1980s) because, first, this will enhance their special status and, second, these are often the only combat stories that have reached their attention in popular culture. When it comes to specific assertions of their profession in the service, such as being a SEAL or Special Forces soldier, they also heavily rely upon publicly available information that is widely known. Their lack of specific knowledge and details of their asserted profession is a sign of a lack of truthfulness.

Another feature is that these stories inevitably put the fake veteran at the center of the action usually with a dramatic retelling. What's notable is the lack of other veterans in the story, which is unusual because combat is a team sport. In a way, this is another example of a lack of detail that should draw additional scrutiny. A lack of knowledge about the military also leads to outlandish claims of medals earned as well. The grim reality is that for most recipients of valorous awards, it is the worst day of their life, and because they are alive to receive the award, there is often a feeling of survivor's guilt since many fellow soldiers were killed in the engagement. There is often a feeling of "why do I deserve this decoration?" which, naturally, causes the recipient to demur when talking about his service in combat. The humility of the recipient and the weight he feels of the human cost of the action prompts an entirely different emotional reaction than boastfulness. Other aspects of stolen valor stories are that they are often "too perfect" and have a logic to them that does not allow for chance or illogical outcomes. They are also implementation-free zones, which is to say they do not account for the practical aspects of combat such as the amount and types of ammunition used, weapons, movement, what other people were doing in the firefight, the time of day, physical features of the terrain, and the like. The stories are also often quite simple, which makes them easier to remember and harder to verify, and, as is usually the case, the fake veteran frequently avoids accounts of combat altogether using the argument his actions were "classified." Finally, when questioned or confronted, many stolen valor and fake veterans become aggressive and angry when, for most war veterans, any questioning of their time in service, especially if they received a valorous decoration, is generally laughed at or ignored; why allow this lesser creature to question your combat veracity—it's the inner confidence of the man who has been in the arena. The ease with which the fake veteran lapses into anger speaks directly to his lack of confidence, reinforced by his lack of any real knowledge and understanding of what he asserts and its deeper meaning.

Conclusion

> *"If people did not benefit from claiming to be military veterans, wounded warriors, or decorated heros* [sic]*, they'd quit doing it. No matter what personal problem, prank, or other motivation starts the fraud, it is fed and maintained by need and greed. . . . The bottom line is they do it because it gives them what they want—and what they need."*
>
> —DOUG STERNER AND PAM STERNER, *RESTORING VALOR: ONE COUPLE'S MISSION TO EXPOSE FRAUDULENT WAR HEROES AND PROTECT AMERICA'S MILITARY AWARDS SYSTEM*, 139

The phenomena of stolen valor and fake veterans is as much an outgrowth of changing conceptions of masculinity in American culture as it is rooted in the normal weaknesses of human nature. While claims have shifted as the nature of warfare has changed and as the U.S. military developed as an institution, the human need to be part of something special, however fraudulently, is so great some people will violate their own oath of service or their own sense of integrity to possess it. The desire to profit off the sanctity of war service is so powerful, whether it is for money, love, prestige, or simply belonging to a group, that people will go to great lengths to perpetuate the fraud. No generation of veterans has been immune to the urge to embellish their military records, and, unfortunately, every generation has those who seek to profit off those who honorably served. For most war veterans, the fake veteran and bogus claims of valor violate not just their sense of integrity but also their feeling of community, of being part of a brotherhood tested in combat, and now being tested in the civilian world. The special bond of trust, of a shared understanding, and a common experience of hardship so bonds other veterans to each other that the creature that is the fake veteran invites the opprobrium of veterans, no matter how harshly delivered. As the current generation of veterans from the wars in Afghanistan and Iraq continue on in their lives, they will encounter more cases of stolen valor as they go to college, start businesses, and serve their communities again. Going forward, it is important to deal firmly and justly with those who perpetuate false claims of valor or military service; the principles real war veterans fought for overseas still require defending here at home.

Veteran Politicians 9

"Status as a veteran is useful in politics."

—WILLARD WALLER, *THE VETERAN COMES BACK*, 179

I T HAS LONG BEEN RECOGNIZED that military service, especially in war, is a highly valued experience to have for an aspiring politician. It speaks volumes of his patriotism, commitment to service, love of country, and, frankly, courage to confront his nation's enemies. Some politicians began as war veterans and eventually decided to run for office, seeking to serve their country once again. Others were perhaps more far-sighted, seeing a brief stint overseas as beneficial to a rise in political circles. As candidates, war veterans are unlike normal politicians. The experience of war and time in the service transforms a civilian into a veteran, and it leaves indelible marks upon his character and fosters new habits and ways of thinking. The communal experience of military service where socio-economic, ethnic, racial, and other differences are partially ameliorated by uniformity of dress, the formality of rank, and the shared experience of military service helps break down barriers among veterans. Further, the practical world of the war veteran is one of having to impose his will on the enemy, take life, experience loss, and witness horrendous things that sharpen as well as harden the veteran to focus on what is important in life; in service to his nation under such conditions, he forges a new and stronger relationship with his country. Additionally, war service forges a type of person who is not reticent to be a bold leader, to take action, and to build a team to achieve a common objective. He knows how to lead under the worst of circumstances, which gives him a perspective and set of skills that translate well into organizing a political campaign. While not all veterans run for office many do or serve in other positions of public responsibility and our nation's leadership, from the White House to the school board, is full of the history of veterans serving their communities once again.

The vast majority of veterans who answered the call to serve their country in war did not set out to eventually run for public office. The predominantly young men who do join in order to fight their country's enemies and defend their nation's interests and values are frequently swept up in patriotic fervor on promises of national support. This particular narrative is true for most of the conventional wars the United States has been involved in. These appeals to patriotism and declarations of resolute support by the government and the American people were especially necessary when the U.S. military was modest in size and relied heavily upon volunteers and conscription to grow its forces quickly. As these appeals to honor, courage, duty, commitment, and country are implemented in practice, the veteran begins to see the gap between the declarations of support and the realities of what he has signed up for in war. Inevitably, a maturation process takes place for these men; they begin to see this divergence between the purity of the cause they signed up for—one they pledged their life to support—and the less than altruistic behavior of many of their countrymen. Additionally, if the war does not go well, if his side loses, he casts about for someone or something to blame. He may even blame his commander in chief, although he is reluctant to do so since he is in charge of the U.S. military and there is great deference to him, but he does throw a wide net of responsibility to include politicians, bureaucrats, and even senior military leaders. This bitterness is strongly felt, and there are many people who fall under his suspicion.

> Let us admit that the veteran, this man disgusted with politics and impatient with argument, has a real, a just grievance—indeed, a whole series of grievances. . . . He comes to believe that he has been swindled, and that belief is rarely without some foundation in fact. We had induced him to risk his neck for patriotism, but allowed others to get rich from his sacrifices. A nation like ours wages war on the basis of an unspoken truce; while the men are fighting we suppose there will be a truce in all our little wars of classes and interests and races and religions and political parties. But there is never any ceasing in these wars and thereby the soldier knows he is betrayed. We have imposed upon the soldier's innocence and generosity; we have taken his youth and give him the memory of horrors; we have taken everything from him and left others at home to get along the better

because he is away. To get his consent to be a soldier, we have promised everything, but usually given very little.[1]

For the war veteran, he is the implementer of political decisions as well as on the receiving end of political decisions. It is likely the first time he has had politics so directly impact his life. He naturally develops some interest in it, if only in the military sphere, and has some strong views since politics affects his life so directly. The veteran is also in some leadership position during his time in uniform; he begins to understand the dynamics of leading people, the nuances of people, and the joys of accomplishing a goal as part of a team and as part of a system. These experiences whet his appetite for additional leadership opportunities upon coming home. How the veteran handles this bitterness or processes the gaps between his patriotism and the behavior of others determines his relationship to politics upon his return.

One of the most profound feelings war veterans have upon returning home is a deep and abiding emotional connection to their country and homeland. It is not an exaggeration to say it is a love affair. The veteran now appreciates on a much deeper level how unique his country is and how special the United States is in the world; his experience has renewed and reimagined his dedication to his country. For many veterans, this serves as a clarion call to serve again, run for office, seek an appointment, or volunteer in their community to help their country live up to the ideals they fought for overseas. Other veterans do not channel their strong views on politics into such constructive outlets. For them, they seek someone to blame for their bitterness and their personal failings, whether it's individuals, groups, or institutions, and, having been away and not involved in politics previously, they do not have as great a stake in the political system as it is. To these veterans, this is the same system that caused them so much pain and recrimination: "Veterans make good revolutionaries. They have learned to hate and to kill. They have been shot over. They have lost their reverence for many of the word symbols that formerly controlled their behavior."[2] He also "feels that he has a score to settle with profiteers, slackers, debunkers, supine stay-at-homes, and sometimes labor leaders who interposed the closed shop in his face. Are these the people that the nation asked him to die for? He begins to see red."[3] Similarly, "[a]s the veterans said in 1919, 'They said when we went away that when we came back nothing would be too good for us, and when we came back that was just what we got, nothing.'"[4] Both kinds of these veterans, and versions of their types in between, seek change in politics. Their goals may sometimes be quite modest, such as making sure wounded veterans are taken care of by the government, but it may also encompass system-wide reforms against those they see as the scapegoats for their pain. The war experience has changed them in profound ways: "One of the more flagrant of dichotomies is that between prewar and postwar Sassoon [WWI veteran and writer], between the 'nice' unquestioning youth of good family, alternately athlete and dreamer, and the fierce moralist of 1917, surging with outrage and disdain."[5]

The veteran returns from war with a number of attributes, character features, and concepts that position him well for elective office. The chief among these is that he has lived in a "communal social order" wherein he has been exposed to Americans of all walks, races, and creeds and worked to achieve a collective goal, under intense strain, through teamwork.[6] These experiences help him relate to his fellow Americans of all backgrounds.

> I confess that a large number of Americans I met in the Army amazed me by their differences. I had not known their like before, nor have I met them since. Nothing else could have made me realize how narrow the circle in which we move in peacetime is. Most of us hardly get an inkling of how ninety per cent of our fellows live or think. Naively we assume that they must be like us or not very different.[7]

In practice, the war veteran is more comfortable with the differences of his countrymen and often sees what unifies Americans more than what divides them. Additionally, he has had to forge a diverse team into a unit that can achieve its purpose in war. This may be only a handful of people or perhaps thousands, but he has been endowed with great authority and responsibility to achieve his goals. The threat of the enemy makes one realize how few differences we have as Americans. In addition, the war veteran has been exposed to a wider world of global affairs, the behaviors of nation-states, and the affairs of men overseas, and he has played a small part in human history. His perspective has been profoundly broadened. This experience endows him with a confidence fired by having succeeded in the most trying of circumstances, and it places the politics of his own country into a larger context that reveals with some certainty its various parochialisms.

The veteran has also developed some insights into human nature, politics, and leadership, which make him stand out from his compatriots on the home front. His preference is for action, he prefers direct communication and fidelity, and he seeks to achieve his objectives in the most direct manner.

By reason of his military service, the moral and political ideas of the veteran differ from those of the balance of society. He is disillusioned about words and men of words; he is immune to many of the words to which civilians respond and thus beyond the control of those who make their living by using such words. He is not interested in certain of the finer moral distinctions, although he admires forcefulness and bravery and loyalty.[8]

Depending upon the circumstances, this can serve as a recipe for success in politics or a source of frustration for the veteran. However, his reference points forged in war make him a somewhat unknown quantity in politics: "When the veteran, the army-made man, returns to civilian society, he understands conflict perfectly, compromise less well, discussion and argument hardly at all. He wants action, dislikes talk, distrusts talkers. He is intolerant of the hypocrisies without which politics is impossible. That is enough to make the veteran politically dangerous."[9] A countervailing tendency among veteran candidates is pragmatism. Most war veterans have had to overcome a number of obstacles on their deployments with whatever they had at hand—whether it's people, equipment, or concepts. Because they had to implement policy and achieve their unit's objectives during a time of war, a flexibility enters their mind about how to achieve things.

The veteran's preference for action also reflects his aversion to words and speeches and his general skepticism of those who rely upon these methods for success. When veterans hear the familiar calls of patriotism on the home front, especially in the context of politics and as part of routinized displays of love of country, they have a mix of reactions. Platitudes ring hollow to him when wielded by those who only know them in the abstract: "In war-time the real meanings of old sayings revive with new force. They were written in times when life and death were not mere amenities."[10] Additionally, the war veteran knows what these words truly mean when he was sent to war—and the gap between their meaning and the reality of the war and the home front—but, similarly, they have been endowed with special meaning due to his war service. The war veteran knows what courage means viscerally, he understands what commitment means, he has internalized the meaning of honor, and he knows love of country like few people on the home front. To him, these ideas have been operationalized by his service overseas, they have been imbued with a special meaning, and they are words of action, not positions to be taken in headlines: "Like all combat veterans, we could not help but agree with Hemingway that 'Abstract words such as glory, honor, courage, or hallow were obscene beside the concrete names of villages, the numbers of roads, the names of rivers, the numbers of regiments and the dates."[11]

> The average soldier is not fond of flag-waving or the oratorical patriotism dear to many civilians. About his cause he has little to say; it is taken for granted, along with his determination to do his best. The balloons of rhetoric are targets too tempting for his crude wit. His view of war is plainly a lowly one—the view of men fighting in the valley rather than directing strategy from the hilltop or writing with the historian's coolness.[12]

This reinterpretation and reimagining of patriotic words serve as part of the rhetorical toolkit the veteran candidate wields in campaigns. His language is one of authority, action, and patriotism in the fullest sense, focused on achieving objectives, and his emotional energy is harnessed to fight for his country once again, this time in the halls of politics.

When the veteran returns home, he inevitably begins his civilian life by perhaps marrying and starting or joining a business, continuing his education, or seeking other avenues of community leadership. He is a natural leader and has been tested in many ways that his civilian counterparts will never know. He is also part of a network of other veterans navigating their own adjustments home, and the bonds of brotherhood forged overseas translate into a base of organization for those veterans who seek public office: "Ernie Pyle, reporter of the human side of the present war [World War II], tells of 'the ties that grow up between men who live savagely and die relentlessly.' 'There is,' he says, 'a sense of fidelity to each other among little corps of men who have endured so long and whose hope in the end can be but so small.'"[13] Further, the veteran finds himself inevitably interested in politics as he navigates his veteran and educational benefits, wrestles with red tape as he starts a business, or confronts how his war experience is portrayed by civilians and politicians. Additionally, the war veteran realizes that society's views of his service have changed now that he is home. He is now seen by many as a victim and somehow unable to take care of himself; he has become a burden on society. "After the war is over, civilian acquaintances and employers, shaking off their bellicose hysteria, begin to pity and patronize [the veteran] as a victim who has been somehow put upon by society."[14] The contrast between the war veteran's inner confidence earned by overcoming incredible odds in combat in service to his nation and the pity and disdain some civilians have for him galls him. Further, some politicians, who did not serve, use the veteran as a political prop, as patriotic bunting to bolster their own careers. These types of attitudes inevitably frustrate and even enrage the war veteran, sometimes prompting him to enter politics and his place as a natural community and political leader.

The war veteran has returned home armed with insights into human nature, comfortable with authority and leading men; he has seen horrendous things and has participated in some of the most consequential historical events of his generation. His relationship to his country is so deep, so unquestioned, that he endeavors to make real its promise to his people. The ceremonies of patriotism that are part of politics are now imbued with a near religious meaning, and the institutions of his government are civic temples to the republic he loves. He is compelled to serve again, to run for office, to serve once more, to fight for the things he defended overseas, and to help his country overcome the parochialisms, petty jealousies, and small tyrannies of narrow-minded men. His reluctance to serve, to enter a new fray, is quickly overcome upon his return, and, as he strides across the public stage, he claims the mantle of responsibility for a new generation.

The Battle of Athens: Veterans Take Action

> *"By making him into a soldier, we have carefully cultivated his sadistic-aggressive impulses, taught him to fight and to kill without mercy, and then done him a series of injustices— should we then be surprised that he fights back? The veteran is accustomed to direct action but not to discussion; he has a pronounced aversion to discussion. He feels intensely but not intelligently, intensely because he has suffered, unintelligently because his political education stopped when he entered the army. He is not afraid to take risks."*

—WILLARD WALLER, *THE VETERAN COMES BACK*, 187

One man and one political machine dominated Tennessee's politics from 1933 to 1948 and continued to exert significant influence even after his sway had been curtailed. The man who wielded such power was Edward Hull Crump, or E. H. Crump; his power base was centered in Tennessee's largest city of Memphis, in Shelby County, with a population of roughly 292,942 people whose votes he controlled. Crump, variously described as an "old fox" who was praised by fellow politicians for his "technical virtuosity," presided over a state-wide "system of shifting alliances with local leaders outside Memphis, alliances that often became relations of subordination."[15] Through an extensive patronage system of city, state, and federal jobs, positions, and favors, voter manipulation, intimidation of the opposition, and a constellation of businesses who supported him, he governed as a political boss. One such local power broker Crump partnered with was a man named Paul Cantrell of McMinn County, approximately 380 miles east of Shelby County, who had variously served as sheriff there from 1938 to 1942 and state senator in the area from 1942 to 1946.[16] In 1946, Cantrell decided to run for sheriff of McMinn County once more, but circumstances had changed; veterans of World War II had returned home.[17]

The political system of McMinn County was democratic in name but authoritarian in nature and in practice. A system had developed over time in which, through voter intimidation and fraud, control of political patronage, and partnerships with gambling and bootlegging interests, corruption was rampant and honest citizens struggled to live their lives unmolested by law enforcement. The sheriff's department was the central point of corruption and enforcement for the political system in the county, but it was buttressed by other local officials and offices. The corrupt machine exerted influence over the county's newspapers, local public-sector hiring such as school teachers, boards of regulations and inspections, and business activity, among many other aspects of civic and political life. One practice the sheriff's department used was the "fee system" wherein sheriff's deputies were paid a fee for every person they arrested.[18] This system was constantly abused, and tourists, out-of-towners, less than compliant (politically and otherwise) local residents, and, eventually, returning World War II veterans were the focus of such efforts. Law enforcement regularly used intimidation tactics such as kidnappings, beatings, and unlawful imprisonment to also intimidate the population. The war veterans of World War II who returned home from victory overseas were immediately confronted by the injustices and authoritarian nature of the system as they stepped off the buses that had taken them directly home to McMinn County following discharge.

The World War II veterans of McMinn County returned home to an authoritarianism they were familiar with from having fought against similar systems overseas. As the veterans celebrated their homecoming at the local bars, the sheriff's deputies harassed, arrested, and beat them. As they sought to start their lives anew, the political machine barred their entry, set up road blocks against employment, and generally sought to exclude them from political and economic life. As the elections of 1946 approached, many of these veterans had had enough. "'It was a dictatorship down here,' said one GI. 'Elections were a farce.'"[19] Another veteran stated, "We just got plain tired of being pushed around by a bunch of thugs."[20] As the August elections approached, the veterans decided they had to act, and at an organizational meeting in May 1946, they agreed to run their own slate of independent veteran candidates.[21] They organized themselves into the GI Non-Partisan League, selected five candidates from both major political parties, and chose as their slogan "Your Vote Will Be Counted as Cast."[22] One veteran put it succinctly: "You want to know how this started. . . . Well, all of us did a lot of thinking over there about the disgraceful way this gang was abusing our people here. When we got back, a group of us got together . . . and decided we couldn't stand for this to go on."[23] As the veterans organized, they counted on approximately three thousand returned GIs to support the effort, roughly 10 percent of the county's population.[24] The veterans were conscious of the methods of the Sheriff's Department and so organized their own security force to deal with the violent depredations of deputies. This "fightin' bunch" was organized "to keep the thugs from beating up GIs and keep them from taking the election."[25] With their slate of candidates selected, their strategy agreed upon, and their security force ready for use, the GI Non-Partisan League was ready for the election in McMinn County. As one veteran put it, "If democracy was good enough to put on the Germans and Japanese . . . it was good enough for McMinn County."[26]

The nefarious machinations of the McMinn County political machine were fully engaged on Election Day, and the World War II veterans of the county were girded for conflict. As the day unfolded, auxiliary sheriff's deputies, many brought in from outside the county, manned each polling station. The veterans also deployed their members as poll watchers to monitor and prevent the corruption of the vote at the ballot box. Inevitably, since the machine relied upon manufacturing democratic legitimacy by vote fraud, conflict erupted over several ballot boxes as specific polling stations were closed by the sheriff's office. No convincing reason had been given for their closure, but conflict erupted as the boxes were retained by sheriff's deputies and, eventually, taken to the county jail. Other violence broke out throughout the day as veteran poll watchers interceded to prevent fraud, and deputies beat and arrested them, taking some to the jail. As violence increased and it became evident the political machine intended to stuff the ballot boxes that had been seized, the veterans went into action. After the veterans' repeated demands for the return of the three ballot boxes the sheriff's deputies had seized, violence escalated.

As the polls closed, the veterans converged on the McMinn County jail in search of the missing ballot boxes. Insisting on transparency in the counting of the ballots, the veterans demanded the boxes be brought out for public inspection. The sheriff and his deputies refused, and the approximately fifty deputies there prevented all efforts by the veterans.[27] Time was of the essence, as the current sheriff, Pat Mansfield, as well as Speaker of the State House of Representatives, George Woods, were present in the jail and constituted a quorum of the election commission and could certify the election results that evening.[28] It is unclear what started the subsequent firefight, but after repeatedly being rebuffed, the veterans, bolstered by privately owned, purchased, and borrowed weapons (some from the local armory), opened fire with small arms on the jail.[29] Using the second floor of a nearby building, the shooting was augmented by Molotov cocktails and, eventually, sticks of dynamite. Some deputies were shot, cars in front of the jail were damaged and flipped by the dynamite, and some structural damage also took place.[30] The veterans were eventually able to gain access to the jail, finding numerous ballots in the process of being marked in favor of machine candidates.[31] The sheriff and the State House Speaker fled in the midst of the firefight, using the ruse of a visiting emergency vehicle to make their escape.[32] Once all the ballots had been completely counted, the reform ticket of World War II veterans had been elected.[33] As the veteran candidates assumed office, reforms were put in place to arrest the corruption of the local system.

The Battle of Athens in Tennessee is one of the more extreme examples of returned U.S. war veterans seeking to change the politics of their community. As a case study, it highlights the preference of veterans for action and their ready-made network of supporters who know how to organize. It also underscores how acutely they feel the difference between the ideals they fought for and the reality of the politics of their communities. Additionally, the veterans are not beholden to local interests or power brokers and use a different yardstick to measure service, honor, commitment, and duty. They are also natural leaders, as well as followers, and know how to executive a plan to achieve a concrete objective. As referenced earlier, the war veterans are revolutionaries in the truest sense, seeking to help the United States live up to its revolutionary principles.

Counterinsurgency Veterans and Politics

As much as war prepares veterans for a new chapter in life of public service to their community, many veterans of counterinsurgency campaigns have additional experiences that make them particularly effective as candidates. Wars of counterinsurgency share many of the attributes of conventional wars—the armed wing of the insurgency must be fought and killed—but at its heart, it is a fundamentally different type of warfare. The focus of counterinsurgency efforts is the population and its support for their government, and the insurgency does everything it can to separate the people from their state. They undertake assassination campaigns to reduce the ability of the government to operate and to demonstrate to the population that the government can't even protect its own members let alone them. They seek to influence the population through robust propaganda efforts and use their armed forces to seize and control territory while administrating a competing form and system of government. A central feature of any successful counterinsurgency campaign is a compelling political strategy to garner the support of the population for their government. Indigenous security forces must also be raised at the local, provincial, and national level to empower the government to confront the insurgency militarily and with security forces. Additionally, robust government services must be provided, such as justice and the rule of law, health and educational services, transportation, and economic development.

The insurgent's preferred strategy is to hide among the population and to eschew the outward appearances of formal security forces. They do not wear uniforms, usually lack heavy weapons, and tend to wear civilian clothing. While the goal of the insurgent is to control the population and implement their governing program, they also seek to outlast counterinsurgent forces, and so they seek to minimize their casualties and use asymmetric tactics to maximize counterinsurgent losses. A common phrase attributed to the Taliban was that while "the U.S. had the watch, the Taliban had the time." Theoretically, insurgent forces can lose each and every military engagement with counterinsurgent forces and still prevail in the long term because they simply survive. The dynamic at play is the degree to which foreign counterinsurgent forces are willing to expend treasure and blood in an overseas conflict versus the insurgent's ability to simply persist. Depending upon the maturity of the insurgency, insurgent fighters may be in small groups of a few dozen or number in the thousands. As an insurgency grows, so, too, does its shadow government—a government in waiting, if you will—that administers territory the movement controls. Insurgents have a robust political arm as well that perpetually seeks to persuade, intimidate, and influence local populations.

Insurgencies are dynamic movements, and successful military veterans of the wars in Afghanistan and Iraq cultivated an insatiable curiosity about them. The veterans of these conflicts undertook a number of tasks not typically associated with U.S. military forces as they bolstered government and security forces and worked with local populations. Many partnered very closely with and forged friendships with local tribal, political, community, and security leaders. They not only planned clearing operations with them to rid districts and cities of insurgents but also planned elections, mediated disputes between community leaders, undertook urban planning, drilled wells in villages, fostered rural development, and acted as honest brokers between different levels of the government. They also served as confidantes, advisors, and colleagues. Veterans of these wars also became incredibly knowledgeable about local culture, history, religion, marriage practices, tribal structures, and farming techniques, among many other subjects, and cultivated a sympathetic understanding of the perspectives of locals. It was not uncommon for U.S. military personnel to rescue villagers stranded by floods in Afghanistan or to deliver food to an isolated valley snowed in by winter. These efforts significantly broadened the experiences of U.S. military veterans to include ostensibly political tasks. Many veterans worked with provincial reconstruction teams, embedded provincial reconstruction teams, and district support teams in both countries, which were expressly designed to partner with local governments to facilitate reconstruction, development, and good governance. These organizations also typically had U.S. Department of State and United States Agency for International Development civilian advisors as well, which further enriched the perspectives of these veterans.

The totality of these experiences means that many veterans of wars of counterinsurgency, and the wars in Afghanistan and Iraq in particular, are largely already accustomed to working with community leaders and contending with local politics. They have gained invaluable experience addressing community problems, have developed an advanced ability to cultivate a sympathetic understanding of local perspectives, and have been immersed in political wrangling, intrigue, and leadership. They have also developed an extremely strong sense of efficacy because they saw results on their tours such as additional schools built, elections held, and communities protected, among so many other indicators. Further, the common struggle of local officials working alongside U.S. military personnel served as an inspiration to run. Far too many of these local officials were killed or assassinated while trying to improve their community. Their examples of truly selfless service also influenced veterans. For these kinds of veterans, seeking public office at home and serving their communities is a natural extension of their war service. The situation is different and the dynamics have changed, but the idea of serving one's community is constant and draws veterans back to serving their country once again.

Presidential War Service

> *"Life in the robe of peace is only too apt to lower the reputation of men that have grown great by arms, who naturally find difficulty adapting themselves to the habits of civil equality. They expect to be treated as the first in the city even as they were in the camp; and on the other hand, men who in war were nobody think it intolerable if in the city at any rate they are not to take the lead. And so when a warrior renowned for victories and triumphs shall turn advocate and appear among them in the forum, they endeavor their utmost to obscure and depress him; whereas, if he gives up any pretensions here and retires, they will maintain his military honor and authority beyond the reach of envy."*

—PLUTARCH, *LIVES OF ILLUSTRIOUS MEN*, 446

As much as war service can enhance a veteran's chances of successfully running for public office, leading a war or playing a central role in its execution at the strategic level can sometimes lead to the highest political office in the United States. Throughout our nation's history, wars have elevated some of our most well-known generals to the White House. The American people like and want victory in war, and they politically reward those who deliver it. The challenge of generals who have participated in wars of counterinsurgency is that these types of conflicts tend to end inconclusively or on a time frame that doesn't provide any political benefits to those who led it. Additionally, wars of insurgency don't generally enlist the great interest of the American people and are not generally seen as existential threats. Their ambiguity prevents narratives of victory, and their lack of conclusive battles robs generals of compelling stories of the enemy being decisively defeated. Approximately 50 percent (twenty-three of forty-six) of presidents have served in uniform as well as in war; of these, eighteen (78 percent) served in the U.S. Army or state militias, and five (22 percent) served in the U.S. Navy. No presidents have served in the U.S. Marine Corps or the U.S. Air Force. Twelve (52 percent) of the twenty-three served as general officers, from one-star to four-star; eleven (48 percent) were officers of lower ranks, from captain (U.S. Army) or lieutenant junior grade (U.S. Navy) to commander (U.S. Navy) or colonel (U.S. Army), and only one president (5 percent) was a former enlisted man who served as a private in his state's militia. Virtually every major conflict the U.S. military has been involved in is represented among the military service of the presidents except for the Korean War, the Vietnam War, the Gulf War, and the wars in Afghanistan and Iraq.

What is notable about these trends is that because the U.S. government typically relied upon volunteer units and state militias until World War II, it frequently created opportunities for enterprising citizens to gain military experience and the political benefits of war service. Additionally, most of these types of conflicts were essentially domestically based, whether it was the Revolutionary War, the Mexican-American War, the Civil War, various campaigns against Native American tribes, or the Spanish-American War. These conflicts tended to maximize the participation of local communities (they were often locally raised volunteer units and state militias) that also became political networks the veteran relied upon to run for office. However, once the current boundaries of the United States were settled and the U.S. War Department did away with volunteer units and its reliance on state militias (although National Guard units are still used extensively)—and following the creation of large, standing military forces after World War II—political opportunities were truncated. However, National Guard general officers still get elected to the U.S. Congress at very high rates. The last president who led a successful military campaign was Dwight D. Eisenhower in the 1950s. Interestingly, presidents who served in the U.S. Navy and in war have dominated the presidency since President Eisenhower stepped down in 1961. The following list details U.S. presidential war service and last rank achieved:

1. George Washington: American Revolution (General of the Armies of the United States)
2. James Monroe: American Revolution (Major)
3. Andrew Jackson: American Revolution, War of 1812, Creek War, First Seminole War (Major General)
4. William Henry Harrison: Northwest Indian War, War of 1812 (Major General)
5. John Tyler: War of 1812 (Captain)
6. Zachary Taylor: War of 1812, Black Hawk War, Second Seminole War, Mexican-American War (Major General)
7. Franklin Pierce: Mexican-American War (Brigadier General)

8. James Buchanan: War of 1812 (Private)
9. Abraham Lincoln: Black Hawk War (Captain)
10. Ulysses S. Grant: Mexican-American War, Civil War (General)
11. Rutherford B. Hayes: Civil War (Major General)
12. James A. Garfield: Civil War (Major General)
13. Chester A. Arthur: Civil War (Brigadier General)
14. Benjamin Harrison: Civil War (Brigadier General)
15. William McKinley: Civil War (Brevet Major)
16. Theodore Roosevelt: Spanish-American War (Colonel)
17. Harry S. Truman: World War I (Colonel)
18. Dwight D. Eisenhower: World War II (General of the Army)
19. John F. Kennedy: World War II (Lieutenant, Navy)
20. Lyndon B. Johnson: World War II (Commander, Navy)
21. Richard M. Nixon: World War II (Commander, Navy)
22. Gerald Ford: World War II (Lieutenant Commander, Navy)
23. George H. W. Bush: World War II (Lieutenant Junior Grade, Navy)[34]

War Service of Major Party Presidential Candidates

While half of successful presidential candidates have served with the U.S. military in war, many major party presidential candidates who did not win also had impressive military war records. Twelve major party nominees for president have served in the U.S. military in war, with six (50 percent) having served as general officers, four (36 percent) as lower-ranking officers, and two (18 percent) as prior enlisted. Most of the nominees (ten, 83 percent) served with the U.S. Army, and two (17 percent) served in the U.S. Navy. One of the prior U.S. Army service nominees later served in the Korean War with the U.S. Air Force. No major party presidential candidates served in the U.S. Marine Corps. Interestingly, unlike the successful presidential candidates (none of whom served in Korea or Vietnam), four of these candidates served in the Korean and Vietnam wars. The following list outlines the war service of presidential candidates and last rank achieved:

1. Lewis Cass in 1848: War of 1812 (Major General)
2. Winfield Scott in 1852: War of 1812, American Indian Wars, Mexican-American War, Civil War (Brevet Lieutenant General)
3. John C. Fremont in 1856: Mexican-American War, Civil War (Major General)

4. George McClellan in 1864: Mexican-American War, Civil War (Major General)
5. Winfield Scott Hancock in 1880: Mexican-American War, Civil War (Major General)
6. Barry Goldwater in 1964: World War II, Korean War (U.S. Army Air Corps and U.S. Air Force; Major General)
7. George Wallace (American Independent Party) in 1968: World War II (Staff Sergeant)
8. George S. McGovern in 1972: World War II (U.S. Army Air Corps; First Lieutenant)
9. Bob Dole in 1996: World War II (Colonel)
10. Al Gore in 2000: Vietnam (Private)
11. John F. Kerry in 2004: Vietnam (Lieutenant)
12. John S. McCain in 2008: Vietnam (Captain)[35]

Afghan and Iraq Veteran Candidates

Patrick Murphy, who was elected as a Democrat in 2006 to Pennsylvania's Eighth Congressional District, became the first Afghan/Iraq War veteran to serve in the U.S. Congress. Since that time, the number of veterans elected to Congress from these conflicts has soared. The 117th Congress, members who were elected in 2020, will have the highest number of military veterans of the wars in Afghanistan and Iraq since the beginning of operations Enduring Freedom in 2001 and Iraqi Freedom in 2003. In the U.S. House, there are thirty-two members who served in one or both conflicts, and they join four other members who served in the Vietnam or Gulf wars. In the U.S. Senate, there are five veterans of Iraq and Afghanistan who serve alongside three Vietnam or Desert Storm/Gulf War veteran members. These veterans join a long procession of veterans returning home from war and running for office. The initial World War I veteran who was elected to the U.S. House of Representatives in 1919 was a former U.S. Army captain named King Swope, who was elected as a Republican from Kentucky's eighth district in a special election.[36] The first World War II veteran to be elected to Congress was George William Andrews, who was elected from Alabama's third district in 1944.[37] The first Vietnam War veteran was John Murtha, a Marine officer who was elected as a Democrat from Pennsylvania's twelfth district in 1974, and the first Gulf War veteran was Republican Steve Buyer, who served as a U.S. Army captain and was elected from Indiana's fourth district in 1992. As the veterans of the wars in Afghanistan and Iraq return home and seek to serve their communities again, they are increasingly turning to public office as a way to fight for their country once again.

In the last several years, efforts to recruit, train, and support veteran candidates have increased significantly and have moved from ad hoc initiatives to organized support. Within the Republican caucus in the U.S. House of Representatives, there are now twenty-four Republicans who served in the wars in Afghanistan and Iraq, representing 75 percent of all Iraq/Afghan veterans in the U.S. House, which is an 84.6 percent increase over 2016, when there were only thirteen. These members represent constituents in fourteen states, with 83 percent of them coming from the South and Midwest; half served in the U.S. Army, 29.2 percent in the U.S. Navy, 12.5 percent in the U.S. Air Force, and 8.3 percent in the U.S. Marine Corps. Their backgrounds are as varied as their constituencies, with many having served as pilots (fighter, helicopter, cargo) (four), surgeons (three), Judge Advocates General (three), intelligence officers (three), and as members of the infantry (two) and Special Operations Forces (two). Approximately twenty-one (87 percent) of the veterans are officers, with three (12.5 percent) prior enlisted. Of the officers, five (20.8 percent) are former general or flag officers, three (12.5 percent) are former O-6s, one (4.2 percent) is a former O-5, seven (29.2 percent) are former O-4s, and five (20.8 percent) are former O-3s. Among the general officer and flag officers, three served in the National Guard, one served in the U.S. Air Force, and one served in the U.S. Navy.

Within the Democratic caucus, there are eight Iraq/Afghan military veterans, with 50 percent elected from northern states and 50 percent elected from western states. Half are former Marines, two (25 percent) are former members of the U.S. Army, and one each (12.5 percent) are former members of the U.S. Navy and the U.S. Air Force. This represents a 100 percent increase over their 2016 numbers, when there were four Iraq/Afghanistan veterans elected to the U.S. House who, similarly, were all elected from the east or the west. Similar to Republicans, most of the members (six; 75 percent) are former officers and only two (25 percent) are prior enlisted. The highest-ranking officer is an O-6, and only one officer was elected who had been either an O-5 or an O-4. Three (37.5 percent) of the members were O-3s. Most of the members (five; 62.5 percent) served in the infantry, two (25 percent) were pilots, and one (12.5 percent) served in intelligence. The members represent parts of seven different states.

While the veterans are united in service to their country, differences exist with respect to the types of candidates who were elected and their backgrounds. Republican candidates are overwhelmingly from the South and Midwest while the Democrats have no veteran candidates from those regions. Democratic members are evenly split and come from either northern or western states, with only 16.5 percent of Republicans coming from those regions. A number of former general officers and flag officers were also elected as Republicans, and the Democrats did not have any successful candidates with those backgrounds. In total, approximately 44 percent of all Iraq/Afghan veterans from both parties served with the U.S. Army, with 25 percent having served in the U.S. Navy, 18.75 percent serving in the U.S. Marine Corps, and 12.5 percent serving in the U.S. Air Force. Roughly 84 percent of all the members are former officers, and 16 percent had been enlisted. Most members came from the American South (40.6 percent), with the Midwest and the North evenly split at 21.9 percent and the West at 15.6 percent. Fully 50 percent of all elected Iraq/Afghan veterans were O-3s or O-4s, with general/flag officers and prior enlisted coming in second at 15.6 percent, O-6s at 12.5 percent, and O-5s at 6.2 percent.[38]

Conclusion

The returning war veteran gains a deeply personal relationship with his country from his experiences in war and, upon his return, seeks new ways to serve his country once again. He has gained a set of skills that make him forever different from his civilian self and his fellow citizens who did not serve. He is a natural leader, has been hardened by his experiences, and has thoroughly internalized the ethos of his service, his country, and the exigencies of war. He is restless upon his return and seeks to "campaign" again, to enter the arena once more on behalf of his people and his community. His natural abilities of organization, discipline, leadership, forthrightness, and preference for action make him an attractive candidate to voters seeking change. While his knowledge of politics may not be robust, he is a determined learner and readily adjusts to the demands of the campaign trail, embarking yet again on a new campaign on behalf of his country. While not all returned war veterans seek public office, many do, and our nation's politics is better off for their service.

Epilogue

WHEN U.S. MILITARY FORCES INVADED Afghanistan in 2001 and Iraq in 2003, our country was supremely confident in its ability to win but not particularly wise about the culture, challenges, and requirements to prevail in either country. As the logic of both campaigns revealed itself and initial strategies crashed upon the enduring violence of the insurgencies, the beginnings of wisdom began to emerge. The cost of these new perspectives was paid in the blood, mangled bodies, and lives of our men and women. As each year of both campaigns unfolded, and fresh rotations of military forces fought the burgeoning insurgencies, the wars began to leave their imprint on a new generation who had answered the call to serve their nation. Over time, as the deaths of our soldiers, sailors, airmen, and Marines prompted change, new strategies were created, new institutions were established, and new ways of thinking (along with new leaders) emerged. At the same time, as each new unit arrived to do its duty, corporate memory departed with those they replaced, making efforts to adapt that much more difficult. Further, initial strategic decisions in both wars hamstrung future efforts at victory, such as addressing Taliban safe havens in Pakistan and decisions to abolish the Iraqi army, fully de-Baathify the Iraqi government, and not provide enough troops to stabilize postinvasion Iraq, among many other factors. The U.S. military often flirted with wisdom during this time but frequently embraced tragedy until, eventually, the right conditions emerged for the application of that banal phrase "lessons learned." Once pragmatic wisdom had finally arrived, American patience on the home front had worn thin, and ambitious politicians seeking to score points by denigrating efforts to win in both countries gained traction with some elements of the American voting public.

The next several years and decades will greatly influence how veterans of these wars view their experiences. The Biden administration's decision to withdraw U.S. military forces from Afghanistan by August 31, 2021, under the guise of "ending the war," forces a conversation about the global war on terror and how it will be remembered by American culture and society. As with every war, veteran perspectives will change over time, and the endgames in both conflicts haven't yet completely played out. How veterans will view their time overseas will depend, for example, on whether Kabul falls to Taliban forces and whether there will be another catastrophic attack on the U.S. homeland by al-Qaeda or similar groups. Similarly, if ISIS-type forces surge again in Iraq (or if the country descends into anarchy or if some version of dictatorship emerges again), veterans' views of their time there will also be impacted. A preview of these types of sentiments can be seen in how veterans of the war in Iraq responded to the growth of ISIS forces in Syria and Iraq in 2013–2014. There was a mix of indignation, frustration, resignation, and depression, and the question that is asked of every war that has not gone well was expressed: "Was it all worth it?" These sorts of questions may also be asked in the future depending on the course of events in the Middle East and Central Asia in the years to come. However much the future direction of both conflicts is not yet known, some enduring features will remain with those who served there in uniform.

The military veterans of Iraq and Afghanistan grew up in the shadow of the legacy of the Vietnam War as well as the successes and legends of World War II and the Gulf War, tempered by the tragedy of Somalia and the "Black Hawk Down" incident. They undertook multiple tours in predominantly Muslim countries and conducted both combat and counterinsurgency operations as well as reconstruction, development, and good governance activities. They had extensive experience with and gained knowledge of Islam, tribes, ethnic groups, and the histories of both countries and developed deep relationships with many Afghans and Iraqis. They also mediated tribal disputes; counseled local leaders; built schools, clinics, roads, and government buildings; and became knowledgeable about the farming, justice, administrative, and marriage customs and practices of both countries, among many other aspects of both cultures. They served in a mature and highly institutionalized U.S. military that had many strengths, as well as many organizational blind spots, which made adapting to the unique attributes of insurgency incredibly difficult. It also made understanding the initial strategic dimensions of both conflicts (as well as organizing U.S. forces and policy options accordingly) that much more challenging.

All the veterans of both wars were volunteers and motivated by many things, but patriotism was the strongest following the attacks on our country in 2001. Those who served adapted to the demands of combat and the nature of insurgency warfare as well as to the institution of the U.S. military and living in developing countries for prolonged periods of time. These various adaptations complicated their journeys home to a highly developed, postindustrial society more focused on entitlements and rights than on responsibilities and duty. Further, they returned to a country that is going through a process of reimagining masculinity, where many Americans are supportive of the military but feel no compulsion to join it and where, all too frequently, veterans and civilians see each other as simply the "other." Additionally, as these veterans move on in life, they will leave their own interpretations of their experiences by writing memoirs and fiction, making movies and crafting poetry, serving their communities and running for political office, or founding and building businesses, among so many other endeavors. These and many other efforts will play out in the years ahead and will also leave their imprint on U.S. culture, history, and the lives of the veterans who served.

Was it all worth it? As it is often said, only history will tell, but that is not particularly gratifying to the men and women who died on behalf of a mission they gave their all to—nor is it gratifying to their families. They will make their own determination regarding whether it was worthwhile; they have earned the right to do so. In wars without victory parades, when there is no decisive victory, are veterans ever truly home?

Notes

Chapter 1: No Victory Parades

1. Veterans Administration, "World War II Veterans by the Numbers," VA Fact Sheet, 2003, http://dig.abclocal.go.com/ktrk/ktrk_120710_WWIIvetsfact sheet.pdf (the World War II era is defined as September 16, 1940, through July 25, 1947); War and Navy Departments, "Going Back to Civilian Life," February 1946, 17. "A device of woven material consisting of a lozenge background 1½ inches in height and 3 inches in width, long axis horizontal and the design of the lapel button for service since 8 Sep 1939 in golden yellow. The ring of the design is 1 inch in diameter. The background will be of olive drab for wear on the enlisted man's service coat the other woolen outer garments, and of khaki for wear on the summer shirt" (Institute of Heraldry, "Honorable Service Lapel Button and Honorable Discharge Emblem," accessed April 5, 2021, https://tioh.army.mil /Catalog/Heraldry.aspx?HeraldryId=15753&CategoryId=14&grp=2&menu=Un iformed%20Services&from=search).

2. War and Navy Departments, "Going Back to Civilian Life," February 1946, 17.

3. War and Navy Departments, "Going Back to Civilian Life," February 1946, 17.

4. Institute for Heraldry, "Honorable Service Lapel Button and Honorable Discharge Emblem."

5. E. B. Sledge, *China Marine: An Infantryman's Life after World War II* (Oxford: Oxford University Press, 2002), 131.

6. War Department, "Information for Soldiers: Going Back to Civilian Life," November 1944, iv.

7. War and Navy Departments, "Going Back to Civilian Life," v.

8. Siegfried Sassoon, *Memoirs of an Infantry Officer* (London: Faber & Faber, 1930), 130.

9. A. D. Horne, ed., *The Wounded Generation: America after Vietnam* (Englewood Cliffs, NJ: Prentice Hall, 1981), 163.

10. Willard Waller, *War and the Family* (New York: Dryden Press, 1940), 36.

11. See Jonathan Shay, *Odysseus in America: Combat Trauma and the Trials of Homecoming* (New York: Scribner, 2002), 64.

12. Dixon Wecter, *When Johnny Comes Marching Home* (Cambridge, MA: Houghton Mifflin, 1944), 461.

13. Wecter, *When Johnny Comes Marching Home*, 461.

14. Shay, *Odysseus in America*, 97.

15. Samuel A. Stouffer et al., *The American Soldier: Adjustment during Army Life* (Princeton, NJ: Princeton University Press, 1949), 431.

16. Stouffer et al., *The American Soldier*, 643.

17. Stouffer et al., *The American Soldier*, 430.

18. Stouffer et al., *The American Soldier*, 292.

19. Stouffer et al., *The American Soldier*, 292.

20. Stouffer et al., *The American Soldier*, 642.

21. Veterans Administration, "World War II Veterans by the Numbers."

22. U.S. Department of Veterans Affairs, "Vietnam," Military Health History Pocket Card, 2019, https://www.va.gov/oaa/pocketcard/vietnam.asp.

23. Samuel Hynes, *On War and Writing* (Chicago: University of Chicago Press, 2018), 35.

24. Dan Lamothe, "How 775,000 U.S. Troops Fought in One War: Afghanistan Military Deployments by the Numbers," *Washington Post*, September 11, 2019; Miriam Berger, "Invaders, Allies, Occupiers, Guests: A Brief History of U.S. Military Involvement in Iraq," *Washington Post*, January 11, 2020.

25. Dan Lamothe, "'Maybe This Is How Vietnam Vets Felt': Americans Who Fought in Afghanistan Wait to See How Their War Ends," *Washington Post*, September 10, 2019.

26. National World War II Museum, "Research Starters: U.S. Military by the Numbers," December 12, 2020, https://www.nationalww2museum.org/students-teachers/student-resources/research-starters/research-starters-us-military-numbers.

27. Office of the Chief of Military History, United States Army, "Peace Becomes Cold War, 1945–1950," in *American Military History*, Army Historical Series (Washington, DC: U.S. Army, 1988), https://history.army.mil/books/amh/AMH-24.htm.

28. Mark F. Cancian, "U.S. Military Forces in FY 2020, Army," Center for Strategic and International Studies, October 2019, https://www.csis.org/analysis/us-military-forces-fy-2020-army; Mark F. Cancian, "U.S. Military Forces in FY 2020, Navy," Center for Strategic and International Studies, October 2019, https://www.csis.org/analysis/us-military-forces-fy-2021-navy.

29. Edward L. King, *The Death of the Army: A Pre-Mortem* (New York: Saturday Review Press, 1972), 57, 59. "In 1950–52 hundreds of career officers

anxiously volunteered to go to Korea to serve in the limited war. They volunteered for a variety of reasons, chief among which was to get credit for combat command, or in Army parlance—get another punch on their promotion ticket. Company, battalion, regimental, and division commands were regularly rotated at six- to eight-month intervals to provide more career officers with an opportunity to obtain combat-command credit on their personnel records. Such credit was an essential ticket to future promotion" (King, *The Death of the Army*, 55).

30. See Andrew F. Krepinevich Jr., *The Army and Vietnam* (Baltimore, MD: Johns Hopkins University Press, 1986).

31. Jennifer Mittelstadt, *The Rise of the Military Welfare State* (Cambridge, MA: Harvard University Press, 2015).

32. Mittelstadt, *The Rise of the Military Welfare State*, 7.

33. Mittelstadt, *The Rise of the Military Welfare State*, 4.

34. Mittelstadt, *The Rise of the Military Welfare State*, 4.

35. Mittelstadt, *The Rise of the Military Welfare State*, 19.

36. Mittelstadt, *The Rise of the Military Welfare State*, 19.

37. Mittelstadt, *The Rise of the Military Welfare State*, 8.

38. Joel Stein, "Warriors and Wusses," *Los Angeles Times*, January 24, 2006.

39. Dave Grossman, *On Combat* (n.p.: Warrior Science Publications, 2008).

40. Hynes, *On War and Writing*, 34–35.

41. Wecter, *When Johnny Comes Marching Home*, 300.

42. Willard Waller, *The Veteran Comes Back* (New York: Dryden Press, 1944), 98–99.

43. Sassoon, *Memoirs of an Infantry Officer*, 290.

44. Wecter, *When Johnny Comes Marching Home*, 323.

45. Samuel Hynes, *The Soldiers' Tale: Bearing Witness to Modern War* (New York: Penguin, 1997), 114.

46. William Matthews and Dixon Wecter, *Our Soldiers Speak, 1775–1918* (Boston: Little, Brown, 1943), 144.

47. Sledge, *China Marine*, 127, 129.

48. Ronald Inglehart and Christian Welzel, *Modernization, Cultural Change, and Democracy: The Human Development Sequence* (Cambridge: Cambridge University Press, 2007), 54.

49. Ronald Inglehart, *Modernization and Postmodernization: Cultural, Economic, and Political Change in 43 Societies* (Princeton, NJ: Princeton University Press, 1997), 67.

50. Inglehart and Welzel, *Modernization, Cultural Change, and Democracy*, 52.

51. Studs Terkel, *"The Good War": An Oral History of World War II* (New York: New Press, 1984), 64 (quoting E. B. Sledge).

52. Daniel Bell, *The Coming of Post-Industrial Society: A Venture in Social Forecasting* (New York: Basic Books, 1999), 127.

53. Bell, *The Coming of Post-Industrial Society*, 146.

54. John Bagot Glubb, *The Story of the Arab Legion* (London: Hodder & Stoughton, 1948), 176.

55. Norman Mailer, *An American Dream* (New York: Dial Press, 1965), 75–76, quoted in Paul Fussell, *The Great War and Modern Memory* (Oxford: Oxford University Press, 1975), 110.

56. Terkel, *"The Good War,"* 176.

57. Gary Buiso, "Sgt. 1st Class Dillard Johnson Is the Deadliest US Soldier on Record—with 2,746 Kills," *New York Post*, June 23, 2013.

58. Karl Marlantes, *What It Is Like to Go to War* (New York: Grove Press, 2011), 187.

59. Hynes, *The Soldiers' Tale*, 215.

60. Horne, *The Wounded Generation*, 191.

Chapter 2: The Mind of the War Veteran

1. Chief among these are (1) the rise of the "professional" military state, (2) the shift to an all-volunteer military, (3) the development of a postmodern and postindustrial world, (4) the moral complexities of prolonged counterinsurgency wars in Muslim countries, and (5) the redefinition and de-legitimatization of masculinity.

2. **Operation Enduring Freedom**
   Phase 1: Liberation of Afghanistan: September 11, 2001–November 30, 2001
   Phase 2: Consolidation I: December 1, 2001–September 30, 2006
   Phase 3: Consolidation II: October 1, 2006–November 30, 2009
   Phase 4: Consolidation III: December 1, 2009–June 30, 2011
   Phase 5: Transition I: July 1, 2011–December 31, 2014
   Phase 6: Transition II: January 1, 2015–Present
   Operation Iraqi Freedom
   Phase 1: Liberation of Iraq: March 19, 2003–May 1, 2003
   Phase 2: Transition of Iraq: May 2, 2003–June 28, 2004
   Phase 3: Iraqi Governance: June 29, 2004–December 15, 2005
   Phase 4: National Resolution: December 16, 2005–January 9, 2007
   Phase 5: Iraqi Surge: January 10, 2007–December 31, 2008
   Phase 6: Iraqi Sovereignty: January 1, 2009–August 31, 2010
   Phase 7: Operation New Dawn: September 1, 2010–December 15, 2011
   Operation Inherent Resolve
   Phase 1: Abeyance: June 15, 2014–November 24, 2015
   Phase 2: Intensification: November 25, 2015–April 14, 2017
   Phase 3: Defeat: April 15, 2017–July 1, 2020
   Phase 4: Normalize: July 2, 2020–Present

3. Jonathan Shay, *Odysseus in America: Combat Trauma and the Trials of Homecoming* (New York: Scribner, 2002), 149.

4. Shay, *Odysseus in America*, 64.

5. Willard Waller, *The Veteran Comes Back* (New York: Dryden Press, 1944), 306.

6. Waller, *The Veteran Comes Back*, 18.

7. Waller, *The Veteran Comes Back*, 70.

8. Studs Terkel, *"The Good War": An Oral History of World War II* (New York: New Press, 1984), 61 (quoting E. B. Sledge).

9. William Matthews and Dixon Wecter, *Our Soldiers Speak, 1775–1918* (Boston: Little, Brown, 1943), 355.

10. Waller, *The Veteran Comes Back*, 22.

11. Willard W. Waller, *On the Family, Education, and War: Selected Writings*, ed. William J. Goode, Frank F. Furstenberg Jr., and Larry R. Mitchell (Chicago: University of Chicago Press, 1970), 323.

12. Dan Lamothe, "How 775,000 U.S. Troops Fought in One War: Afghanistan Military Deployments by the Numbers," *Washington Post*, September 11, 2019.

13. Samuel Hynes, *The Soldiers' Tale: Bearing Witness to Modern War* (New York: Penguin, 1997), 22.

14. Charles Edmonds, *A Subaltern's War* (London: Davies, 1929), 128.

15. Brian Castner, "Still Fighting, and Dying, in the Forever War," *New York Times*, March 9, 2017.

16. Benedict Carey, "Those with Multiple Tours of Wars Overseas Struggle at Home," *New York Times*, May 29, 2016.

17. Nolan Peterson, *Why Soldiers Miss War: The Journey Home* (Philadelphia: Casemate, 2019), xxviii.

18. Gary W. Gallagher, ed., *Fighting for the Confederacy: The Personal Recollections of General Edward Porter Alexander* (Chapel Hill: University of North Carolina Press, 1989), xviii.

19. E. B. Sledge, *China Marine: An Infantryman's Life after World War II* (Oxford: Oxford University Press, 2002), 122.

20. Shay, *Odysseus in America*, 57.

21. Dixon Wecter, *When Johnny Comes Marching Home* (Cambridge, MA: Houghton Mifflin, 1944), 321 (quoting a veteran in *The Home Sector*, early in 1920).

22. Waller, *On the Family, Education, and War*, 326.

23. Shay, *Odysseus in America*, 30.

24. Waller, *The Veteran Comes Back*, 140.

25. Hervey Allen, *Toward the Flame* (New York: Doran, 1926), 114.

26. James Gibson, ed., *Let the Poet Choose* (London: Harrap, 1973), 37 (quoting Edmund Blunden); Paul Fussell, *The Great War and Modern Memory* (Oxford: Oxford University Press, 1975), 256.

27. Peterson, *Why Soldiers Miss War*, xxviii.

Chapter 3: Camaraderie, Love, and Humor

1. "After the warrior returns home from the initiation of combat, he becomes a member of 'the Club' of combat veterans" (Karl Marlantes, *What It Is Like to Go to War* [New York: Grove Press, 2011], 208).

2. J. Glenn Gray, *The Warriors: Reflections on Men in Battle* (Lincoln: University of Nebraska Press, 1959), 15.

3. Willard Waller, *The Veteran Comes Back* (New York: Dryden Press, 1944), 22.

4. Gray, *The Warriors*, 26–27.

5. Samuel Hynes, *The Soldiers' Tale: Bearing Witness to Modern War* (New York: Penguin, 1997), 9.

6. Gray, *The Warriors*, 26–27.

7. Studs Terkel, *"The Good War": An Oral History of World War II* (New York: New Press, 1984), 60 (quoting E. B. Sledge).

8. Waller, *The Veteran Comes Back*, 39.

9. See Robert Wright, *Non-Zero: The Logic of Human Destiny* (New York: Pantheon, 2000); Robert Wright, *The Moral Animal: Why We Are the Way We Are: The New Science of Evolutionary Psychology* (New York: Vintage, 1994); Edward O. Wilson, *On Human Nature* (Cambridge, MA: Harvard University Press, 1978); Edward O. Wilson, *Sociobiology: The New Synthesis* (Cambridge, MA: Harvard University Press, 2000).

10. Wright, *Non-Zero*, 23.

11. Wright, *The Moral Animal*, 158.

12. Wright, *Non-Zero*, 60–61.

13. Wright, *The Moral Animal*, 198.

14. Wright, *Non-Zero*, 21.

15. Wright, *Non-Zero*, 58.

16. Wright, *Non-Zero*, 56–57.

17. Wright, *The Moral Animal*, 191.

18. Waller, *The Veteran Comes Back*, 63.

19. See also Sebastian Junger, *Tribe: On Homecoming and Belonging* (New York: Twelve, 2016).

20. Waller, *The Veteran Comes Back*, 124.

21. Waller, *The Veteran Comes Back*, 24.

22. Willard Waller, *War and the Family* (New York: Dryden Press, 1940), 13.

23. Please see the 2011 novel by Siobhan Fallon titled *You Know When the Men Are Gone* (New York: Amy Einhorn Books, 2011), which is about civilian communities of military spouses whose husbands have deployed, as well as the 2014 memoir by Angela Ricketts, *No Man's War: Irreverent Confessions of an Infantry Wife* (New York: Counterpoint, 2014).

24. Waller, *War and the Family*, 3.

25. Waller, *The Veteran Comes Back*, 14.

26. Gray, *The Warriors*, 61.

27. Waller, *War and the Family*, 36.

28. Harold Shapiro, *What Every Young Man Should Know about War* (New York: Knight, 1937), 112.

29. Australian War Memorial, Social Hygiene Division, United States of America, "A German Bullet Is Cleaner Than a Whore!" poster, 1918, https://www.awm.gov.au/collection/C102773.

30. Shapiro, *What Every Young Man Should Know about War*, 108.

31. See Ann Scott Tyson, *American Spartan: The Promise, the Mission, and the Betrayal of Special Forces Major Jim Gant* (New York: Morrow, 2014).

32. Dixon Wecter, *When Johnny Comes Marching Home* (Cambridge, MA: Houghton Mifflin, 1944), 461.

33. Willard W. Waller, *On the Family, Education, and War: Selected Writings*, ed. William J. Goode, Frank F. Furstenberg Jr., and Larry R. Mitchell (Chicago: University of Chicago Press, 1970), 338.

34. Chris Hedges, *War Is a Force That Gives Us Meaning* (New York: Anchor, 2003), 100–101.

35. Shapiro, *What Every Young Man Should Know about War*, 17; see also the memoir by Tom Carhart, *The Offering: A Generation Offered Their Lives to America in Vietnam—One Soldier's Story* (New York: Morrow, 1987), 95–104.

36. Hedges, *War Is a Force That Gives Us Meaning*, 167–68.

37. Waller, *On the Family, Education, and War*, 322.

38. Waller, *War and the Family*, 19.

39. Waller, *On the Family, Education, and War*, 323.

40. Waller, *War and the Family*, 36.

41. Waller, *The Veteran Comes Back*, 140.

42. Waller, *War and the Family*, 33.

43. Waller, *The Veteran Comes Back*, 58.

44. Waller, *The Veteran Comes Back*, 120.

45. Marlantes, *What It Is Like to Go to War*, 190.

46. Waller, *War and the Family*, 48 (quoting from Calvin Hall, "The Instability of Post-War Marriages," *Journal of Social Psychology* 5 [1934]: 523–30).

47. Waller, *On the Family, Education, and War*, 324.

48. William Matthews and Dixon Wecter, *Our Soldiers Speak, 1775–1918* (Boston: Little, Brown, 1943), 355.

49. Matthews and Wecter, *Our Soldiers Speak, 1775–1918*, 356–57.

50. Katherine E. Brown and Elina Penttinen, "'A "Sucking Chest Wound" Is Nature's Way of Telling You to Slow Down . . .': Humor and Laughter in War Time," *Critical Studies on Security* 1, no. 1 (2013): 126.

51. There are several versions of these laws, but those used for this section come from the humor website https://mirth.fandom.com/.

Chapter 4: Zombies, Movies, and Video Games

1. Willard Waller, *The Veteran Comes Back* (New York: Dryden Press, 1944), 63.

2. Waller, *The Veteran Comes Back*, 24.

3. Waller, *The Veteran Comes Back*, 70.

4. "All-Time Top-Grossers," *Variety*, January 18, 1950, 18; "Upped Scale Films Cop 'Win, Place, Show' Spots in Gross Sweepstakes," *Variety*, January 7, 1948, 63.

Chapter 5: War Memoirs

1. Frances Houghton, *The Veterans' Tale: British Military Memoirs of the Second World War* (Cambridge: Cambridge University Press, 2019), 36.

2. Houghton, *The Veterans' Tale*, 51.

3. Mark Rawlinson, *British Writing of the Second World War* (Oxford: Oxford University Press, 2000), 43.

4. Houghton, *The Veterans' Tale*, 47–48.

5. Samuel Hynes, *The Soldiers' Tale: Bearing Witness to Modern War* (New York: Penguin, 1997), 6.

6. Houghton, *The Veterans' Tale*, 43–44.

7. Gary W. Gallagher, ed., *Fighting for the Confederacy: The Personal Recollections of General Edward Porter Alexander* (Chapel Hill: University of North Carolina Press, 1989), xvi.

8. Houghton, *The Veterans' Tale*, 35.

9. Hynes, *The Soldiers' Tale*, 4.

10. Philip Caputo, *A Rumor of War* (Austin, TX: Holt, Rinehart and Winston, 1977), xi, quoted in Hynes, *The Soldiers' Tale*, 3.

11. Hynes, *The Soldiers' Tale*, 145.

12. "The stories that soldiers tell are small-scale, detailed, and confined—'very local, limited, incoherent,' as Edmund Blunden put it—and necessarily so, for that is the way they see war" (Hynes, *The Soldiers' Tale*, 12).

13. J. Glenn Gray, *The Warriors: Reflections on Men in Battle* (Lincoln: University of Nebraska Press, 1959), 29.

14. Gray, *The Warriors*, 29.

15. Hynes, *The Soldiers' Tale*, 19.

16. Paul Fussell, *The Great War and Modern Memory* (Oxford: Oxford University Press, 1975), 326–27.

17. Hynes, *The Soldiers' Tale*, 26.

18. Hynes, *The Soldiers' Tale*, 134.

19. Hynes, *The Soldiers' Tale*, 2.

20. Samuel Hynes, *On War and Writing* (Chicago: University of Chicago Press, 2018), 32.

21. Hynes, *On War and Writing*, 242.

22. Houghton, *The Veterans' Tale*, 10.

23. See Fussell, *The Great War and Modern Memory*.

24. Fussell, *The Great War and Modern Memory*, 174.

25. Hynes, *The Soldiers' Tale*, 72.

26. Fussell, *The Great War and Modern Memory*, 314.

27. I created a database of these memoirs from which this data is drawn. The information is current as of March 2021 and will be updated regularly.

28. Hynes, *The Soldiers' Tale*, 223, 127.

29. Hynes, *The Soldiers' Tale*, 128 (referring to Richard Hillary's *The Last Enemy* [New York: Macmillan, 1942]).

30. War memoirs published by military veterans of the wars in Afghanistan and Iraq (year/#) are as follows: 2004 (three), 2005 (four), 2006 (six), 2007 (four), 2008 (ten), 2009 (seven), 2010 (four), 2011 (nine), 2012 (eleven), 2013 (eleven), 2014 (thirteen), 2015 (seven), 2016 (thirteen), 2017 (twelve), 2018 (eleven), 2019 (twenty-one), 2020 (seventeen), 2021 (five as of July 2021).

31. For a comprehensive list of fiction written by Afghan and Iraq veterans, see "Iraq and Afghanistan War Fiction, Poetry, and Film 2020," *Time Now: The Iraq and Afghanistan Wars in Art, Film, and Literature* (blog), December 31, 2020, https://acolytesofwar.com/2020/12/31/iraq-and-afghanistan-war-fiction-poetry -and-film-2020/.

32. The Colby Award and Norwich University Military Writers' Symposium, "2021 William E. Colby Award," accessed July 9, 2021, https://www.norwich .edu/colby/colby-award.

Chapter 6: The Vietnam War

1. See Linda Robinson, *One Hundred Victories: Special Ops and the Future of American Warfare* (New York: PublicAffairs, 2013), and Daniel R. Green, *In the Warlords' Shadow: Special Operations Forces, the Afghans, and Their Fight against the Taliban* (Annapolis, MD: Naval Institute Press, 2017).

2. The information for this section was taken from my PhD dissertation in political science. Daniel R. Green, "First among Equals: The History and Politics of Choosing the Chairman of the Joint Chiefs of Staff" (PhD diss., George Washington University, 2012). It explains how the chairman of the Joint Chiefs of Staff is selected, which, of necessity, required an understanding of the development of the Joint Chiefs of Staff as an institution as well as the impact of various conflicts on it and its decision-making processes. It is also based on the writings of Mark Perry's books *Four Stars* (New York: Houghton Mifflin Harcourt, 1989) and *Partners in Command* (New York: Penguin, 2007), David Halberstam's *The Best and the Brightest* (New York: Random House, 1972), and Tom Rick's *The Generals* (New York: Penguin, 2012), among many other sources.

3. Short-termism also impacts the U.S. political system, as most elected federal officials face voters regularly every two years; it is hard to have strategic patience under these sorts of conditions.

Chapter 7: Militaria

1. Samuel Hynes, *The Soldiers' Tale: Bearing Witness to Modern War* (New York: Penguin, 1997), 156.

2. Dixon Wecter, *When Johnny Comes Marching Home* (Cambridge, MA: Houghton Mifflin, 1944), 311.

3. James J. Fahey, *Pacific War Diary, 1942–1945* (Boston: Houghton Mifflin, 1963), 229–30, quoted in Hynes, *The Soldiers' Tale*, 170–71.

4. Hynes, *The Soldiers' Tale*, 192.

5. Kaufman's Army & Navy, "A Short History of the 'Military Goods Business' in America," poster, August 1, 2019.

6. Relic Record, "Francis Bannerman Military Surplus," accessed July 9, 2021, https://relicrecord.com/blog/francis-bannerman-military-surplus/.

7. Relic Record, "Francis Bannerman Military Surplus."

8. Relic Record, "Francis Bannerman Military Surplus."

9. Hynes, *The Soldiers' Tale*, 29.

10. J. Glenn Gray, *The Warriors: Reflections on Men in Battle* (Lincoln: University of Nebraska Press, 1959), 28.

Chapter 8: Stolen Valor and Fake Veterans

1. Quoted in Doug Sterner and Pam Sterner, with Michael Mink, *Restoring Valor: One Couple's Mission to Expose Fraudulent War Heroes and Protect America's Military Awards System* (New York: Skyhorse, 2014), 4–5.

2. Sterner and Sterner, *Restoring Valor*, 5, 7; Major Charles V. Mugno, "Maintaining the Quality of Our Military Awards System," *Marine Corps Gazette*, March 1994, 77.

3. Sterner and Sterner, *Restoring Valor*, 5, 7; Mugno, "Maintaining the Quality of Our Military Awards System," 77.

4. Mugno, "Maintaining the Quality of Our Military Awards System," 77.

5. Mugno, "Maintaining the Quality of Our Military Awards System," 77.

6. Mugno, "Maintaining the Quality of Our Military Awards System," 3; Arthur E. Du Bois, "The Heraldry of Heroism," *National Geographic Magazine* 84, no. 4 (October 1943): 411.

7. Mugno, "Maintaining the Quality of Our Military Awards System," 3, 5.

8. Mugno, "Maintaining the Quality of Our Military Awards System," 3.

9. Mugno, "Maintaining the Quality of Our Military Awards System," 5; Colonel Robert E. Wyllie, "The Romance of Military Insignia: How the United States Government Recognizes Deeds of Heroism and Devotion to Duty," *National Geographic Magazine* 36, no. 6 (December 1919): 472.

10. Wyllie, "The Romance of Military Insignia," 472.

11. Wyllie, "The Romance of Military Insignia," 472.

12. Wyllie, "The Romance of Military Insignia," 472.

13. Gregg S. Clemmer, *Valor in Gray: The Recipients of the Confederate Medal of Honor* (Staunton, VA: Hearthside, 1998), xv.

14. Clemmer, *Valor in Gray*, xv.

15. Clemmer, *Valor in Gray*, xix.

16. Clemmer, *Valor in Gray*, xviii.

17. Clemmer, *Valor in Gray*, xx–xxi.

18. Clemmer, *Valor in Gray*, xxi.

19. *Encyclopedia Britannica*, "Brevet: Military Rank," December 10, 2020, https://www.britannica.com/topic/brevet.

20. John E. Strandberg and Roger James Bender, *The Call of Duty: Military Awards and Decorations of the United States of America* (San Jose, CA: Bender, 1994), 14; Wyllie, "The Romance of Military Insignia," 472.

21. Wyllie, "The Romance of Military Insignia," 475.

22. Mugno, "Maintaining the Quality of Our Military Awards System," 79.

23. Sterner and Sterner, *Restoring Valor*, 6.

24. Sterner and Sterner, *Restoring Valor*, 63.

25. Jennifer Mittelstadt, *The Rise of the Military Welfare State* (Cambridge, MA: Harvard University Press, 2015), 4.

26. John McCarthy, "Stolen Valor: Imposters Touting Military Accolades an Ongoing Problem," *Press Journal*, March 2, 2020, 1A, 6A. The article references a 2010 report in *Military History* magazine that cited a *Harper's New Monthly Magazine*, which, in turn, had referenced a January 1893 report.

27. Sterner and Sterner, *Restoring Valor*, 6.

28. Sterner and Sterner, *Restoring Valor*, 7.

29. Sterner and Sterner, *Restoring Valor*, 6–7.

30. Wyllie, "The Romance of Military Insignia," 478.

31. Wyllie, "The Romance of Military Insignia," 478; Sterner and Sterner, *Restoring Valor*, 7. In 1942, the U.S. Navy reversed the order of precedence of the Distinguished Service Medal and the Navy Cross.

32. Sterner and Sterner, *Restoring Valor*, 7.

33. Sterner and Sterner, *Restoring Valor*, 7.

34. Wyllie, "The Romance of Military Insignia," 478–79.

35. Dixon Wecter, *When Johnny Comes Marching Home* (Cambridge, MA: Houghton Mifflin, 1944), 314.

36. Sterner and Sterner, *Restoring Valor*, 7–8.

37. Sterner and Sterner, *Restoring Valor*, 7–8.

38. See Pyramid of Honor after the title page in Sterner and Sterner, *Restoring Valor*.

39. U.S. Air Force Personnel Center, "Distinguished Flying Cross," August 4, 2010, https://www.afpc.af.mil/About/Fact-Sheets/Display/Article/421931/distinguished-flying-cross/.

40. George C. Marshall Foundation, "4-225 Memorandum for the President, February 3, 1944," accessed July 9, 2021, https://www.marshallfoundation.org/library/digital-archive/memorandum-for-the-president-107/.

41. Studs Terkel, *"The Good War": An Oral History of World War II* (New York: New Press, 1984), 176 (quoting U.S. Marine and World War II veteran Roger Tuttrup).

42. E. B. Sledge, *China Marine: An Infantryman's Life after World War II* (Oxford: Oxford University Press, 2002), 131.

43. National World War II Museum, "Research Starters: U.S. Military by the Numbers," December 12, 2020, https://www.nationalww2museum.org/students-teachers/student-resources/research-starters/research-starters-us-military-numbers.

44. Office of the Chief of Military History, United States Army, "Peace Becomes Cold War, 1945–1950," in *American Military History*, Army Historical Series (Washington, DC: U.S. Army, 1988), https://history.army.mil/books/amh/AMH-24.htm.

45. A. D. Horne, ed., *The Wounded Generation: America after Vietnam* (Englewood Cliffs, NJ: Prentice Hall, 1981), 191 (quoting Vietnam veteran Sam Brown).

46. McCarthy, "Stolen Valor," 1A, 6A.

47. McCarthy, "Stolen Valor," 1A, 6A.

48. McCarthy, "Stolen Valor," 1A, 6A.

49. Jonn Lilyea, "What Is 'Stolen Valor'?" Valor Guardians, October 14, 2015, https://www.valorguardians.com/blog/?p=62317.

50. Lilyea, "What Is 'Stolen Valor'?"

51. Rachael Monroe, "How to Spot a Military Imposter," *New Yorker*, October 26, 2020; see Don Shipley, "Phony Naval SEALs Verifications," accessed June 15, 2021, http://www.extremesealexperience.com/Fake-Navy-Seal-Verification.

52. Shipley, "Phony Naval SEALs Verifications."

53. Valor Guardians, "Valor Vultures," accessed June 15, 2021, https://valorguardians.com/blog/?cat=391.

54. B. G. Burkett and Glenna Whitley, *Stolen Valor: How the Vietnam Generation Was Robbed of Its Heroes and Its History* (Dallas, TX: Verity Press, 1998), 352.

55. Sterner and Sterner, *Restoring Valor*, 45 (109th Congress).

56. Sterner and Sterner, *Restoring Valor*, 139.

57. Stephen Braun, "A Parade of Fake War Heroes," *Los Angeles Times*, May 31, 1992.

58. Siegfried Sassoon, *Memoirs of an Infantry Officer* (London: Faber & Faber, 1930), 290.

59. Richard Hillary, *The Last Enemy* (New York: Macmillan, 1942), 21, quoted in Samuel Hynes, *The Soldiers' Tale: Bearing Witness to Modern War* (New York: Penguin, 1997), 126.

60. Sterner and Sterner, *Restoring Valor*, 48 (quoting George Washington University law professor Jonathan Turley).

Chapter 9: Veteran Politicians

1. Willard Waller, *The Veteran Comes Back* (New York: Dryden Press, 1944), 186.

2. Waller, *The Veteran Comes Back*, 111.

3. Dixon Wecter, *When Johnny Comes Marching Home* (Cambridge, MA: Houghton Mifflin, 1944), 464.

4. Waller, *The Veteran Comes Back*, 186.

5. Paul Fussell, *The Great War and Modern Memory* (Oxford: Oxford University Press, 1975), 90.

6. Waller, *The Veteran Comes Back*, 22.

7. J. Glenn Gray, *The Warriors: Reflections on Men in Battle* (Lincoln: University of Nebraska Press, 1959), 15.

8. Waller, *The Veteran Comes Back*, 187.

9. Waller, *The Veteran Comes Back*, 185–86.

10. Hervey Allen, *Toward the Flame* (New York: Doran, 1926), 84.

11. A. D. Horne, ed., *The Wounded Generation: America after Vietnam* (Englewood Cliffs, NJ: Prentice Hall, 1981), 163.

12. William Matthews and Dixon Wecter, *Our Soldiers Speak, 1775–1918* (Boston: Little, Brown, 1943), 352–53.

13. Waller, *The Veteran Comes Back*, 39.

14. Wecter, *When Johnny Comes Marching Home*, 464.

15. V. O. Key Jr., *Southern Politics in State and Nation* (New York: Knopf, 1949), 59, 62.

16. Stephen C. Byrum, *McMinn County* (Memphis, TN: Memphis State University Press, 1984), 115.

17. Byrum, *McMinn County*, 115–16.

18. Byrum, *McMinn County*, 116.

19. Chris DeRose, *The Fighting Bunch: The Battle of Athens and How World War II Veterans Won the Only Successful Armed Rebellion since the Revolution* (New York: St. Martin's Press, 2020), 2.

20. DeRose, *The Fighting Bunch*, 2.

21. Byrum, *McMinn County*, 117.

22. Byrum, *McMinn County*, 117.

23. DeRose, *The Fighting Bunch*, 3–4.

24. Byrum, *McMinn County*, 117.

25. Bill White, "An Interview with Bill White for the Veteran's Oral History Project, Center for the Study of War and Society, Department of History, the University of Tennessee Knoxville," interviewed by G. Kurt Piehler and Brandi Wilson (Athens, TN, July 20, 2000), 19.

26. DeRose, *The Fighting Bunch*, 3–4.

27. Byrum, *McMinn County*, 118.

28. Byrum, *McMinn County*, 118.

29. Bill White, "An Interview with Bill White for the Veteran's Oral History Project," 19–22.

30. Lones Seiber, "The Battle of Athens," *American Heritage*, February–March 1985.

31. Kate William, "Riots in Tennessee," Tennessee State Library and Archives, January 10, 2013.

32. Lones Seiber, "The Battle of Athens," *American Heritage*, February–March 1985.

33. Seiber, "The Battle of Athens."

34. See https://en.wikipedia.org/wiki/List_of_presidents_of_the_United _States_by_military_service.

35. See https://en.wikipedia.org/wiki/List_of_United_States_presidential _candidates.

36. "In the spring of 1919, Dallas reported the first soldier-mayor from over-seas. In August, Kentucky sent the first World War soldier to Congress, King Swope. Young Jacob L. Mulligan, twice gassed in the Argonne, was elected later in the year to Congress on a Democratic pro-League platform" (Wecter, *When Johnny Comes Marching Home*, 371).

37. Don Gonyea, "Congress Says Goodbye to Its Last World War II Vets," NPR, December 9, 2014, https://www.npr.org/sections/itsall politics/2014/12/09/369663245/congress-says-goodbye-to-its-last-world-war -ii-vets.

38. This information was compiled by the author using data obtained from https://www.house.gov.

Bibliography

Allen, Hervey. *Toward the Flame*. New York: Doran, 1926.

Australian War Memorial, Social Hygiene Division, United States of America. "A German Bullet Is Cleaner Than a Whore!" Poster, 1918. https://www.awm.gov.au/collection/C102773.

Bell, Daniel. *The Coming of Post-Industrial Society: A Venture in Social Forecasting*. New York: Basic Books, 1999.

Berger, Miriam. "Invaders, Allies, Occupiers, Guests: A Brief History of U.S. Military Involvement in Iraq." *Washington Post*, January 11, 2020.

Bowlby, Alex. *The Recollections of Rifleman Bowlby*. Rev. ed. London: Cooper, 1989.

Braun, Stephen. "A Parade of Fake War Heroes." *Los Angeles Times*, May 31, 1992.

Brown, Katherine E., and Elina Penttinen. "'A "Sucking Chest Wound" Is Nature's Way of Telling You to Slow Down . . .': Humor and Laughter in War Time." *Critical Studies on Security* 1, no. 1 (2013): 124–26.

Buiso, Gary. "Sgt. 1st Class Dillard Johnson Is the Deadliest US Soldier on Record—with 2,746 Kills." *New York Post*, June 23, 2013.

Burkett, B. G., and Glenna Whitley. *Stolen Valor: How the Vietnam Generation Was Robbed of Its Heroes and Its History*. Dallas, TX: Verity Press, 1998.

Byrum, Stephen C. *McMinn County*. Memphis, TN: Memphis State University Press, 1984.

Cancian, Mark F. "U.S. Military Forces in FY 2020, Army." Center for Strategic and International Studies, October 2019. https://www.csis.org/analysis/us-military-forces-fy-2020-army.

———. "U.S. Military Forces in FY 2020, Navy." Center for Strategic and International Studies, October 2019. https://www.csis.org/analysis/us-military-forces-fy-2021-navy.

Caputo, Philip. *A Rumor of War*. Austin, TX: Holt, Rinehart and Winston, 1977.

Carey, Benedict. "Those with Multiple Tours of Wars Overseas Struggle at Home." *New York Times*, May 29, 2016.

Carhart, Tom. *The Offering: A Generation Offered Their Lives to America in Vietnam—One Soldier's Story*. New York: Morrow, 1987.

Castner, Brian. "Still Fighting, and Dying, in the Forever War." *New York Times*, March 9, 2017.

Churchill, Winston. "War Decorations and Medals." Speech to the House of Commons, March 22, 1944. Hansard, accessed July 13, 2021. https://api .parliament.uk/historic-hansard/commons/1944/mar/22/war-decorations -and-medals.

Clemmer, Gregg S. *Valor in Gray: The Recipients of the Confederate Medal of Honor*. Staunton, VA: Hearthside, 1998.

The Colby Award and Norwich University Military Writers' Symposium. "2021 William E. Colby Award." Accessed July 9, 2021. https://www.norwich.edu /colby/colby-award.

DeRose, Chris. *The Fighting Bunch: The Battle of Athens and How World War II Veterans Won the Only Successful Armed Rebellion since the Revolution*. New York: St. Martin's Press, 2020.

Du Bois, Arthur E. "The Heraldry of Heroism." *National Geographic Magazine* 84, no. 4 (October 1943).

Edmonds, Charles. *A Subaltern's War*. London: Davies, 1929.

Encyclopedia Britannica. "Brevet: Military Rank." December 10, 2020. https:// www.britannica.com/topic/brevet.

Fahey, James J. *Pacific War Diary, 1942–1945*. Boston: Houghton Mifflin, 1963.

Fallon, Siobhan. *You Know When the Men Are Gone*. New York: Amy Einhorn Books, 2011.

Fussell, Paul. *The Great War and Modern Memory*. Oxford: Oxford University Press, 1975.

Gallagher, Gary W., ed. *Fighting for the Confederacy: The Personal Recollections of General Edward Porter Alexander*. Chapel Hill: University of North Carolina Press, 1989.

George C. Marshall Foundation. "4-225 Memorandum for the President, February 3, 1944." Accessed July 9, 2021. https://www.marshallfoundation.org /library/digital-archive/memorandum-for-the-president-107/.

Gibbs, Philip. *Now It Can Be Told*. Garden City, NY: Garden City Publishing, 1920.

Gibson, James, ed. *Let the Poet Choose*. London: Harrap, 1973.

Glubb, John Bagot. *The Story of the Arab Legion*. London: Hodder & Stoughton, 1948.

Gonyea, Don. "Congress Says Goodbye to Its Last World War II Vets." NPR, December 9, 2014. https://www.npr.org/sections/itsallpolitics/2014 /12/09/369663245/congress-says-goodbye-to-its-last-world-war-ii-vets.

Graves, Robert. *Good-Bye to All That*. New York: Vintage, 1998.

Gray, J. Glenn. *The Warriors: Reflections on Men in Battle*. Lincoln: University of Nebraska Press, 1959.

Green, Daniel R. "First among Equals: The History and Politics of Choosing the Chairman of the Joint Chiefs of Staff." PhD diss., George Washington University, 2012.

———. *In the Warlords' Shadow: Special Operations Forces, the Afghans, and Their Fight against the Taliban*. Annapolis, MD: Naval Institute Press, 2017.

Grossman, Dave. *On Combat*. N.p.: Warrior Science, 2008.

Halberstam, David. *The Best and the Brightest*. New York: Random House, 1972.

Hedges, Chris. *War Is a Force That Gives Us Meaning*. New York: Anchor, 2003.

Hillary, Richard. *The Last Enemy*. New York: Macmillan, 1942.

Houghton, Frances. *The Veterans' Tale: British Military Memoirs of the Second World War*. Cambridge: Cambridge University Press, 2019.

Horne, A. D., ed. *The Wounded Generation: America after Vietnam*. Englewood Cliffs, NJ: Prentice Hall, 1981.

Hynes, Samuel. *On War and Writing*. Chicago: University of Chicago Press, 2018.

———. *The Soldiers' Tale: Bearing Witness to Modern War*. New York: Penguin, 1997.

Inglehart, Ronald. *Modernization and Postmodernization: Cultural, Economic, and Political Change in 43 Societies*. Princeton, NJ: Princeton University Press, 1997.

Inglehart, Ronald, and Christian Welzel. *Modernization, Cultural Change, and Democracy: The Human Development Sequence*. Cambridge: Cambridge University Press, 2007.

Institute for Heraldry. "Honorable Service Lapel Button and Honorable Discharge Emblem." Accessed April 5, 2021. https://tioh.army.mil/Catalog/Heraldry.aspx?HeraldryId=15753&CategoryId=14&grp=2&menu=Uniformed%20Services&from=search.

"Iraq and Afghanistan War Fiction, Poetry, and Film 2020." *Time Now: The Iraq and Afghanistan Wars in Art, Film, and Literature* (blog), December 31, 2020. https://acolytesofwar.com/2020/12/31/iraq-and-afghanistan-war-fiction-poetry-and-film-2020/.

Junger, Sebastian. *Tribe: On Homecoming and Belonging*. New York: Twelve, 2016.

Kaufman's Army & Navy. "A Short History of the 'Military Goods Business' in America." Poster. August 1, 2019.

Key, V. O., Jr. *Southern Politics in State and Nation*. New York: Knopf, 1949.

King, Edward L. *The Death of the Army: A Pre-Mortem*. New York: Saturday Review Press, 1972.

Kirkbride, Alec. *An Awakening: The Arab Campaign, 1917–1918*. London: University Press of Arabia, 1971.

Krepinevich, Andrew F., Jr. *The Army and Vietnam*. Baltimore, MD: Johns Hopkins University Press, 1986.

Lamothe, Dan. "How 775,000 U.S. Troops Fought in One War: Afghanistan Military Deployments by the Numbers." *Washington Post*, September 11, 2019.

————. "'Maybe This Is How Vietnam Vets Felt': Americans Who Fought in Afghanistan Wait to See How Their War Ends." *Washington Post*, September 10, 2019.

Lartéguy, Jean. *The Centurions*. New York: Penguin Classics, 2015.

Lilyea, Jonn. "What Is 'Stolen Valor'?" Valor Guardians, October 14, 2015. https://www.valorguardians.com/blog/?p=62317.

Mailer, Norman. *An American Dream*. New York: Dial Press, 1965.

Marlantes, Karl. *What It Is Like to Go to War*. New York: Grove Press, 2011.

Matthews, William, and Dixon Wecter. *Our Soldiers Speak, 1775–1918*. Boston: Little, Brown, 1943.

McCarthy, John. "Stolen Valor: Imposters Touting Military Accolades an Ongoing Problem." *Press Journal*, March 2, 2020, 1A, 6A.

Mittelstadt, Jennifer. *The Rise of the Military Welfare State*. Cambridge, MA: Harvard University Press, 2015.

Monroe, Rachael. "How to Spot a Military Imposter." *New Yorker*, October 26, 2020.

Mugno, Charles V. "Maintaining the Quality of Our Military Awards System." *Marine Corps Gazette*, March 1994.

National World War II Museum. "Research Starters: U.S. Military by the Numbers." December 12, 2020. https://www.nationalww2museum.org/students-teachers/student-resources/research-starters/research-starters-us-military-numbers.

Office of the Chief of Military History, United States Army. "Peace Becomes Cold War, 1945–1950." In *American Military History*. Army Historical Series. Washington, DC: U.S. Army, 1988. https://history.army.mil/books/amh/AMH-24.htm.

Perry, Mark. *Four Stars*. New York: Houghton Mifflin Harcourt, 1989.

————. *Partners in Command*. New York: Penguin, 2007.

Peterson, Nolan. *Why Soldiers Miss War: The Journey Home*. Philadelphia: Casemate, 2019.

Plutarch. *Lives of Illustrious Men*. Boston: Little, Brown, 1880.

Rawlinson, Mark. *British Writing of the Second World War*. Oxford: Oxford University Press, 2000.

Relic Record. "Francis Bannerman Military Surplus." Accessed July 9, 2021. https://relicrecord.com/blog/francis-bannerman-military-surplus/.

Remarque, Erich Maria. *All Quiet on the Western Front*. Boston: Little, Brown, 1929.

Ricketts, Angela. *No Man's War: Irreverent Confessions of an Infantry Wife*. New York: Counterpoint, 2014.

Ricks, Tom. *The Generals*. New York: Penguin, 2012.

Robinson, Linda. *One Hundred Victories: Special Ops and the Future of American Warfare*. New York: PublicAffairs, 2013.

Sassoon, Siegfried. *Memoirs of an Infantry Officer*. London: Faber & Faber, 1930.

Seiber, Lones. "The Battle of Athens." *American Heritage*, February–March 1985.

Shapiro, Harold. *What Every Young Man Should Know about War*. New York: Knight, 1937.

Shay, Jonathan. *Odysseus in America: Combat Trauma and the Trials of Homecoming*. New York: Scribner, 2002.

Shipley, Don. "Phony Naval SEALs Verifications." Accessed June 15, 2021. http://www.extremesealexperience.com/Fake-Navy-Seal-Verification.

Sledge, E. B. *China Marine: An Infantryman's Life after World War II*. Oxford: Oxford University Press, 2002.

Stein, Joel. "Warriors and Wusses." *Los Angeles Times*, January 24, 2006.

Sterner, Doug, and Pam Sterner, with Michael Mink. *Restoring Valor: One Couple's Mission to Expose Fraudulent War Heroes and Protect America's Military Awards System*. New York: Skyhorse, 2014.

Stouffer, Samuel A., et al. *The American Soldier: Adjustment during Army Life*. Princeton, NJ: Princeton University Press, 1949.

Strandberg, John E., and Roger James Bender. *The Call of Duty: Military Awards and Decorations of the United States of America*. San Jose, CA: Bender, 1994.

Terkel, Studs. *"The Good War": An Oral History of World War II*. New York: New Press, 1984.

Tyson, Ann Scott. *American Spartan: The Promise, the Mission, and the Betrayal of Special Forces Major Jim Gant*. New York: Morrow, 2014.

U.S. Air Force Personnel Center. "Distinguished Flying Cross." August 4, 2010. https://www.afpc.af.mil/About/Fact-Sheets/Display/Article/421931/distinguished-flying-cross/.

U.S. Department of Veterans Affairs. "Vietnam." Military Health History Pocket Card, 2019. https://www.va.gov/oaa/pocketcard/vietnam.asp.

Valor Guardians. "Valor Vultures." Accessed June 15, 2021. https://valorguardians.com/blog/?cat=391.

Variety. "Upped Scale Films Cop 'Win, Place, Show' Spots in Gross Sweepstakes." January 7, 1948.

———. "All-Time Top-Grossers." January 18, 1950.

Veterans Administration. "World War II Veterans by the Numbers." VA Fact Sheet, 2003. http://dig.abclocal.go.com/ktrk/ktrk_120710_WWIIvetsfactsheet.pdf.

Waller, Willard. *On the Family, Education, and War: Selected Writings*. Edited by William J. Goode, Frank F. Furstenberg Jr., and Larry R. Mitchell. Chicago: University of Chicago Press, 1970.

———. *The Veteran Comes Back*. New York: Dryden Press, 1944.

———. *War and the Family*. New York: Dryden Press, 1940.

War and Navy Departments. "Going Back to Civilian Life." February 1946.

War Department. "Information for Soldiers: Going Back to Civilian Life." November 1944.

Wecter, Dixon. *When Johnny Comes Marching Home*. Cambridge, MA: Houghton Mifflin, 1944.

White, Bill. "An Interview with Bill White for the Veteran's Oral History Project, Center for the Study of War and Society, Department of History, the University of Tennessee Knoxville." Interviewed by G. Kurt Piehler and Brandi Wilson. Athens, TN, July 20, 2000.

William, Kate. "Riots in Tennessee." Tennessee State Library and Archives, January 10, 2013.

Wilson, Edward O. *On Human Nature*. Cambridge, MA: Harvard University Press, 1978.

———. *Sociobiology: The New Synthesis*. Cambridge, MA: Harvard University Press, 2000.

Wright, Robert. *The Moral Animal: Why We Are the Way We Are: The New Science of Evolutionary Psychology*. New York: Vintage, 1994.

———. *Non-Zero: The Logic of Human Destiny*. New York: Pantheon, 2000.

Wyllie, Robert E. "The Romance of Military Insignia: How the United States Government Recognizes Deeds of Heroism and Devotion to Duty." *National Geographic Magazine* 36, no. 6 (December 1919).

Index

About the Author

Daniel R. Green, PhD, is a commander in the U.S. Navy Reserve and has mobilized four times for service in the wars in Afghanistan and Iraq. He also served with the U.S. Department of State as the political advisor to a provincial reconstruction team in southern Afghanistan. He is the author of *The Valley's Edge: A Year with the Pashtuns in the Heartland of the Taliban* and *In the Warlords' Shadow: Special Operations Forces, the Afghans, and Their Fight against the Taliban*, as well as coauthor of *Fallujah Redux: The Anbar Awakening and the Struggle with Al-Qaeda*. He has also served as the deputy assistant secretary of defense for strategy and force development (2019–2021) with the Office of the Secretary of Defense at the U.S. Department of Defense. He is a recipient of the Secretary of Defense Medal for Outstanding Public Service (2021), the Office of the Secretary of Defense's Exceptional Public Service Award (2009), the U.S. Department of State's Superior Honor Award (2005), and the U.S. Army's Superior Civilian Honor Award (2005).

CPSIA information can be obtained
at www.ICGtesting.com
Printed in the USA
BVHW071725071021
618383BV00001B/1